George H. Horn

A synopsis of the Halticini of Boreal America

George H. Horn

A synopsis of the Halticini of Boreal America

ISBN/EAN: 9783741129803

Manufactured in Europe, USA, Canada, Australia, Japa

Cover: Foto ©Thomas Meinert / pixelio.de

Manufactured and distributed by brebook publishing software
(www.brebook.com)

George H. Horn

A synopsis of the Halticini of Boreal America

A synopsis of the HALTICINI of Boreal America.

BY GEORGE H. HORN, M. D.

The insects which constitute the study in the following pages have never been dealt with in any systematic manner. The nearest approach was by Mr. Crotch (Proc. Acad. 1873), whose object seemed to be rather the description of some of the more striking forms than a conscientious study of the material before him.

The European species have been the subject of distinct studies by Allard, Foudras and Kutschera, while at the present time a fourth work is in progress by Weise (Insecten Deutschl. vol. vi) and now nearly completed. While all of these have great merit, the last named author has been enabled to profit by the studies of his predecessors in a manner that leaves but little to be desired regarding the species of central Europe.

Our species have been dealt with in an isolated manner, a few having been described at a time by Fabricius, Olivier, Illiger, Say, Melsheimer and LeConte, while in the work of Crotch, supplemented by the Check List, gave, in accessible form, the approximately correct generic position of the species which had nearly all been described as Haltica.

Chapuis has given (Genera xi) an interesting account of the development of the tribe from the first suggestion of Altica by Geoffroy to his own time, to which those interested may refer, it being deemed unnecessary in an essay purely faunal to repeat what he has so well said.

The Halticini constitute a portion of a larger tribe, and are defined by the structure of the posterior femora, which are more or less dilated, often greatly so, giving to its possessors the power of jumping, from which the older authors adopted the designation *Saltatoria*.

The subdivision of the genera into groups is practically that adopted by Chapuis, although certain changes have been made by the partition of several of his groups, which will be explained in their proper places. Of the nineteen groups suggested five only lack representation in our fauna (*Elithiites, Amphimelites, Acrocryptites, Oxygonites* and *Nonarthrites*), while three additional groups are suggested : *Pseudolampses, Disonycha* (by division of Halticæ) and *Systena* (by division of Crepidoderæ).

Probably the most important character for the subdivision of the groups is found in the structure of the anterior coxal cavities, whether open behind or closed. This seems to divide the entire series in two cohorts containing in each genera which form parallels and agree in the possession of characters of secondary importance. As an illustration we have the Monoplati, Crepidoderæ and Chætocnemæ with closed cavities, and Pseudolampses, Lacticæ and Aphthonæ with closed cavities.

The character used by Chapuis for the definition of his Amphimelites (the insertion of the antennæ against the inner border of the eye) is open to some objection, as the same is observed in Psylliodes, of which no mention has been made. The latter genus he erroneously places among those with open front coxal cavities.

A striking character, in a few (in our fauna) genera, is the abrupt inflation of the last joint of the hind tarsi. In this case the claws are usually smaller and more slender than on the four front feet, and at times simple, while the others may be broadly appendiculate at base. In the vast majority of our genera the claws are appendiculate, but in the group Aphthonæ they are simple ; rarely (*Blepharida*) the claws are bifid.

As a rule the posterior tibia, at least, has a terminal spur, although several genera are mentioned by Chapuis without, these are not represented in our fauna. It is almost as rare to find genera with spurs to all the tibiæ. On this point Chapuis seems to have been confused, as on p. 68 he says of *Cæporis:* "this character is not otherwise known in the entire subtribe," while on p. 11 he instances *Cæporis* and *Xuthea*, and on p. 21 a group is formed on this character alone, Diamphidiites. Among our genera *Blepharida* and *Hemiglyptus* have spurs to all the tibiæ.

A character of no small importance is found in the impressed lines at the base of the thorax. Here Chapuis has been especially vague, and it has been found extremely inconvenient to retain his groups Halticæ and Crepidoderæ as constituted each to contain genera without the least trace of a groove.

The other characters made use of in the following tables seem sufficiently plain without further explanation.

From what has been observed in the study of our genera it is evident that some of Chapuis' groups must be modified as to their composition. *Homopharta* should certainly not remain with the Œdionyches nor *Phrynocepha* with Halticæ, and the two have the essential characters of the Aspicelæ. The Monoplati contains in Chapuis thirty-nine genera; one of these (Pachyonychis ‡ *Clk.* = *Hamletia* Cr.) has the anterior coxal cavities open behind, and is a true Œdionychide, and from the fact that in our fauna a genus has occurred which might readily be placed in the group by its facies and with open front coxal cavities, it seems very probable that a second careful examination would show that some of the genera at present placed in Monoplatites should be removed.

The entire tribe is one which presents many difficulties in its study. The characters of taxonomic importance are few, and these are so often interlinked as to make it almost impossible to decide to which priority of importance should be given.

At this point I desire to acknowledge the kind assistance of friends in the preparation of the work.

The Museum of Comparative Zoology at Cambridge contains the types of Melsheimer, Ziegler and LeConte; these I have been permitted to examine carefully during a recent visit to the Museum.

The National Museum at Washington has added vastly to the series examined.

To Messrs. Ulke and Schwarz, of Washington, I am indebted for the loan and gift of much valuable material not elsewhere accessible.

To Messrs. Angell and Roberts, of New York, I owe important data in distribution obtained from a loan of their material.

To Mr. Henshaw, of Boston, and Blanchard, of Lowell, I am indebted for a knowledge of the species of the New England region.

In this city the Wilt collection, now the property of the American Entomological Society, contains the most extensive material examined, although a little less rich in species than the LeConte cabinet.

From Messrs. Wenzel and Liebeck much information of value has been obtained regarding the species of the vicinity of Philadelphia.

My own cabinet needs scarcely more than half a dozen species to make it complete.

From the large material examined I have been enabled to determine the limits of the species from numbers of specimens, and it is *extremely rarely* that I have ventured to indicate species on unique examples, and then only when the characters have been so pronounced as to warrant it.

It may be the cause of surprise to some readers that more mention has not been made of the habits of the species and their food plants, as they are all more or less injurious to vegetation, and the economic literature contains considerable information on this point.

In explanation of this it may be stated that the various collectors are not in agreement as to specific names in their collections, and I have preferred to give only such information as has been supplied with specimens and have not trusted to their economic literature unless confirmed by positive data.

————o————

Analytical Table of Groups of Halticini.

Last joint of hind tarsi globosely inflated..2.
Last joint of hind tarsi not globosely inflated, usually slender, but sometimes thickened when viewed laterally..3.

2.—Anterior coxal cavities closed behind, elytra punctate-striate.
                                        II. MONOPLATI.

Anterior coxal cavities open behind.
    Elytra punctato-striate ; surface pubescent ; thorax much narrower than the elytra...**III. PSEUDOLAMPSES.**
    Elytra with confused punctuation ; surface glabrous ; thorax very little narrower than the elytra ....**IV. ŒDIONYCHES.**

3.—Anterior coxal cavities open behind...4.
Anterior coxal cavities closed behind..8.

4.—Mesosternum very short, nearly concealed by the approximation of the pro and metasterna ; body orbicular or hemispherical......**VII. MNIOPHILÆ.**
Mesosternum always visible, usually moderately long......................5.

5.—Prothorax without transverse ante-basal impression............................6.
Prothorax with transverse ante-basal impression ....7.

6.—Posterior tibiæ broadly sulcate on the posterior edge and with a more or less elevated margin each side, obliquely sinuate on the outer margin near the apex ; last joint of posterior tarsi thickened.................**V. ASPICELÆ.**
Posterior tibiæ faintly or not grooved, without sinuation ; last joint of hind tarsus slender.
    First joint of hind tarsus short as compared with the tibia and rather broad ; claws appendiculate ; species of moderate or larger size.
                                    VI. DISONYCHÆ.
    First joint of hind tarsus slender and long ; claws simple ; species of small size ....**XV. APHTHONÆ.**

7.—Transverse impression usually feeble, not limited at each extremity.
                                        VIII. HALTICÆ.
Transverse impression deep, limited at each end by a longitudinal plica.
                                        IX. LACTICÆ.

Group I.—BLEPHARIDÆ.

Antennæ 11-jointed, rather distant at base. Thorax without basal impressions. Anterior coxal cavities closed behind. Last joint of posterior tarsi rather slender, the claws bifid. Form short, robust as in many Chrysomelæ.

This group, as constituted by Chapuis, contains four genera, but one having representation in our fauna. In the generic description which follows certain characters are mentioned which may require a modification of those of the group when the other genera have been studied a little more closely.

BLEPHARIDA Rogers.

Head broadly oval, moderately deeply inserted, front vertical, broad, not carinate, the tubercles flat, widely separated, clypeus truncate. Labrum transverse, arcuate in front; maxillary palpi slender, moderately long, the joints cylindrical, the terminal longer than the third, acute at tip. Antennæ rather widely distant at base, slender, half as long as the body, first four joints glabrous, outer joints opaque and finely pubescent, first joint clavate, second oval, half as long, third and fourth slender, each longer, five to ten broader than fourth and gradually very slightly shorter, eleventh longer, apparently constricted at apex, but actually with a small terminal, articulated joint. Eyes oval, prominent, narrower above. Thorax transverse, narrowed in front, base arcuate, apex feebly emarginate. Elytra a little wider at base than the thorax, oval, widest at middle, surface regularly punctato-striate. Prosternum rather widely separating the coxæ, as elevated as they, dilated at apex, and with the epimera closing the cavities behind. Mesosternum narrowly visible, vertical in front; ventral segments free, the first as long as the next three, these nearly equal, fifth nearly as long as the preceding two. Legs rather short and robust, posterior femora moderately inflated. Tibiæ gradually broader to apex, each with a short terminal spur, anterior tibia not sinuate near apex, middle and posterior tibia with a distinct sinuation bordered with short ciliæ, limited above by a distinct angulation, the posterior deeply grooved on posterior edge at apex; tarsi stout, first joint broadly triangular, second narrower, third broadly bilobed, fourth slender, terminated by bifid claws. Form robust, glabrous, winged (Pl. vii, fig. 18).

The various opinions which have been emitted regarding the position of Blepharida have been dwelt upon in considerable detail by Chapuis (Genera xi, p. 33), and need not be repeated here.

Several points in the organization seem to have been passed over. The antennæ are really 12-jointed (Pl. vii, fig. 18), the terminal piece of the eleventh joint being distinctly articulated and movable. All the tibiæ have a distinct terminal spur, and, in such a large insect, it is remarkable that this should have been passed over.

The male has the first joint of the anterior and middle tarsi more widely dilated than the female. The last ventral segment is sinuate each side, the median lobe transversely impressed near the margin.

But one species is known in our fauna.

B. rhois Forst —Form short, robust oval, convex, beneath rufotestaceous, above yellowish testaceous, elytra irregularly variegated with rufocastaneous. Antennæ with four basal joints rufotestaceous, the outer joints piceous or nearly black. Head entirely yellow, sparsely coarsely punctate on the vertex. Thorax more than twice as wide as long, narrowed in front, sides regularly arcuate, anterior angles prominent anteriorly, hind angles obtuse, lateral margin thickened, limited within by a row of punctures, disc convex, sparsely finely punctured, a few coarse punctures at the middle of the declivity. Elytra scarcely wider at base than the thorax, humeri broadly rounded, sutural angle rather obtuse, disc convex, with nine feebly impressed striæ; striæ with coarse, deep, but not closely placed punctures, an extremely fine puncture between the larger ones, intervals broad, scarcely convex. Abdomen finely punctate and pubescent. Legs rufotestaceous. Length .20—.26 inch; 5—6.5 mm.

This species is variable in the coloration of the elytra; sometimes
these are in great part yellow, with a few scattered, small, rufocastaneous spots, or they may be irrorate with that color, or finally the
entire disc may be rufocastaneous with the sides and apex broadly
yellow. Those variations as remarked by Mr. W. F. Rogers amply
account for the many synonyms.

Occurs from Massachusetts to Montana, and from these points
south to Florida and Texas.

<h2>Group II.--MONOPLATI.</h2>

Antennæ 11-jointed. Prothorax usually narrower at base than
the elytra, either with or without ante-basal transverse impression.
Anterior coxal cavities closed behind. Last joint of posterior tarsi
globosely inflated at tip, the claws appendiculate in our genera.

Two characters neatly define this group, the closure of the anterior
coxal cavities and the globosely inflated apex of the last joint of
hind tarsi. The first of these characters will be found in many
groups, the latter only otherwise in the Œdionyches and Pseudolampses, both of which have the coxal cavities open.

The following genera occur in our fauna:

Maxillary palpi slender; thorax not impressed at base; posterior tibiæ with a
    double terminal spur...**Phædromus.**
Maxillary palpi stout; posterior tibiæ with one spur.
    Posterior tibiæ longitudinally bicarinate; thorax transversely impressed at
    base; body glabrous.. **Pachyonychus.**
    Posterior tibiæ feebly unicarinate; thorax not impressed; body hairy.
                                                              Hypolampsis.

These genera all belong to the Atlantic region.

<h3>PHÆDROMUS Clark.</h3>

Head short, transverse. Labrum rounded in front; maxillary
palpi slender, second joint obconical, third twice as long, slightly
broader at tip, fourth very small, more slender, acute at tip. Eyes
large, globular. Antennæ filiform, but rather stout, first joint
clavate, arcuate, second short, oval, third shorter than first, joints
following gradually shorter, the last acuminate. Prothorax transverse, apex squarely truncate, sides angularly dilated in front of
middle, disc little convex, subdepressed at base, without ante-basal
impressions; scutellum very small. Elytra a little wider than the
thorax, sides subparallel, moderately convex, finely punctate. Legs

moderate, posterior thighs oval, tibiæ slightly incurved, slightly thickened, the posterior edge depressed and margined, the edges slightly sinuate toward the apex, without trace of tooth, but forming at apex a double shortened spine. Tarsi with first joint subdilated, second short, third large, orbicular, fourth elongate, swollen, globular, with appendiculate claws.

P. Waterhousei Clark.—Oblong, subdepressed, glabrous, shining. Thorax yellow, impunctate. Elytra oblong, parallel, finely punctato-striate, the striæ nearly obsolete toward apex, color black, shining. Body beneath and antennæ black. Legs pale. Length .25 inch.; 7 mm, nearly.

This insect was described by Clark from a specimen obtained from Mr. George R. Waterhouse, said to be from South Carolina. The specimen in the British Museum carries the label "Carolina."

No specimen has ever been seen in any American collection, and there is consequently a suspicion that the locality given may be erroneous. The above description will enable it to be recognized when seen.

PACHYONYCHUS Chev.

Head broadly oval, not deeply inserted; eyes free, clypeus truncate, front short, very obtusely carinate, the tubercles large, flat, oblique; labrum transverse, entire. Eyes oval, moderately prominent, finely granulated. Maxillary palpi short, very robust, second joint conical, third very short, obconical, fourth as broad at base as the third, closely articulated with it and longer, obtusely oval at tip; these two joints apparently form a flattened ovate club to the second joint. Antennæ a little longer than half the body, not thickened externally, first joint clavate, second and third short, nearly equal in length, together longer than the first, but shorter than the fourth, the latter a little longer than the first; joints 4–10 equal, shorter than the fourth, eleventh longer, constricted at tip. Thorax broader than long, apex truncate, base truncate at middle, obliquely sinuate each side, disc convex, with a deep ante-basal transverse impression. Elytra oblong, emarginate at base, disc punctato-striate. Prosternum moderately separating the coxæ, dilated behind them and with the epimera closing the coxal cavities. Mesosternum moderate in length. Ventral segments free, the first and fifth longer, the intermediate equal. Legs moderate in length. Tibiæ slightly broader toward apex, the posterior broadly sulcate, carinate each side and terminated by a single spur; tarsi moderately long, the first two joints triangu-

lar, the first longer, third broader and bilobed, the fourth on the
posterior legs globosely inflated at apex. The claws appendiculate.
Form oblong, surface glabrous, body winged.

This genus is now for the first time fully described, although
Melsheimer described the species on which it is based in 1847. The
question of the validity of Pachyonychus and Pachyonychis has
been amply discussed by Crotch (Proc. Acad. 1873, p. 58), and by
Jacoby and myself (Trans. Am. Ent. Soc. xv, pp. 302–304), and
will not be dwelt upon at this time. At that time the suggestion was
made that it might be related to Cerichrestus, which now seems to
me not well founded. At present I am unable to suggest any special
relationship for it, although by the table given by Chapuis it must
be placed near Omototus and Hypolampsis.

One species is known to me.

P. paradoxus Mels.—Oblong, nearly parallel, rufotestaceous, shining,
elytra piceous, the margin narrowly, the suture broadly rufotestaceous. Antennæ
black, the three basal joints rufotestaceous. Head smooth, shining. Thorax
more than one-half broader than long, not narrowed in front, sides feebly arcuate, margin thickened at front angles, posterior angles rather acute, disc convex,
irregularly sparsely punctate, the ante-basal impression deep, extending from
side to side within the angles. Elytra wider at base than the thorax, humeri
obtusely prominent, umbone distinct, base emarginate at middle, sides feebly
arcuate, apical angles well defined, disc moderately convex, regularly punctato-
striate, striæ not deeply impressed, punctures moderately coarse and closely
placed, intervals slightly convex, broader than the striæ, each with a row of
very fine punctures. Abdomen sparsely punctate and slightly pubescent.
Length .12–.18 inch.; 3—4.5 mm. Pl. vii, fig. 1.

No sexual characters have been observed in the seven specimens
before me.

Occurs in the Middle States region; sometimes abundant in District of Columbia (Ulke).

HYPOLAMPSIS Clark.

Head moderately deeply inserted, the eyes free, clypeus somewhat
prolonged, truncate, front very obtusely carinate, the tubercles distinct. Eyes oval, convex, coarsely granulated. Labrum transverse,
slightly emarginate. Antennæ rather stout, not longer than half the
body, the five outer joints rather abruptly broader, forming an elongate club which is opaque, and with dense fine pubescence, first five
joints not densely pubescent, shining; first joint clavate, second oblong oval, as stout as first, but shorter, third more slender, longer

than second, 4–5–6 gradually shorter, 7–10 quadrate or more transverse, eleventh longer, oval, obtuse at tip. Maxillary palpi stout, second joint clavate, third ovate, fourth conical, acute and scarcely longer. Thorax quadrate, not narrowed in front, apex truncate, base arcuate, without ante-basal discal impressions. Elytra wider at base than the thorax, oblong oval, widest at middle, surface coarsely and densely striato-punctate, with a more or less distinct oblique impression on each elytron. Prosternum rather narrow between the coxæ, dilated behind them, the cavities rather widely closed behind. Mesosternum distinct, oblique. Abdominal segments free, 2–3–4 equal in length. Legs moderately stout, the posterior femora broadly oval. Anterior and middle tibiæ scarcely wider at tip, the posterior tibiæ with the posterior edge rounded, dilated at tip, a small tooth above the dilatation, the apex distinctly prolonged beyond the insertion of the tarsus and with a small spur. Posterior tarsi nearly as long as the tibia, first joint obconical, very narrow at base, second smaller in front, but more depressed, third elongate oval, not bilobed, fourth nearly as long as the preceding, abruptly inflated at apex, the claws toothed at middle. Claws of anterior and middle tarsi bifid, the inner division shorter and curved inward. Body pubescent and with erect hairs.

The above description is drawn from our species alone. Chapuis remarks that the species are often quite dissimilar, and their study, from a generic standpoint, of some difficulty. Some differences have been observed between his generic description, and that above given for our species, more, however, in the omissions in preceding descriptions to mention especially the form of the hind tibiæ at apex and the form of the claws. As Hamlet Clark, the author of the genus, has seen our species and considered it a true Hypolampsis, I feel unwilling to do more than say that the species seem to need more careful study generically.

Two species are known to me in our fauna :

Thorax roughly punctured, wider than long; elytra not striate...........**pilosa.**
Thorax evenly punctured, as long as wide; elytra broadly striate........**Mellyi.**

H. pilosa Illig. Oblong oval, convex, opaque, variable in color from testaceous to piceous black ; surface with recumbent pubescence and more sparsely placed erect hairs. Antennæ rufotestaceous or brownish, the outer five joints always darker, sometimes black. Head densely punctate and rugose, the tubercles alone smooth. Thorax quadrate, very little wider than long, not narrowed in front, sides straight or slightly sinuous, anterior angles obtuse to the front, base arcuate, disc convex, very coarsely and closely punctate, surface irregular and with two distinct callosities slightly in front of middle. Elytra wider at base than the thorax, rather broadly emarginate at middle, humeri obtusely prominent, umbone moderately prominent, disc convex, with a faint oblique impression from the humerus to suture, ending in a more or less defined fovea on the first and second striae, a little in front of middle, the striae composed of very coarse and deep punctures, closely placed, the intervals not wider than the distance between the punctures very minutely punctulate, the surface not densely clothed with fine recumbent pubescence, usually intermixed with brown and gray, the scutellum whitish, the two foveae and often two others more posterior black. Body beneath similar in color to the upper surface, shining; the abdomen very sparsely punctate. Legs usually a little paler than the under surface. Length .07--.16 inch; 2—4 mm.

In the male the last ventral segment is truncate, shorter than in the female and more convex.

This species is probably more variable than any other Halticide in our fauna. The size is noted above, and when the small one is pale rufotestaceous and the large one almost black, the contrast is very striking. With the color of the surface the pubescence varies so that the black forms from the Southern States have entirely black pubescence, those from the Middle States with brown color are variegated. In the very small specimens the thoracic callosities are not evident, and there seems to be vague median impression. The oblique impression of the disc of the elytra may be distinct or not, and the punctures round or more crowded and quadrate.

The sufficiently abundant material before me proves the necessity of uniting some of the forms mentioned by Crotch under one name. The species since described by LeConte does not belong to the group.

Occurs from the Hudson's Bay region to Florida, and from Massachusetts to Oregon, a sufficiently wide distribution to admit of great climatic variation.

11. Mellyi Cr.--Elongate, moderately convex, pale brown, feebly shining, sparsely clothed with grayish pubescence and with sparse erect hairs. Antennae brownish, joints 3 4-5 paler. Head pale brown, front testaceous, occiput closely punctate. Thorax as long as wide, quadrate, anterior angles obliquely truncate, sides slightly coarctate behind the middle, disc moderately convex, a vague transverse depression in front of base, surface densely, but not roughly punctate. Elytra nearly twice as wide at base as the base of the thorax, the disc with rather broad, but not deep striae, the punctures rather coarse and closely placed, intervals distinctly convex and finely punctulate. Body beneath pale fuscous, the abdomen sparsely punctate and with few hairs. Legs pale yellow. Length .12 inch; 3 mm.

Of this species I have seen but the single specimen in the cabinet of Dr. LeConte. The surface sculpture is less rough than in *pilosa*, although here the striae are well marked. It differs especially from that species in having the thorax less roughly punctured, and in shape nearly as long, if not longer than wide.

One specimen, Kansas.

Group III.--PSEUDOLAMPSES.

Antennæ 11-jointed. Thorax much narrower than the elytra. Anterior coxal cavities open behind. Posterior tibiæ not sulcate, apex with small spur. Last joint of posterior tarsus globosely inflated, the claws appendiculate. Body pubescent, elytra punctato-striate.

In this group we have a structure intermediate between the Monoplati and Œdionyches, with a greater resemblance to the former from the pubescent surface and striate elytra as well as the form.

From the discovery of this form it may be questioned whether all the genera now placed in the Monoplati really belong there. Already one genus, Pachyonychis *Clk.*, has been found to be incorrectly placed there, and it seems to me possible that some of those with slender palpi might be placed in this group.

One genus is known to me.

PSEUDOLAMPSIS n. g.

Head broad, rather deeply inserted, eyes free, front not carinate, tubercles small and indistinct, clypeus slightly prolonged, truncate. Labrum arcuate. Eyes oval, prominent, rather coarsely granulated ; maxillary palpi slender, second joint slightly thicker toward apex, third much shorter, obconical, fourth more slender, but as long, acute at tip. Antennæ half as long as the body, gradually thicker toward apex, first joint elongate oval, second ovate, half as long as first, third slender, as long as the second, joints 4–10 nearly equal in length, but gradually broader, eleventh longer, the tip broadly conical. Thorax a little wider than long, not narrowed in front, lateral margin entirely obliterated ; scutellum small. Elytra nearly twice as wide at base as the thorax, humeri prominent, sides feebly arcuate, very little wider at middle than at base, disc convex, a distinct post-basal impression extending obliquely backward from the suture to the sides, surface punctato-striate. Prosternum moderately separating the coxæ, very slightly dilated at apex, the coxal cavities rather widely open behind. Mesosternum distinct, oblique. Ventral segments free, the first longer, next three equal, fifth longer. Legs moderate, anterior and middle tibiae scarcely broader at apex, outer edge rounded. Posterior femora broadly thickened, posterior tibiae very little broader at apex, the outer edge faintly unicarinate, obliquely truncate at apex, without sinuation or tooth, terminated by a small spur; tarsi moderate in length, first joint slightly broader externally, second equally broad, triangular, fourth deeply bilobed. Last joint of posterior tarsi globosely inflated at apex, claws appendiculate at base. Form short, like a robust *Lema*, body above finely pubescent.

This genus is suggested for a small species described by Dr. Le-Conte as *Hypolampsis guttata*, but the open anterior coxal cavities not only forbid its retention in that genus, but in the group to which it belongs.

There seems to be a parallel arrangement of groups of genera in which the anterior coxal cavities are either open or closed, each group possessing in turn an added character alike in the two series. The Monoplati have closed cavities, and the inflated fourth tarsal joint. In the present genus we have the open cavities and inflated joint. In the Œdionyches we have open cavities and inflated joint, but the surface is glabrous, elytra confusedly punctate and thorax not much narrower than the elytra. There still remains to be discovered an Œdionychoid genus with closed coxal cavities.

P. guttata Lec.—Form rather robust, piceous, feebly shining, clothed with fine fulvous pubescence, forming an irregular pattern. Antennae pale yellowish brown. Head reddish yellow, rather coarsely and closely punctate. Thorax quadrate, slightly broader than long, sides feebly arcuate, base arcuate at middle, very slightly oblique each side, disc convex, densely not coarsely punctate; finely pubescent. Elytra nearly twice as wide at base as the thorax, humeri obtusely prominent, umbone moderately prominent, disc convex, a vague oblique impression on each elytron, moderately deeply punctato-striate, the punctures moderately coarse and serrate, intervals convex, scarcely wider than the striae, extremely finely punctulate; surface with fulvous pubescence forming a broad space at apex, and on the disc a humeral space, an oblique band in the depression and an oval space behind it. Body beneath rufescent, abdomen paler, with close, fine punctuation and pubescence. Legs yellowish testaceous. Length .08 inch.; 2 mm.

In the male the last ventral segment is broadly emarginate at middle.

The form of this insect resembles Hypolampsis somewhat, but more closely some of the short Lema, or even certain of our Xylophilus.

Occurs near New Orleans, Louisiana.

Group IV.--ŒDIONYCHES.

Antennæ 11-jointed, usually slender. Prothorax without trace of ante-basal transverse impression. Anterior coxal cavities open behind. Elytra glabrous and with confused punctuation. Last joint of hind tarsus globosely inflated at apex.

These few words define this group with sufficient sharpness to enable any of its members to be recognized, and it seems to me that the characters should be strictly applied, so that no genus without *globosely* inflated claw joint to the posterior tarsus should be admitted here; consequently, Homophœta has been excluded. Chapuis notes the close resemblance between some Aspicelites and members of the present group without realizing the necessity of a rearrangement of the two groups.

Two genera are known in our fauna separated in the following manner:

First joint of hind tarsus short and broad; four anterior claws feebly appendiculate, the posterior slender and simple........................**Hamletia.**
First joint of hind tarsus moderately long and slender, claws all appendiculate.
                   Œdionychis.

The first of these genera was placed by Chapuis in the Monoplati under the name *Pachyonychis.*

HAMLETIA Crotch.

Head not deeply inserted in the thorax, occiput oblique, front vertical, labrum transverse, slightly sinuous at middle. Maxillary palpi stout, the penultimate joint obconical, a little longer than wide at apex, last joint acutely conical. Antennæ 11-jointed, separated at base by an obtuse frontal carina, joints 5–11 equal in width, broader than those which precede, third and fourth joints nearly equal in length. Thorax a little wider at base than long, very feebly emarginate at apex, sides subangulate at middle, base truncate, distinctly sinuate at the hind angles. Elytra distinctly wider at base than the thorax, humeri rounded; anterior coxal cavities open behind, angulate externally, the trochantin visible. Posterior tibiæ rather deeply sulcate on the outer edge and with a distinct sinuation and small tooth above the insertion of the tarsus. First joint of posterior tarsi short and rather stout, the claw joint globosely inflated, the claws slender and simple. First joint of front tarsi broadly triangular, the claws of this and middle tarsi feebly appendiculate.

From the description which Chapuis gives of this insect under the name *Pachyonychis* (Genera xii, p. 100) it is very evident that he has not seen the insect, otherwise it would never have been placed in the Monoplati from the open front coxal cavities. With the limited material in our fauna it is better to place the genus with the Œdionyches, although it might well constitute a tribe intermediate between that and Monoplati. The fact of the dissimilarity of the claws seems to have escaped notice, those of the hind tarsi being absolutely simple and slender, those of the front and middle are slightly appendiculate in the usual manner. This fact is sufficient to indicate the tribe, together with the dissimilarity in the form of body from any of the Œdionyches, approaching somewhat certain Monoplati as Tetragonotes.

The reasons for adopting this name for the genus have been fully given by Mr. Jacoby, who has also shown the incorrect position of the genus by Chapuis (Trans. Am. Ent. Soc. 1888, p. 302).

II. dimidiaticornis Crotch.—Elongate oval, subdepressed, feebly shining, beneath almost entirely piceous, legs yellow, above black, elytra blue-green Antennæ a little longer than half the body, the three basal and half the fourth, also the three terminal joints pale, the intermediate piceous. Head black, smooth, frontal tubercles distinct and with a transverse depression above them. Thorax a little wider at base than long, narrower in front, apex scarcely emarginate, sides obtusely angulate at middle, the margin very narrow, front angles not dentiform, base sinuate each side, the hind angles moderately prominent. surface black, shining, not punctate. Elytra wider at base than the thorax, humeri rounded, umbone distinct, limited within by a slight depression. surface bluish green, relatively coarsely and closely punctate, but much smoother near the apex. Body beneath black. Abdomen piceous, the last segment yellow. Legs pale yellow. Length .13 inch.; 3.25 mm. Plate VI, fig. 9.

The specimen before me is a male, and has the last segment subtruncate and with a slight impression at middle, in length the segment nearly equals the two preceding, and in the female is probably longer.

This insect seems to be one of the rarest of our Halticides. I have seen but three specimens,—one in my cabinet and that of LeConte, from Georgia, the third in the British Museum from an unknown locality. As the latter came from the Dejean collection it is probably also from Georgia.

ŒDIONYCHIS Latr.

Head inserted in the prothorax to the posterior border of the eyes front variable, either regularly declivous from the occiput with mouth more anterior, or abruptly vertical from the insertion of the antennæ so that the mouth is more inferior, the carina usually obtuse, the tubercles usually feebly developed. Antennæ approximate at base, slender. Thorax always much broader than long, deeply emarginate in front, the margin more or less dilated, often widely, the front angles dentiform or not, base arcuate, more or less obliquely sinuate near the posterior angles. Elytra oval, the margin often explanate the humeri not prominent. Prosternum not depressed between the coxæ, moderately wide between them, dilated behind, the cavities open behind, angulate externally, exposing the trochantin. Metathoracic parapleuræ rather wide, parallel and always more roughly sculptured than the adjacent part of the sternum. Legs short and robust, the anterior and middle femora fusiform, the tibiæ slightly broader at apex, the outer edge deeply grooved, ciliate along the edges; tarsi with first joint oblong, triangular, second smaller and narrower, third subbilobed, fourth with the claws divaricate and appendiculate at base. Posterior femora very stout and thick, sometimes nearly as wide as long, deeply grooved beneath for the tibiæ these short feebly grooved on the posterior edge, which has a sinuation just above the insertion of the tarsi and limited above by a small acute tooth ; a single slightly curved spur at the tip of the tibia. Tarsi more slender than in front, the claw joint globularly swollen, the claws small and appendiculate. Plate VII, fig. 11.

In a study of the comparatively small number of species two forms of head were observed with other characters in association. As a rule, the outline of the head when viewed laterally forms a regular curve from the occiput to the mouth. In our smaller and more depressed species, the front below the insertion of the antennæ is nearly vertical, so that the mouth is somewhat retracted and opens inferiorly, while in the larger species the mouth is anterior. When the front is regularly arcuate, the antennæ are somewhat stouter and rarely reach the middle of the body, the front between the eyes has not the deep transverse groove, while the tubercles are rather more distinct. In those with the vertical front the antennæ are slender and usually longer than half the body, the interocular groove is deep, while the tubercles are not distinct. The species of the first series are larger and convex, those of the second smaller and more depressed.

The oblique sinuation of the base of the thorax although fairly well marked in the majority of the species is very variable, and in many of the species of the second series not at all evident. The extent of the expansion of the lateral margins of both thorax and elytra is purely a specific matter, and will be referred to in the descriptions.

The epipleuræ show two fairly distinct forms. In those species which have no expansion of the margin of the elytra, the epipleuræ are always very narrow at apical half, while in those with explanate elytra the epipleuræ are broad until very near the apex.

The sexual characters (if they have not escaped observation) have never been referred to in print. The first joint of the anterior tarsus is always more broadly dilated in the male; the last ventral segment has on each side a deep sinuation, the space between forming a prominent oval lobe which has a finely impressed line at middle. The last ventral of the female is entirely simple. Among the different males no part in analysis can be taken from the sexual differences as the variation is too slight.

In one species (*tenuilineata*) it will be observed that the male is shorter, the thorax scarcely wider at base than at middle, while in the female the form of thorax is that usual in the genus. In *miniata* also the males are shorter and more convex than the females. As far as my observation goes the females are fully four times as numerous as the males.

As *Œdionychis* is so well known and abundantly represented by species, it will be used as the centre of comparison for allied genera. Attention is directed, however, to the fact that about the only character separating *Physodactyla* is in the present genus purely sexual, that is, all male *Œdionychis* would be *Physodactyla*.

The species with a single exception belong to the Atlantic region, several reaching Arizona ; *violascens* is the only one at present known from the Pacific slope.

Based on the notes always given it is proposed to divide our species into two series in the following manner :

Antennæ stout, scarcely as long as half the body ; species larger and convex ; front oblique, interocular impression never very distinct, usually obliter ated by punctures : thorax rarely widely margined ; elytra never explanate ....SERIES A.

Antennæ slender, as long as, or longer than half the body ; species small, much depressed, front vertical, a deep, transverse, interocular depression : elytra usually explanate ....SERIES B.

SERIES A.

Elytra *entirely* unicolorous, either bright metallic blue, dull violaceous, or nearly
   black, margin never pale... ....2.

Elytra bicolored, either with a pale margin or with the disc vittate (in *fimbriata*
   sometimes entirely pale) ....6.

2.—Body never entirely black beneath..3.

   Body and legs entirely black...5.

3.—Elytra brilliant blue or green, thorax smooth, body beneath entirely pale.
                                                        1. **gibbitarsa.**

   Elytra dull violaceous or greenish black, thorax more or less punctate, body
      beneath in greater part dark..4.

4.—Elytral punctures distinct, often coarse and close; thorax at least bordered
      with pale ....4. **vians.**

   Elytral punctures obsolete, thorax black . ...5. **concinna.**

5.—Surface rather shining, punctures very distinct.............. 6. **violacens.**

   Surface dull black, impunctate.................................... 7. **lugens.**

6.—Elytra violaceous or bluish, margin pale.

   Thorax and elytra coarsely and closely punctate.......... 3. **thoracica.**

   Thorax and elytra indistinctly punctate, elytra brilliant violaceous.
                                                       2. **flavocyanea.**

   Elytra distinctly punctured, a short yellow vitta just within the hu-
      meral umbone...var. **brevilineata.**

   Elytra entirely testaceous, vittate or maculate.

   Elytra entirely testaceous,.................................... **fimbriata** var.

   Elytra blue, green or violaceous, disc with a yellow vitta, usually in form
      of **!**; sometimes entire................. 8. **interjectionis.**

   Elytra yellow, with dark vittae..7.

   Elytra brown, with large pale spots...................17. **Jacobiana.**

7.—Three vittæ on each elytron, sutural median and submarginal................8.

   Two vittæ, sutural and median..9.

8.—Form oblong oval, anterior angles of thorax not dentiform.

   Body beneath and legs black, elytral punctuation very indistinct, the
      vittæ blue.. .... 10. **æmula.**

   Body beneath (except metasternum) and legs pale; elytral punctuation
      distinct and moderately close, vittæ piceous.... ....9. **fimbriata.**

   Form oval, anterior angles of thorax dentiform.

   Elytral vittæ broad, antennæ piceous...... ....11. **petaurista.**

   Elytral vittæ very narrow, the three basal and the terminal joint of an-
      tennæ pale ....12. **tenuilineata.**

9. Elongate oblong; elytra, especially posteriorly, asperate punctate.
                                                       16. **longula.**

   Oval, or oblong oval, elytra impresso-punctate...... ....10.

10.—Antennæ with fourth joint distinctly longer than third......13. **miniata.**

   Antennæ with joints 3 and 4 equal.

   Elytra coarsely and closely punctate................ ....14. **Horni.**

   Elytra sparsely, finely and indistinctly punctate................15. **Ulkei.**

1. **Œ. gibbitarsa** Say.--Oval, slightly oblong, moderately convex, honey-yellow, elytra brilliant cobalt-blue or green, thorax with four piceous spots, often more or less confluent, tibiæ and tarsi piceous. Antennæ scarcely half as long as the body, piceous. Frontal carina very flat, two feeble tubercles, not transversely impressed between the eyes, a few punctures in a transverse row, others near the eye, vertex and occiput smooth. Thorax more than twice as wide as long, gradually arcuately narrowed from base to apex, margin moderately explanate, but not translucent, surface smooth, with four piceous spots, the middle pair larger, more or less confluent; scutellum black. Elytra slightly wider at base than the thorax, humeri obtuse, umbone moderately prominent, smooth, surface sparsely indistinctly punctulate, epipleuræ concolorous. Abdomen shining, sparsely punctate with very sparse short hairs. Length .18--.28 inch.: 4.5--7 mm.

This species shows no great variation; sometimes the thoracic spots are confluent in a broad transverse band. The elytral variation from blue to green is usual in that color, and it has been observed that the more northern specimens are the more green.

Occurs from the Middle States to Missouri and Texas.

2. **Œ. flavocyanea** Crotch.--Form rather broadly oval, subdepressed, shining, bright yellow, thorax with a discal spot, elytra violet-blue, the entire margin pale. Antennæ half as long as the body, third and fourth joints about equal, piceous, three basal joints testaceous, terminal joint usually paler than those which precede. Head reddish yellow, frontal carina tuberculiform, the tubercles distinct, vertex coarsely, closely and deeply punctured, especially near the eyes. Thorax more than twice as wide as long, sides arcuately narrowing to the front, the margin moderately wide, especially in front, not translucent, base nearly regularly arcuate, the usual sinuation near the angles scarcely evident, surface sparsely, but very distinctly punctate, color yellow, with a median piceous spot, sometimes forming a very broad transverse band. Elytra not wider at base than the thorax, humeri obliterated, umbone scarcely prominent, disc indistinctly sparsely punctate near base, almost smooth at middle, a region of coarse punctures beginning at the base just within the umbone, extending one-fourth the length of the elytra; epipleuræ yellow, the inner half piceous at the dilated basal portion. Body beneath entirely yellow, abdomen shining, very indistinctly sparsely punctate. Legs yellow, the anterior and middle pair slightly darker. Length .20--.24 inch.; 5--6 mm.

This species has much the form and general coloration of *gibbitarsa*, but may be distinguished by the entirely pale lateral border of the elytra. The discal black spot of the thorax does not seem to be made up of the union of many, but is unique.

Occurs in Texas.

3. **Œ. thoracica** Fab.-- Oblong oval, feebly convex, reddish yellow, elytra piceous with blue, violaceous or slightly greenish lustre, the sides narrowly margined at basal half with pale. Antennæ half as long as the body, piceous; third and fourth joints equal. Head pale, occiput bordered with piceous, frontal carina obtuse, tubercles distinct, surface rather coarsely and closely punctate,

except at the middle of the occiput. Thorax rather more than twice as wide as long, arcuately narrowing to the front, margin narrow, disc rather coarsely, not densely punctate, color reddish, with piceous spots, two in the anterior row, four in a posterior arcuate row; these are usually more or less confluent or forming a zigzag band. Elytra a little wider at base than the thorax, humeri rounded, umbone distinct, smooth, surface closely and moderately coarsely punctate. Epipleuræ pale nearly their entire length. Body beneath and legs reddish yellow, the tibiæ and tarsi piceous. Abdomen shining, indistinctly sparsely punctate. Length .20—.26 inch ; 5—6.5 mm.

The sculpture of the upper surface resembles the most coarsely punctate forms of *vians*, which it also resembles in general appearance. The under surface is always entirely reddish yellow. There is very little variation, except in surface color of the elytra and the greater or less confluence of the thoracic spots.

Widely distributed over the entire region east of the Rocky Mountains.

4. **Œ. vians** Illig.—Oblong oval, moderately convex, very shining. Antennæ black, scarcely as long as half the body, third joint longer than fourth. Head black, sometimes with a pale vertical spot, frontal carina obtuse, tubercles distinct, vertex rather closely punctate. Thorax twice as wide at base as long, narrowed in front, sides nearly straight, margin narrow, surface distinctly punctate, either rather coarsely or moderately finely, color usually yellowish with five piceous spots confluent and forming the letter M or extending into a large discal spot, so that only the margins are narrowly pale; scutellum black. Elytra a little wider at base than the thorax, humeri distinct, umbone moderately prominent, smooth, surface usually closely punctate, although variable in distinctness, color black, with a slight violet lustre. Epipleuræ concolorous; prothorax beneath yellow, meso- and metasternum black. Abdomen piceous at middle, broadly yellow at sides and apex, surface shining, very sparsely punctate. Legs entirely black. Length .16—.28 inch ; 4—7 mm.

This species varies in the color of the thorax, as stated above, those with the large discal space being the typical *vians*, while those with the M shaped mark are *scripticollis* Say. The sculpture of the surface may be rather fine or moderately coarse. The abdomen also varies in the extent of the yellow color, sometimes only the middle of the first two segments is piceous.

Occurs nearly everywhere east of the Rocky Mountains

5. **Œ. concinna** Fab.—Oblong oval, moderately convex, feebly shining, black, elytra slightly greenish or blue, abdomen yellow at apex. Antennæ black, not half as long as the body, third joint longer than fourth. Head black, frontal carina indistinct, tubercles well marked, a distinct concavity of the vertex, which is coarsely closely punctate. Thorax twice as wide at base as long, narrowed in front, sides straight or feebly arcuate, the margin moderate, surface

alutaceous, sparsely moderately punctate; scutellum black. Elytra a little wider at base than the thorax, humeri very obtuse, umbone feebly prominent, surface distinctly alutaceous, punctuation very indistinct, visible near base only, Epipleuræ black. Body beneath black. Abdomen at apex, and often at sides, yellow; the surface shining, very sparsely punctate. Legs entirely black. Length .24—.30 inch.; 6--7.5 mm.

This species resembles *vians*, but is always more elongate, and the elytra are almost entirely without the punctuation so evident even in the smoothest forms of that species. The thorax is here always completely black, both above and beneath and never so in *vians*. The species seems to me abundantly distinct, although Crotch suppressed the older name in making *concinna* a synonym of *vians*.

Occurs in Georgia and Texas.

6. **Œ. violascens** Lec.—Form rather broadly oval and less convex, violaceous blue, feebly shining. Antennæ short and stout, nearly black, third and fourth joints equal. Head cribrately punctate at sides, smoother at middle of occiput, tubercles obliterated, frontal carina very indistinct. Thorax twice as wide at base as long, distinctly narrowed in front, sides feebly arcuate, front angles slightly everted, disc moderately convex, surface shining, punctures sparse, not deep, a little closer along the base and hind angles, these rather acute. Elytra scarcely wider at base than the shorax, oval, broadest behind the middle, surface coarsely and closely punctate as in the rougher forms of *thoracica*. Body beneath more shining than above, abdomen very sparsely and indistinctly punctate. Length .24 inch.; 6 mm.

This species is rather more broadly oval than several in this part of the series. The color is very nearly that of *thoracica*, and the elytral sculpture rather coarser and deeper. The legs are entirely blue-black.

A specimen in my cabinet, from Nevada, which may be a variety of the above, is slightly bronzed and with less pronounced sculpture.

Two specimens from Fort Tejon, Cala.

7. **Œ. lugens** Lec.—Oblong oval, feebly convex, dull black, opaque. Antennæ shorter than half the body, third and fourth joints equal. Head coarsely and deeply punctured, densely between the eyes, frontal carina very short and obtuse, tubercles very flat and indistinct. Thorax twice as wide as long, sides arcuately narrowing to the front, margin very narrow, surface moderately closely punctate, more coarsely near the sides. Elytra a little wider at base than the thorax, humeri obtuse, umbone not distinct, surface opaque, very minutely alutaceous, without trace of punctuation. Body beneath and legs entirely black. Abdomen shining, the punctuation coarse, but obsolete. Length .18—.22 inch. 4.5--5.5 mm.

The opaque and totally black surface will enable this species to be readily recognized. It is even more elongate and depressed than *concinna*.

Occurs in New Mexico and Arizona.

8. **Œ. interjectionis** Crotch.—Elongate oval, moderately convex, shining. Antennæ brown, half the length of body. third joint a little longer than fourth. Head bicolored, front yellow, occiput piceous, frontal carina indistinct, tubercles feeble, vertex coarsely punctured between the eyes. Thorax twice as wide as long, feebly, arcuately narrowed to the front, lateral margin distinct, color pale yellow, surface smooth, shining. Elytra a little wider at base than the thorax, humeri rounded, umbone distinct, disc finely punctate, smoother near apex, piceous with blue or green lustre, margin narrowly yellow, disc with an interrupted vitta near the suture in a general form like an exclamation mark (!). Epipleuræ pale, the inner half near the base piceous. Body beneath reddish yellow, the metasternum posteriorly piceous Anterior and middle legs and posterior tibiæ brownish. Abdomen shining, very sparsely punctate. Length .23—.25 inch.; 6—6.5 mm. Plate V, fig. 6.

This species is very constant. I have one specimen in which the anterior portion of the vitta is indistinct. The specimen described by Crotch was plainly immature, as it shows none of the metallic surface of all the other specimens examined.

Œ. gracilis Jacoby (Biol. Cent. Am. vi, i, p. 420, pl. xxiv, fig. 14), is merely a variety of this species with the subsutural white vitta entire. According to Mr. Jacoby the elytra may be entirely blue-green, without vitta.

Occurs in Texas (Waco, Belfrage) and Mexico.

9. **Œ. fimbriata** Illig.—Oblong oval, moderately convex, feebly shining, yellowish white, thorax maculate, elytra vittate or not. Antennæ half as long as the body, piceous, scape often paler. third joint a little longer than fourth. Head variable in color, coarsely and closely punctate between the eyes, frontal carina obtuse, tubercles distinct. Thorax more than twice as wide as long, feebly arcuately narrowed to front, margin narrow, front angles not dentiform, disc finely alutaceous, moderately coarsely punctate, color yellowish with five piceous spots usually more or less confluent; scutellum black. Elytra scarcely wider than the thorax, humeri rounded, umbone not prominent, surface closely punctate, more finely at apex, color either entirely yellow or with the three piceous vittæ, sutural, median and marginal, with intergrades. Epipleuræ variable. Body beneath entirely pale, except the sides and posterior portion of metasternum, which are brown or piceous. Abdomen shining, sparsely punctate, distinctly pubescent. Legs yellow, tibiæ and tarsi piceous. Length .20—.30 inch.; 5—7.5 mm. Plate V, fig. 8.

This species presents two ultimate varieties, the vittate and the entirely pale. In the vittate form the stripes are never sharply defined, the median especially shading off indefinitely, while the sutural and lateral are often more like stains than vittæ.

In the typical or vittate form the head is partly black, the front being nearly always pale. The sutural vitta is extremely narrow, the median broad, but variable in width, sometimes not wider than the yellow on each side, or so wide that the yellow is nearly linear. The marginal vitta is also very narrow, and is at the extreme edge of the elytra, the epipleuræ are therefore black at apical half and pale at base.

The pale variety has an entirely pale head. The elytra are entirely yellow, except an extremely narrow sutural stripe. This form resembles, at first sight, similar variations which occur in *Disonycha quinquelineata*.

Occurs from North Carolina to Florida and Texas.

10. **Œ. remula** n. sp.—Oblong oval, moderately convex, feebly shining, beneath black, above yellow, thorax maculate, elytra each with three vittæ with bluish green surface lustre. Antennæ piceous, not as long as half the body, third joint longer than the fourth. Head black, frontal spot yellow, coarsely and deeply punctured, frontal carina obtuse, the tubercles indistinct. Thorax more than twice as wide as long, sides arcuately narrowing to the front, margin narrow, disc somewhat irregular, sparsely obsoletely punctate, color yellow, with five piceous spots more or less confluent in the form of ʍ. Elytra a little wider at base than the thorax, humeri rounded, umbone not prominent, surface indistinctly alutaceous, sparsely, very indistinctly punctate, color yellow, with the sutural, median and submarginal vittæ piceous with blue-green lustre, the submarginal not reaching the humerus. Epipleuræ pale, the inner border piceous. Prothorax beneath yellow, body black, abdomen black, the last segment yellow, the surface shining, coarsely sparsely punctate. Legs entirely black. Length .18—.22 inch.; 4.5–5.5 mm. Plate V. fig. 7.

This insect so resembles a Disonycha of the *caroliniana* series that on first impression it would be placed among them. Its facies will enable it to be at once known, together with the fact that in no other vittate species are the legs and underside black. It varies in having the median vitta narrower.

Occurs in Arizona, special region unknown.

11. **Œ. petaurista** Fab.—Oval, sometimes slightly oblong, convex, shining, above yellow, thorax with a variable central spot, elytra each with three black vittæ. Antennæ half as long as the body, piceous, the basal joints usually paler. Head reddish brown, cribrately punctate, a moderately deep longitudinal and feebler transverse groove, frontal carina short, tuberculiform, tubercles distinct, but flat. Thorax more than twice as wide as long, sides arcuately narrowing to the front, margin moderately wide, anterior angles dentiform, disc sparsely punctate, yellow, a central spot, piceous, of variable size and form; scutellum black. Elytra scarcely wider at base than the thorax, humeri rounded, surface always distinctly punctate, but variable in degree, color yellowish, with three piceous vittæ, sutural, median and submarginal. Epipleuræ testaceous, the inner edge

at basal half piceous. Body beneath and legs reddish yellow, the anterior and
middle tibiae and tarsi brownish. Abdomen shining, very sparsely punctate.
Length .22—.31 inch.; 5.5—8.5 mm. Plate V. figs. 1—5.

This is the largest species in our fauna, and one of the most variable. The variations are in form, sculpture and coloration.

The usual form of this species is oval, usually rather broadly, but
occasionally oblong. The elytral sculpture may be as coarse and
dense as in *thoracica*, or comparatively smooth. The median vitta
is usually equal in width to the yellow on either side of it, but may
become broader, and specimens have been seen in which the sutural
and median vittae are confluent. A specimen in my cabinet from
Georgia has the submarginal vitta extremely narrow, while another
from Florida has the median vitta slender and broadly interrupted
at middle. The discal spot of the thorax is variable, but never large,
and does not often form a transverse band.

A remarkable variety has been observed, which, for convenience,
I call *brevilineata* (Plate V, fig. 4), in which, with an entirely pale
margin, the disc is black or slightly bluish, with a short yellow vitta
beginning within the humeral umbone. Another variety in the
cabinet of Mr. H. A. Kelley has the median vitta almost entirely
obliterated.

The intrahumeral impression at the base of the elytra is usually
feeble, and the punctures in the vicinity not more conspicuous. Two
specimens in my cabinet have the depression deep, and from it pro-
ceed coarse punctures extending at least one-fourth the length of the
elytra. These also agree in having the submarginal vitta very narrow. It is quite possible that this vitta may disappear, in which case
the specimens would agree very well with Harold's description of
Horni.

Occurs from North Carolina to Texas.

12. **Œ. tenuilineata** n. sp.—Broadly oval, moderately convex, shining,
reddish yellow beneath, pale above, elytra with very slender vittæ, sutural, median and marginal. Antennæ scarcely half as long as the body, piceous, the
three basal joints paler, terminal joint partly ♂, or entirely yellow ♀. Head
reddish yellow, smooth at middle, coarsely cribrate at the sides, frontal carina
very short and obtuse, tubercles distinct. Thorax more than twice as wide as
long, widest at base ♀, or not wider at base than middle ♂, sides arcuate, margin rather widely explanate, anterior angles distinctly dentiform, surface smooth,
shining, with scarcely any evidence of punctures, color pale yellow with faint
traces of five darker spots. Elytra scarcely wider than the thorax, the humeri
obtuse, umbone scarcely prominent, a slight impression within it, disc moderately coarsely, not closely punctate near the base, gradually more finely to apex.

the coarsest punctures are close to the margin and extend around the apex; color pale yellow, sutural vitta narrow, entire, median vitta very narrow, submarginal also narrow, curving at base around the umbone, nearly joining the median. Epipleuræ pale, narrowly piceous within. Body beneath and legs reddish yellow. Abdomen shining, sparsely punctate, more coarsely at the sides. Length .25—.28 inch.; 6.5—7 mm. Pl. V, fig. 14.

This species is remarkable in the very slender elytral vittæ, being in this genus the analogue of *tenuicornis* in Disonycha. The thoracic margin is more widely explanate than usual in this series. The male is shorter and broader, the thorax at base not wider than at middle. In the female the terminal joint of the antennæ is entirely pale, in the male only the apex of the joint.

Occurs in southern Arizona (Morrison).

13. **Œ. miniata** Fab.—Oval, convex, sometimes slightly oblong, moderately shining, ferruginous beneath, yellow above, thorax with a brown fascia, elytra with a sutural and median vitta. Antennæ not as long as half the body, piceous, three basal joints paler, third joint a little shorter than the fourth. Head ferruginous, carina tuberculiform, the tubercles distinct, vertex and occiput coarsely punctured, closely near the eyes. Thorax three times as wide as long, sides arcuately narrowed to the front, lateral margin moderately explanate, front angles dentiform, disc sparsely punctate, yellow, a brownish central space usually forming a broad fascia; scutellum black. Elytra scarcely wider at base than the thorax, humeri rounded, umbone distinct, smooth, surface variably punctate, either moderately coarse and dense, or fine and indistinct. with all intergrades; color yellow, with the sutural black vitta entire, a median vitta beginning at the umbone and nearly reaching the tip. Epipleuræ pale, narrowly piceous within. Body beneath and legs reddish brown, the anterior and middle tibiæ and tarsi darker. Abdomen shining, coarsely sparsely punctate and with few hairs. Length .20 –.25 inch.; 5—6.5 mm. Plate V, fig. 13.

This species shows the same style of variation as in *petaurista*. As a rule the males are less frequent than the females, and their form shorter and more convex than the other sex. The punctuation varies in degree, some few being quite as in *vians* (var. *scripticollis*), although less dense, while in others the punctuation is more sparse, less distinct, and near the apex quite obliterated. The median vitta is usually as wide as the yellow space next the suture, but in others either broader or narrower.

After a study of the material before me I am satisfied that *jocosa* Harold is founded on a male of this species. The thorax is apparently less than three times as wide as long and scarcely punctate, but in the series before me from all parts of our country, numbering thirty-six, I can find no reason for recognizing the form as distinct.

Occurs everywhere east of the Mississippi and in Texas.

14. **Œ. Horni** Harold.—Oval, moderately shining, head ferruginous, thorax and elytra testaceous, the former with a piceorufous fascia, the latter densely and coarsely punctured, sutural vitta rather wide, vitta broad and apparently closely to the lateral margin, beneath piceous, legs rufopiceous. Length 6 mm.

Of somewhat broadly oval form, moderately convex, not feebly shining from the dense punctuation. Head rusty red, front in the middle smooth, around coarsely punctured. Thorax moderately coarsely punctate, more finely at middle, the front angles dentiform; color reddish yellow, with a transverse reddish brown fascia; scutellum black, shining. Elytra densely, equally and moderately coarsely punctured; umbone not prominent; color yellow, a broad sutural vitta gradually narrower posteriorly and a second equally broad, which approaches closely to the lateral border, the yellow space between these vittae equally broad from base to apex, but narrower than the lateral black vitta; underside brownish black, legs reddish brown, also prosternum. Antennæ dark brown, basal joints scarcely paler, joints 3 and 4 usually long. Epipleuræ yellow, brown within.

Baron Harold compares this with *miniata*, and says that the most nearly approaching specimen of that is much more finely punctured. I have not seen any specimens which I can safely refer to this.

Occurs in Texas.

15. **Œ. Ulkei** n. sp.—Rather broadly oval, convex, moderately shining, beneath pale reddish brown, above yellow, thorax with a broad pale brown band, elytra with the sutural and a rather broad median brown vitta. Antennæ half as long as the body, piceous, three basal joints paler, third and fourth joints equal in length. Head brownish, coarsely punctured between the eyes, occiput smooth, frontal carina tuberculiform, tubercles distinct. Thorax three times as wide as long, sides arcuately narrowed to the front, lateral margin rather narrow, anterior angles distinctly dentiform, surface alutaceous, distinctly, but sparsely punctate, color yellow, with a broad brownish median fascia; scutellum piceous. Elytra a little wider at base than the thorax, humeri distinct, but obtuse, umbone moderately prominent and smooth, surface moderately finely, not closely punctate, smoother near the apex; color yellow, with a brown sutural vitta, broader at base, median vitta broad, the outer edge parallel with the lateral margin, the inner arcuate, the vitta becoming gradually wider from base beyond the middle, then rapidly narrower to apex. Epipleuræ pale, narrowly piceous within. Abdomen shining, moderately coarsely and closely punctate. Length .18—.20 inch.; 4.5—5 mm   Pl. V, fig. 15.

This species is the smallest in the present series. At first glance it resembles small specimens of *Calligrapha elegans*. It is allied to *miniata*, but is smaller, with a smoother head and differing in the proportion of the third and fourth joints of the antennæ; here these joints are equal in length, in *miniata* the fourth is very plainly longer.

Œ. Horni Har. is also related, but is described as having the median fascia close to the margin and the elytra densely punctured.

Occurs in Florida. I am indebted to Mr. H. Ulke for the specimen in my cabinet.

16. **Œ. longula** Harold.—Elongate oblong, ferruginous, thorax yellow, obsoletely punctate, with a ferruginous band ; elytral humeri not sulcate within, roughly rather densely punctate, suture and discoidal vitta ferruginous brown. Epipleuræ yellow, ferruginous within ; antennæ brownish, three basal joints paler, third joint distinctly shorter than the fourth. Length 6.5 mm.

Baron Harold compares this species with *umbratica*, which is much larger. I have not seen anything in any of our cabinets which can be identified with this species, although I suspect it may be a *petaurista* of the more elongate forms in which the submarginal vitta has been lost. A specimen of that species is now before me with the submarginal vitta so narrow that it would readily escape notice. The comparison with *umbratica* adds a little to the probability of the correctness of my surmise.

Occurs, according to Harold, in California. This seems to me very doubtful.

17. **Œ. Jacobiana** n. sp.—Oval, slightly oblong, surface shining, beneath entirely pale reddish yellow, thorax yellowish, immaculate, elytra pale brown, with large yellow spots. Antennæ not reaching the middle of the body, piceous, the three basal joints and half the fourth pale, the terminal also yellow. Occiput piceous, front pale, frontal carina moderately prominent, tubercles distinct, a well marked impressed line between the eyes, a few coarse punctures on each side near the eyes. Thorax more than twice as wide as long, narrowed in front, base scarcely wider than middle, margin rather broad, reticulate when viewed with transmitted light, anterior angles dentiform, surface almost absolutely smooth, yellow, immaculate; scutellum piceous. Elytra a little wider at base than the thorax, humeri obtuse, umbone moderately prominent, smooth, limited within by a rather deep impression, lateral margin narrowly explanate, surface shining, sparsely rather finely punctate near base, smooth at apex, color pale brown with large yellow spots, the first basal of irregular outline, leaving the umbone brown, behind this two smaller oval spots, followed by a broad sinuous fascia interrupted by the suture, near the apex a spot of semi-oval form. Abdomen shining, sparsely, obsoletely, coarsely punctate. Legs entirely reddish yellow. Length .25 inch.; 6.5 mm. Plate V, fig. 16.

Of this species I have seen but one male. The thorax is similar in form to that of the male of *tenuilineata*, and it is probable that in the other sex the thorax is widest at base. It is remarkable that in the two species with this form of thorax in the male the terminal joint of the antennæ should be pale. The latter character, together with the style of elytral ornamentation, will render this species easily known.

Occurs in southern Arizona.

Series B.

Elytra without explanate margin, the epipleuræ very narrow and vertical poste-
    riorly..2.
Elytra with explanate margin, the epipleuræ wide and horizontal..................4.
  2.—Elytra blue, head and thorax dull red, form oblong .....19. **indigoptera.**
    Elytra never blue...3.
  3.--Form oblong.
    Body above and beneath cream-yellow, surface smooth and shining.
                                      18. **flavida.**
    Elytra yellowish, with a narrowly oval sutural space with irregular
    margins, and which sometimes divides into vittæ........20. **texana.**
    Form oval.
    Elytra yellow, with on oval discal black space, with regular borders, and
    which never reaches the tips of suture; head always yellow.
                                        21. **thyamoides.**
  4.—Elytra broadly oval, sides much arcuate, coarsely punctate, entirely dirty
    yellow, with indistinct vittæ, or with the disc entirely black, margin
    only pale..22. **limbalis.**
    Elytra with sides feebly arcuate, or nearly parallel; the surface yellow,
    with piceous or brown spots, or bands, or with the disc entirely pi-
    ceous ....5.
  5.--Thorax very coarsely punctured ; elytra with a more or less evident costa
    from the humeri to apex......................23. **sexmaculata.**
    Thorax finely sparsely punctate, or smooth ....6.
  6.—Head coarsely closely punctate....................24. **suturalis.**
    Head sparsely punctate, or almost smooth........................7.
  7.—Smaller species, usually with the elytra in great part piceous.
                                        25. **quercata.**
    Larger, elytra yellow, ornamented with black spots tending to form trans-
    verse bands..26. **scalaris.**

18. **Œ. flavida** n. sp.—Oblong, depressed, scarcely at all oval, shining, beneath reddish yellow, above yellowish white. Antennæ slender, a little longer
than half the body, testaceous, slightly darker externally, third joint very
little shorter than the fourth. Head entirely smooth, a deep transverse impression between the eyes. Thorax two and a half times as wide as long, very little
wider at base, sides arcuate, margin explanate and anteriorly reflexed, front angles not dentiform, disc polished. Elytra oblong, sides scarcely arcuate, humeri
obtuse, margin not explanate, umbone not prominent, surface smooth, with
scarcely any trace of even fine punctures. Abdomen smooth, impunctate.
Length .18--.22 inch. ; 4.5—5.5 mm.

There is no species known to me in our fauna so completely deprived of surface sculpture as this one. This, with the oblong form
and ivory-yellow color, will enable the species to be at once known.
Occurs at El Paso, Texas (G. W. Dunn).

19. **Œ. indigoptera** Lec.—Oblong oval, subdepressed, reddish brown,
feebly shining, elytra entirely blue. Antennæ slender, longer than half the
body, rufescent, darker externally, third and fourth joints equal. Head sparsely

punctate, a moderate interocular depression. Thorax not twice as wide as long, arcuately narrower to apex, margin moderately explanate, the front angle dentiform, surface distinctly alutaceous, sparsely, finely punctate. Elytra oval, slightly oblong, humeri obtuse, margin not explanate, umbone not prominent, disc moderately coarsely and closely, not deeply, punctate, surface alutaceous, entirely blue or bluish green. Epipleuræ piceous, narrow at apical half. Abdomen shining, sparsely punctate. Length .12--.16 inch.; 3--4 mm.

Similar in form to *thyamoides*, but differs in color. The sinuation of the outer edge of the posterior tibiæ is quite feeble and must be looked for with some care.

Occurs in Georgia and Florida.

20. **Œ. texana** Crotch.—Elongate oval, subdepressed, moderately shining, beneath reddish yellow, above pale yellow, each elytron with the sutural and median vitta. Antennæ slender, longer than half the body, outer half piceous, basal five joints paler, third and fourth joints equal. Head reddish yellow punctate, a deep impression from eye to eye, frontal carina obtuse, tubercles indistinct. Thorax not quite twice as wide as long, very little wider at base than apex, sides arcuate, margin moderately explanate, anterior angles slightly dentiform, surface finely alutaceous, sparsely punctate; scutellum black. Elytra not wider at base than the thorax, oblong oval, humeri obliterated, umbone not distinct, margin not explanate, moderately coarsely, not densely punctate, smooth near apex, color pale yellow, normally with the sutural vitta entire, a median vitta exactly parallel not reaching the apex. Epipleuræ pale. Body beneath and posterior legs reddish yellow, front and middle legs paler. Abdomen shining, very coarsely punctured. Length .16--.18 inch.; 4--4.5 mm. Plate V, figs. 9--12.

This species is very like a *Systena* in form and coloration, being but little broader.

The markings vary notably. The vitta normally are as described, extending from the basal edge. Specimens occur in which the median vittæ do not reach the base; others again have the vittæ confluent in a discal space, in which, however, the edges are irregular. Still more rarely the sutural vitta alone remains. The head may be fuscous.

The only species with which some varieties of this might be confounded is *thyamoides*, which is broader, the sides of elytra distinctly explanate, and the discal spot regularly oval, not reaching the apex.

Occurs in Texas (Dallas).

21. **Œ. thyamoides** Crotch.—Oval, subdepressed, moderately shining, reddish yellow beneath, pale yellow above, elytra with a broadly oval, common, black spot. Antennæ slender, longer than half the body, piceous, three or four basal joints paler, third and fourth equal. Head pale, occiput slightly darker, finely alutaceous, sparsely punctate, a deep, transverse, interocular impression, frontal carina obtuse, the tubercles indistinct. Thorax more than twice as wide

as long, distinctly broader at base than apex, sides arcuate, margin rather broadly explanate, front angles dentiform, surface finely alutaceous, sparsely indistinctly punctulate; scutellum black. Elytra oval humeri rounded, margin narrowly explanate and slightly reflexed, surface rather coarsely and closely punctate, smoother near the apex, color yellow, with a common discal black space, never reaching the apex, variable in extent. Epipleuræ pale. Body beneath and legs reddish yellow, abdomen smooth, sparsely indistinctly punctate. Length .15--.18 inch.; 4--4.5 mm. Plate VI, fig. 8.

This species resembles, in minature, *Disonycha discoidea*. It varies but little, except in the extent of the black discal space, which at times leaves but a narrow pale border, while it may become so narrow as to occupy but half the space between the suture and margin on each side.

Occurs west of the Mississippi River from Dakota to Texas.

22. Œ. limbalis Mels.—Broadly oval, subdepressed, moderately shining, yellowish testaceous, darker beneath, elytra with short fuscous vittæ, often confluent in a large discal spot. Antennæ slender, longer than half the body, testaceous, darker externally, third and fourth joints equal. Head pale, occiput darker, fuscous, never piceous. surface alutaceous, sparsely punctate, a deep interocular impression. Thorax nearly three times as wide as long, widest at base, sides arcuate, margin broadly explanate, front angles not dentiform, surface alutaceous, obsoletely, sparsely punctulate. Elytra broadly oval, margin explanate and slightly reflexed, umbone moderately prominent, slightly impressed within, surface moderately, coarsely and closely punctate, with fuscous vittæ as follows : a very narrow sutural vitta, not reaching the base, a short oblique vitta each side of scutellum, a slightly oblique vitta beginning at the umbone extending two-thirds to apex, a shorter vitta from the umbone parallel with the lateral margin ; these vittæ may be one or all absent, or all confluent in a large discal space. Epipleuræ yellow, wide. Body beneath darker than above, sometimes pale brown. Abdomen shining, sparsely punctate. Length .14--.20 inch.; 3.5--5 mm. Plate VI, fig. 7.

This is the most broadly oval species in our fauna. The elytral sculpture varies in degree from relatively fine to coarse. The markings vary as indicated above. This species is closely related to *oculata* and *sublineata*, which occur south of our fauna, in both of which there is a similarity of style of elytral marking. Ours is especially related to *oculata* as figured, but which seems to me doubtfully determined in Biol. Cent. Am.

The typical specimen described by Melsheimer is one of those in which the elytra are black, with the outer and apical border narrowly pale, resembling *thyamoides*, and also *quercata*. From the former it may be distinguished by the epipleural structure and from the latter by the more oval (not quadrate) elytra with much more

evident punctuation. The striped form, which, for convenience, may
be known as *subvittata*, seems the more abundant, and it is remarkable that it has not received a name.

Occurs from Massachusetts to Iowa, Georgia and Texas, and intermediate localities.

23. **Œ. sexmaculata** Illig.—Oblong oval, depressed, not shining, above
reddish yellow, thorax and elytra with piceous spots. Antennæ slender, longer
than half the body, yellowish testaceous, third and fourth joints equal. Head
reddish yellow, occiput piceous, alutaceous, coarsely sparsely punctate, a short,
moderately deep, transverse impression between the eyes, frontal carina obtuse,
tubercles not distinct. Thorax twice as wide as long, arcuately, but slightly
narrowing to apex, margin widely explanate, anterior angles feebly dentiform,
surface alutaceous, coarsely not closely punctate, color reddish yellow with a
large brown space each side. Elytra a little wider at base than the thorax, humeri obtuse, umbone moderately prominent, smooth, a distinct, rather long
sulcus within it and a distinct costa or plica extending from the umbone nearly
to the apex, margin distinctly explanate, surface coarsely, deeply and moderately
closely punctate, color reddish yellow, with piceous or black spots as follows:
one at umbone, a second posteriorly near the side margin, a third between these,
but near the suture, these are often connected, forming a broad X, behind the
middle an irregular transverse fascia, broadest at the suture. Epipleuræ pale,
broad in the entire length. Prothorax beneath pale. Meso-metasternum piceous, abdomen reddish, usually darker at middle, surface finely alutaceous, sparsely
punctate, with few hairs. Legs rufotestaceous. Length .14—.16 inch.; 3.5—4
mm. Plate VI, fig. 3.

While this species varies considerably in the extent of its elytral
markings it is readily known by the very coarse punctuation of the
entire upper surface and the costa which extends from the umbone
to near the apex. There is often a second short costa within this
near the apex.

Occurs from the New England States westward to Missouri and
south to Florida.

24. **Œ. suturalis** Fab.—Oblong oval, depressed, feebly shining, pale yellow,
base of elytra, suture and spots on each side brown. Antennæ longer than half
the body, slender, testaceous, third joint very slightly shorter than the fourth.
Head yellow in front, vertex and occiput brown, coarsely and sparsely punctate,
a deep transverse depression between the eyes, frontal carina short and obtuse,
the tubercles smooth. Thorax more than twice as wide as long, sides arcuately
narrowed to apex, margin broadly explanate, front angles dentiform, color yellow, immaculate, alutaceous, sparsely and very indistinctly punctate. Elytra
not wider than the thorax, humeri obtuse, umbone moderate, limited within by
a distinct sulcus, margin distinctly explanate, surface coarsely and moderately
closely punctate, smoother at apex, color pale yellow, the base between the umbones, suture three-fourths to apex, and often two spots on each elytron brown.
Epipleuræ broad, pale. Body beneath and legs pale. Abdomen shining, sparsely
punctate. Length .14—.16 inch.; 3.5 -4 mm. Plate VI, fig. 5.

It is remarkable that this species should have been made a synonym of *quercata* after the good description and figure by Olivier. The brown color on the elytra extends along the base between the umbones on each of which it forms a slight hook. The lower edge curves inward and downward along the suture, at the middle of the suture it is angulate, opposite which is a round spot, extending to three-fourths the band terminates abruptly with an angulation opposite which is another spot. Either one or both of the spots may be wanting.

Occurs in Georgia and Florida.

25. **Œ. quercata** Fab.—Oval, depressed, piceous, thorax entirely or with the sides pale, elytra with pale border, surface moderately shining. Antennae slender, longer than half the body, pale yellowish, the outer joints often darker, third joint slightly shorter than the fourth Head piceous, front paler, a very few indistinct punctures posteriorly, interocular depression deep, frontal carina obtuse, tubercles not distinctly separated. Thorax more than twice as wide as long, arcuately narrower to apex, margin widely explanate, disc finely alutaceous, obsoletely, finely, sparsely punctate, anterior angles dentiform, color often entirely yellow (*quercata*), sometimes piceous with the border yellow (*obsidiana*). Elytra not wider at base than the thorax, humeri rounded, umbone distinct, within sulcate, margin explanate, disc distinctly punctate, smoother near apex, color piceous, the entire margin pale, narrower along the sides, wider at apex, Epipleuræ broad, pale. Body beneath and posterior legs piceo-rufous, front and middle legs pale. Abdomen shining, sparsely, indistinctly punctate. Length .14–.15 inch; 3.5–4 mm. Plate VI, figs. 1-2-4.

In addition to the two varieties above indicated, a specimen (Pl. VI, fig. 4) from Illinois varies in a peculiar way. The elytra are dark brown, the entire limb as usual pale and with a transversely oval spot at basal third, another behind the middle, these broadly united along the suture. No other differences can be detected, and I therefore consider it merely a variation.

Widely distributed in the entire eastern United States.

26. **Œ. scalaris** Mels.—Oval, slightly oblong, depressed, shining. Antennae slender, half as long as the body, piceous, basal joints paler, third and fourth equal. Head in great part pale, piceous along the middle, very indistinctly punctate, interocular depression deep, frontal carina obtuse, tubercles distinct. Thorax more than twice as wide as long, arcuately narrowed to the front, margin widely explanate, anterior angles dentiform, surface alutaceous, very sparsely and finely punctate, color yellow, with a brownish spot on each side, sometimes forming a large discal space. Elytra not wider at base than the thorax, humeri rounded, umbone distinct, limited within by a distinct sulcus, margin moderately explanate, surface rather coarsely punctate near the base, smoother at tip, general color yellow, a broad basal black fascia of irregular form enclosing a pale

spot each side of scutellum, an oblique band extends from umbone toward the suture and at middle of elytra bends abruptly outward toward the margin, a transverse fascia at apical third tridentate on front and posterior borders, extending narrowly along the suture in front. Epipleuræ pale, broad. Body beneath piceous. Abdomen brown, paler at apex, finely alutaceous, sparsely punctate. Legs entirely pale. Length .18—.20 inch.; 4.5—5 mm. Pl. V, figs. 17–20.

The above description of elytral markings is such as will be found in the majority of specimens. There is, however, very great variation in the extent of the black markings by increase or decrease of the style described.

A specimen in my cabinet from North Carolina has the elytra nearly as in *quercata*, except that there is a small oblique pale spot on each side slightly in front of middle and nearer the suture.

A specimen from Texas has much smoother elytra and with the black reduced to spots placed as follows: one on umbone, a second posterior and more internal, third at middle and larger, a fourth smaller, between this and apex, near the margin are small spots, one between the first two, a second opposite the large spot. With more specimens to prove its constancy this latter may be found specifically distinct. Unless there are some well defined structural characters it is far better to allow doubtful uniques to remain unnamed, especially in Chrysomelidæ.

Occurs from the Middle States to Kansas, Georgia and Texas.

Group V.—ASPICELÆ.

Antennæ 10-jointed. Prothorax transverse, without discal impressions at base. Anterior coxal cavities open behind. Mesosternum distinct. Tibiæ (especially the posterior) broadly grooved on their outer edge for nearly their entire length, the groove limited each side by a ridge. Last joint of posterior tarsi not globoso-inflated, although at times thickened.

This group occupies nearly an intermediate position between the Œdionyches and Disonychæ, differing from the former in the absence of the inflated joint and from the second by the broadly grooved tibiæ.

Two genera are known in our fauna :

Antennæ filiform ; last joint of hind tarsus gradually thicker toward apex ; posterior tibiæ sinuate on the outer edge near the apex..........**Homophœta.**
Antennæ flattened, broader at middle, slender at tip ; last joint of hind tarsus slender ; tibiæ not sinuate.. ....**Phydanis.**

With Homophœta I have united Asphæra, as there does not seem to be any *structural* character separating them. It will be observed that Mr. Jacoby places them side by side in the " Biologia," while in the " Genera" Chapuis placed them in separate tribes. The species belonging to this tribe are all from the southwest, from the Rio Grande region.

HOMOPHŒTA Chev.

The differences between this genus and Œdionychis reside entirely in the fact that the claw joint of the posterior tarsus is not abruptly globularly dilated, but is gradually expanded toward the tip in an ovate manner. This, too, is somewhat variable, and while well marked in *æquinoctialis* and *abdominalis* is scarcely more dilated in *lustrans* than in Disonycha. The posterior tibiæ are grooved on the outer edge and above the insertion of the tarsi is sinuate and with the small tooth as will be observed in Œdionychis. Pl. VII, fig. 12. Under the above name I have united species which are now placed in two genera: *Homophœta* and *Asphæra*. I find it impossible to define these genera, much less to place them in separate tribes, and I am forced to believe that many of the genera of Halticini have no other basis than cabinet convenience without structural difference.

The species known to me are :

Elytra blue, or violet-black, with large yellowish white spots; head in great part black ; abdomen yellow ....**æquinoctialis.**
Elytra bright blue, smooth ; head almost entirely yellow; abdomen yellow.
lustrans.
Elytra dull blue, distinctly punctate; head entirely black; abdomen piceous, vaguely paler at apex and sides ....**abdominalis.**
These species are all from our southwestern limits.

H. æquinoctialis Linn. – Oval, slightly oblong, surface shining, thorax yellow, elytra violet-black, with four more or less oval, yellow-white spots on each side and a short submarginal stripe. Antennæ slender, more than half the length of the body, piceous, underside of two basal joints testaceous. Head b'ack, frontal spot and clypeus yellow, labrum black, frontal tubercles indistinct, surface smooth, a few punctures near the eyes. Thorax not twice as wide as long, very little wider at base than apex, sides arcuate, margin narrowly ex- planate, anterior angles not dentiform, surface smooth and shining. Elytra scarcely wider at base than the thorax, humeri rounded, umbone not prominent, surface smooth, shining, violet-black, with yellow-white spots arranged as fol lows: one on each side of scutellum, one transversely near the side, one at middle near the suture, somewhat oblique, a transversely oval spot near the apex, a short subhumeral stripe. Epipleuræ black. Body beneath entirely reddish yellow. Anterior and middle legs entirely piceous, posterior femora yellow, tibiæ and tarsi piceous. Length .30 inch.; 7.5 mm.

The conspicuous marking on the elytra render this an easily known species. As far as specimens have been examined it is practically invariable in its markings.

Occurs quite commonly in Texas near the Rio Grande, extending through Mexico to Brazil.

II. lustrans Crotch.—Oval, moderately shining, beneath in great part yellow, head and thorax yellow, elytra cobalt-blue. Antennæ half as long as the body, piceous; underside of two basal joints pale. Head entirely yellow, except a narrow fuscous band between the eyes, frontal tubercles distinct, a transverse impression above them, surface entirely smooth. Labrum piceous. Thorax twice as wide as long, widest at base, sides slightly arcuate, margin not explanate, anterior angles simple, color yellow, smooth and impunctate. Elytra a little wider at base than the thorax, humeri rounded, umbone moderately distinct, limited within by a slight impression, surface smooth, almost absolutely impunctate. Epipleuræ black Body beneath and abdomen entirely yellow, the sides of the metasternum sometimes piceous. Femora yellow, the anterior and middle tibiæ and tarsi piceous, sometimes paler on the inner side, posterior tibiæ piceous near the tip. Abdomen shining, sparsely punctate. Length .26 inch.; 6.5 mm.

This insect bears a very close resemblance to *Dison. varicornis*. The claw joint of the posterior tarsus is still less thickened than in either of the species of this genus, and, by the systems of classification, would be very difficult to place generically. It is not, however, a true Œdionychis, and the only course to adopt is that suggested by Harold.

Occurs in Texas.

II. abdominalis Chev. Oval, feebly shining, beneath piceous, thorax yellow, elytra blue, or blue-black Antennæ half as long as the body, piceous, third joint slightly shorter than the fourth. Head black, shining, frontal tu bercles moderately distinct, a transverse depression above them, surface smooth, a few punctures near the eyes. Thorax twice as wide as long, distinctly broader at base, sides arcuate, margin moderately explanate, front angles not dentiform, color yellow, surface smooth and impunctate. Elytra a little wider at base than the thorax, humeri rounded, umbone moderate, limited within by a distinct depression, surface closely punctate, more coarsely and densely in the female. Epipleuræ black. Body beneath black, shining, abdomen black, the apex and sides indeterminately rufous, surface sparsely punctate. Femora of all the legs yellow, tibiæ and tarsi black. Length .30—.40 inch.; 7.5—10 mm.

The elytral sculpture is very like that of *Œd. thoracica* in the female, but in the male the punctures are finer and apparently less closely placed.

The specimens marked Texas in my own and the LeConte cabinet were from the old Berlandiere collection, and are open to some doubt as to locality. It is common in the adjacent regions of Mexico.

PHYDANIS n. g.

Head oval, inserted as far as the eyes, front oblique, the carina short, obtuse, bifurcate in front, forming an elevated margin, which extends to the sides of the buccal cavity, the tubercles distinct, separated by a deeply impressed line, sides of head in front of eyes deeply concave, forming a lodgement for the first antennal joint. Labrum transverse, entire, the basal membrane visible. Maxillary palpi short and stout, second joint conical, third obovate, truncate, fourth conical and slightly longer. Eyes oval, not prominent. Antennæ a little longer than half the body, flattened, more slender to apex, first joint moderately long and stout, the underside broadly flattened and smooth as well as concave longitudinally, second joint oval, narrower than the first and not more than one-third as long, third joint longer and broader, wider at apex, fourth joint similar, 5–7 equal in length, a little shorter than fourth and gradually narrower, 8–10 gradually longer and less flattened, eleventh longer, slender, the apex prolonged. Thorax very broad, broadly emarginate at apex, the anterior angles obtuse in front, sides feebly arcuate, narrowly margined, hind angles distinct, base arcuate, more lobed at middle, a distinct basal marginal line, but no discal impressions. Elytra not wider than thorax, sides feebly arcuate, disc convex with confused punctuation, but with coarser punctures forming indistinct striæ near the base. Prosternum moderately separating the coxæ, nearly as elevated, apex not broader, the coxal cavities rather widely open behind. Mesosternum distinct, oblique. Ventral segments all free. Legs rather stout, the tibiæ all broader toward apex, their outer edge rather broadly and deeply sulcate, with an elevated margin each side. Posterior tibiæ obliquely truncate, with a short terminal spur. Anterior and middle tarsi with first joint oval, second shorter and narrower, third bilobed, fourth slender. Posterior tarsi with first joint slender, a little shorter than the following joints together. Claws on all the feet distinctly appendiculate. Form oblong oval, glabrous, body winged.

After as careful a search of the literature as possible no genus has been found to which the above description will apply. The antennal characters do not seem to be at all like this in any other Halticide.

The first joint when in repose is folded obliquely downward and backward in front of the eye resting in a broad and deep concavity between the eye and the lateral border of the mouth, the bifid frontal carina forming the anterior border of the concavity. The first antennal joint is broadly flattened beneath and bent to conform to the curve of the side of the head. The third and fourth joints are the broadest, and from this they gradually narrow to apex. When the antennæ are viewed on their narrow edge all the joints are equally thick, but when seen from above are as described. The legs are all rather stout, the four anterior femora being slightly swollen also, the posterior are broadly oval and but feebly sulcate for the tibiæ.

These rather peculiar characters make the genus not an easy one to place satisfactorily, but taking the other characters in reference to their importance in other genera—the open coxal cavities, the non-impressed thorax and the broadly sulcate and margined tibiæ— no other course remains than to place it in the Aspicelites of Chapuis.

P. bicolor n. sp.—Oblong oval, moderately convex; beneath head and thorax reddish yellow, elytra bluish (not unlike in form and color to *Gastroidea polygoni*). Antennæ brownish, three basal joints rufotestaceous. Head sparsely, very finely punctate. Thorax nearly three times as wide as long, slightly narrowed in front, sides feebly arcuate, disc moderately convex, with two or three vague depressions at the declivity, surface finely, indistinctly punctate Elytra not wider at base than the thorax, humeri broadly rounded, umbone not prominent, sides feebly arcuate, disc moderately convex, the punctures moderately fine and closely placed, with coarse punctures forming indistinct striæ, which extend nearly to middle. Abdomen punctate and wrinkled, sparsely pubescent. Length .14 -.16 inch.; 3.5—4 mm. Plate VI, fig. 10.

The male has the first joint of the anterior tarsi more dilated than the female. The last ventral sinuate each side, the middle lobe narrow and short.

As remarked above the first appearance of this insect recalls *Gastroidea polygoni*, but it is less convex and with finer punctuation.

Occurs in southwestern Texas; collected by Mr. S. F. Aaron.

Group VI.--DISONYCHÆ.

Antennæ 11-jointed. Thorax with base arcuate at middle, more or less obliquely sinuate each side. Anterior coxal cavities open behind. Posterior tibiæ usually feebly sulcate near the apex. Claw joint of hind tarsus not inflated, the claws appendiculate.

This group has been separated from the Halticites of Chapuis in consequence of the absence of any ante-basal impression of the thorax. It has been found very inconvenient to retain the group as constituted by Chapuis from the fact that the definition should include the statement that an ante-basal impression is present, and to admit an exception in which the most conspicuous species are included would be, at least, confusing.

Two genera are known to me as occurring in our fauna :

Thorax with an oblique sinuation each side of base; prosternum moderately separating the coxae and not depressed between them ; second joint of antennae much shorter than third........ ....**Disonycha.**
Thorax regularly arcuate at base; prosternum very narrow between the coxae and depressed between them ; second joint of antennae very little shorter than third.. ....**Hemiphrynus.**

The latter genus is instituted for *Phrynocepha intermedia* Jacoby and some allied forms which cannot remain as placed. Phrynocepha, having *pulchella* as the type, has broadly sulcate and bicarinate hind tibiae, and must be placed in the *Aspicelites*. It is remarkable that so obvious a character should have escaped notice.

DISONYCHA Chev.

Head inserted as far as the eyes, front declivous, frontal carina distinct, sometimes acute, joining the thickened border of the clypeus in front, above the end of the carina are two tubercles usually well marked, separated by a fine line. Antennae slender, rarely longer than half the body, the fourth joint longer than the third, except in the species with blue elytra, where they are about equal. Thorax as wide at base as the elytra, narrowed in front, the apex truncate, or feebly emarginate ; anterior angles not prominent, base either rounded at middle or slightly emarginate opposite the suture, the sides obliquely sinuate, although at times feebly ; disc convex, without distinct ante-basal transverse depression in any of our species. Scutellum triangular, broader than long. Elytra oblong, or oval ; the epipleurae gradually narrower from base to apex. Prosternum variable in width between the coxae, usually narrow, the cavities open behind, angulate externally, exposing the trochantin. Metasternal side pieces moderate in width, with parallel sides. Legs moderate, posterior thighs fusiform, grooved beneath ; tibiae more or less distinctly bisulcate on the outer face without trace of sinuation or tooth above the tarsi, terminated by a moderate spur (Plate VII, fig. 16). Tarsi slender, moderately long, the first joint of the posterior pair as long as the next two ; claws appendiculate at base.

In the males the last ventral segment is truncate, the pygidium vertical and convex ; in the female the last ventral is oval and the pygidium horizontal.

As represented in our fauna, Disonycha is far more homogeneous than Œdionychis, the species not exhibiting any marked structural differences among themselves, consequently any attempt at tabulation is more or less based on coloration, which seems to be quite constant as to type, but variable in degree.

The genera with which Disonycha is associated are extremely difficult to separate by sharply drawn characters. The species of Haltica have the tibiæ longitudinally sulcate, but in a less marked degree The base of the thorax, although generally regularly arcuate, is in some species quite oblique each side as in Disonycha. Phrynocepha is especially indistinct, the more so when we consider the species at present referred to it.

The species at present known to me may be separated by the following table, the arrangement in a sequence by facies is shown by the numbers :

Form elongate, parallel, elytra subsulcate ; thorax rather irregularly convex ; elytra yellow, with black vittæ..............1. **pennsylvanica.**
Form more or less oval, elytra even : thorax regularly convex.................2.
2.—Elytra vittate..3.
    Elytra with large discal spot black..........10. **discoidea.**
    Entire body above black, subopaque.................11. **funerea.**
    Elytra dark violet, blue or green...............8.
3.—Elytra with a submarginal vitta......4
    Elytra without submarginal vitta............7.
4.—Abdomen densely punctured, subopaque, the pubescence conspicuous........5.
    Abdomen very sparsely punctured and shining, pubescence scarcely visible..6.
5.—Head coarsely punctured from side to side, occiput piceous or brown.
        2. **quinquevittata.**
    Head smooth at middle.
    Elytral vittæ rather broad, head and metasternum more or less fuscous or piceous, labrum piceous.............. 3. **crenicollis.**
    Elytral vittæ narrow, head and body beneath always pale yellow; labrum pale ....4. **caroliniana.**
6.—Thorax distinctly punctured.
    Head smooth at middle ; epipleuræ pale...........5. **arizonæ.**
    Head with coarse, deep punctures: epipleuræ black........6. **maritima.**
    Thorax smooth ; head rough; epipleuræ black...........7. **glabrata.**
7.—Median elytral vitta broad ; antennæ normal ; thorax not spotted.
        8. **abbreviata.**
    Median vitta extremely narrow ; antennæ slender, three-fourths the length of body ; thorax with two spots...........9. **tenuicornis.**

8.—Body beneath and legs entirely black; thorax with three spots in triangle;
    elytra punctate ....12. **triangularis.**
  Body beneath and legs in part at least yellow................................9.
9.—Posterior femora entirely or in part piceous.
  Body beneath entirely yellow.
    Head entirely yellow; antennæ with four basal and one or two terminal
    joints yellow, femora (except posterior at apex) yellow; tibiæ and
    tarsi black; elytra bright violaceous blue.........15. **varicornis.**
    Head piceous; antennæ piceous; legs entirely black; elytra blue-black,
    rather dull..14. **cervicalis.**
  Abdomen alone entirely yellow, hind femora bicolored, or entirely black;
    head piceous; elytra blue-black............13. **xanthomelæna.**
  Abdomen piceous at middle, apex and sides yellow, legs bicolored; head
    bicolored; elytra brilliant blue.....................16. **politula.**
  Posterior femora entirely yellow; abdomen piceous, apex and sides yellow;
    head bicolored.
    Elytra blue or violet, form of body oval, as in *xanthomelæna.*
                                                            17. **mellicollis.**
    Elytra bright green, form more oblong....................18. **collata.**

1. **D. pennsylvanica** Illig.—Oblong, nearly parallel. Antennæ a little
longer than half the body, moderately stout, black, except usually the underside of three basal joints. Head black, front yellow, surface nearly smooth, except a small group of punctures near each eye. Labrum piceous or brown.
Thorax more than twice as wide as long, slightly narrower in front, disc convex,
somewhat uneven, a very indistinct, oblique impression beginning at the front
angles extending toward the middle, behind which is a more or less developed
umbone; lateral margin rather wide, the submarginal impression deep, surface
shining nearly smooth, the punctures very fine and indistinct; color pale yellow,
with black spots varying in size and number. Scutellum black. Elytra yellow,
or yellowish white, with the suture, a marginal vitta (these rarely joining at
apex) and a median vitta not reaching the apex, black; surface subsulcate, especially near the sides, punctuation variable, either quite distinct or entirely obsolete. Body beneath nearly entirely black, side margin of elytra and outer side
of epipleuræ yellow, the inner margin usually piceous. Abdomen densely punctured and finely pubescent. Legs variable in color from black to rufescent.
Length .26—.30 inch.; 6.5—7.5 mm.

As might be expected in a species of such wide distribution, there
is considerable variation, the types of which will be considered separately.

Limbicollis Lec.—Antennæ entirely black. Thorax with the spots
confluent in a large discal black space having a comparatively narrow yellow border. Thorax beneath black, narrowly margined with
yellow. Body beneath and legs black.

Pennsylvanica Illig.—Head in part yellow. Prothorax reddish
yellow, with a central black spot, round in front and gradually narrowed posteriorly, beneath entirely yellow. Body beneath black,

abdomen at sides and apex paler. Legs in great part black. The two described as *uniguttata* Say and *vicina* Kby. are synonyms of this variety.

Pallipes Crotch agrees with the preceding, except that the legs are reddish yellow and the tibiæ slightly darker, tarsi piceous.

Conjugata Fab.—In this form the usual black of the surface is replaced by rufous, and the legs, even to the tarsi, reddish yellow.

In addition to the above a form occurs in Florida and Louisiana somewhat smaller, with the entire head, antennæ, underside and legs black. The black vittæ of the elytra are also unusually broad, so that the pale yellow is reduced to a narrow thread.

The normal marking of the thorax consists of five spots, two forming an anterior row slightly behind the anterior margin, three forming a posterior arcuate row. Often the spots forming the central triangle are confluent, and the lateral spots wanting, while in the var. *limbicollis* they are all fused, forming a large discal space. Varieties often occur with the thorax immaculate, giving the species again an entirely different aspect, but the form is well recognized as a mere variety.

Among the species with vittate elytra this one is known by the parallel form, subsulcate elytra and almost entirely black head.

This species occurs all over the United States and Canada, but is more especially the species of the northern region, that is to say, it extends east and west north of the fortieth parallel of latitude.

2. **D. quinquevittata** Say.—Oblong oval. Antennæ a little longer than half the body, piceous, the under and posterior side of the first three joints testaceous. Head yellow, and, except in rare instances, with the occiput piceous, vertex with coarse and deep punctures extending from one side to the other, frontal carina broad and obtuse, the tubercles well marked. Labrum black. Thorax twice as wide as long, narrowed in front, anterior angles distinctly prominent, sides feebly arcuate, the margin narrower, disc not evenly convex usually a slight umboue at the position of the outer dark spot, surface very minutely and sparsely punctate; color yellow, normally with five spots arranged in an anterior row of two and a posterior of three, often with the two spots only. Scutellum black. Elytra distinctly wider at base than the thorax, humeri obtuse, umbone moderately prominent, surface sparsely finely punctulate, yellow, a narrow sutural stripe, a submarginal line often incomplete at base and not joining the sutural at apex, a very narrow median vitta. Epipleuræ pale. Body beneath reddish yellow, metasternum usually piceous. Abdomen densely punctured, the pubescence close and conspicuous. Legs reddish yellow, the tibiæ at tip darker, tarsi piceous. Length .22—.36 inch.; 5.5—9 mm.

This species exhibits very nearly as much variation as *pennsylva-nica*, while preserving a facies which enables it to be quite readily recognized.

In the normal form the five spots on the thorax are well marked, and the metasternum entirely or in great part piceous. The spots may become obliterated until only the two anterior ones remain. Specimens from near Fort Yuma have the underside entirely yellow, while the thoracic spots may be well developed. These have been described as *pura* Lec.

Rarely individuals occur with the median elytral vitta entirely wanting, still more rarely the submarginal vitta is wanting.

The median vitta is usually very narrow, but specimens from Missouri in my cabinet have all the vitta a little wider, so that the yellow space on either side of the median vitta is not wider than the vitta.

The oblong form of this species makes it intermediate between the parallel form of *pennsylvanica* and the more truly oval form of those which follow.

From the two species which follow, having the abdomen densely punctured, it may be known by the coarsely punctured vertex; *caroliniana* has a pale head and labrum, *crenicollis* has a more oval form, wider vittæ and the sutural and marginal unite at apex.

This insect has long borne the name *alternata* in our cabinets through an erroneous interpretation of Illiger. It cannot be *alternata* because that species is described from Carolina and Pennsylvania, and it is quite unlikely that Illiger could have had specimens of an essentially western species in his hands in 1807. Moreover, Illiger describes *alternata* as having a pale head. It is more than probable that *alternata* is a synonym of *caroliniana*, as will be seen by reference to remarks under that species.

From the fact that the name given by Say is now disposable I have used it in preference to any of the names which have been given in more recent times.

The present species is especially that of the entire region west of the Mississippi River, extending from our northern boundary to Mexico and from the Mississippi to the Pacific. Single specimens are in my cabinet from Illinois, Virginia and Massachusetts.

3. **D. crenicollis** Say.—Oval, slightly narrower in front. Antennæ half the length of the body, black, the three basal joints pale on the under and posterior side. Head either entirely yellow or with the occiput piceous, frontal carina very obtuse, the tubercles feeble or absent, surface smooth, a feebly punc-

tured depression at the upper inner angles of the eye. Labrum always black.
Thorax twice as wide as long, narrower in front, sides feebly arcuate or nearly
straight, the margin narrower, disc convex, smooth, nearly impunctate, yellow
or slightly reddish, usually with three piceous spots placed in a triangle, the
anterior pair oval and larger, the posterior linear, rarely with a lateral spot on
each side. Scutellum black. Elytra scarcely wider than the thorax at base,
humeri rounded, the umbone not distinct, surface smooth or indistinctly punctulate, color yellow ; suture, submarginal vitta (these united at apex) and median
vitta black, this as wide as the yellow space on either side, extreme margin of
elytra and outer side of epipleurae yellow, inner side piceous. Prothorax beneath
yellow. Metasternum usually black, abdomen yellowish or pale brown, densely
punctured and with very conspicuous silken pubescence. Femora reddish yellow, piceous along the upper edge, tibiae and tarsi piceous. Length .22 -.26 inch. ;
5.5 -6.5 mm.

This species is closely related to *caroliniana*, and is difficult to distinguish by description. The labrum is here always piceous, the
metasternum in great part piceous, except in rare examples; the
legs are always darker, the abdomen more densely punctured and
the pubescence more abundant. It is also observed that *crenicollis*
has the median elytral vitta as wide or wider than the yellow on each
side and in the vast majority of specimens the sutural and marginal
vittae join at the tip, while in *caroliniana* the reverse is the case in
both characters.

Occurs from New York to southwestern Texas and Mexico.

4. **D. caroliniana** Fab —Oval, slightly narrower in front. Antennae half
the length of the body, piceous, the underside of three basal joints pale. Head
entirely yellow, entirely smooth, except a punctured fovea at the upper inner
border of the eye, frontal carina obtuse, tubercles small. Labrum always pale.
Thorax convex, more than twice as wide as long, distinctly narrowed in front,
sides feebly arcuate, margin narrow, surface polished with very indistinct, sparse
punctures, two piceous spots of variable size behind the apical border, these are
rarely absent. Scutellum black. Elytra scarcely wider at base than the thorax.
humeri indistinct, yellow (when recent slightly reddish), a narrow sutural black
border, a marginal line not covering the edge, which very rarely joins the sutural.
a median vitta narrower than the yellow spaces on either side, surface usually
impunctate, rarely obsoletely punctulate. Body beneath reddish yellow. Epi
pleurae internally piceous, sometimes entirely yellow. Abdomen closely punctate, pubescence distinct. Legs reddish yellow, tibiae at tip and tarsi piceous.
Length .20 -.26 inch. ; 5 -6.5 mm.

Very little variable, except as noted above. In the Florida specimens before me the epipleurae are entirely pale.

With this species I have united *alternata* Illig. as a synonym.
From Illiger's description (Magaz. vi, p. 144) of *caroliniana* it is
evident that he had not seen the Fabrician type, and the description

is made up entirely of a rescript of those of Fabricius and Olivier, while the supposed differences are diagnosed from the figure given by the latter author. *D. pulchra* Casey is described from a very fresh specimen.

Occurs from Pennsylvania to Florida. A specimen from Missouri in my cabinet is doubtful as to locality.

5. **D. arizonæ** Casey.—Oval, slightly narrower in front. Antennæ scarcely half the length of body, black, the underside of three basal joints pale. Head entirely reddish yellow, frontal carina and tubercles indistinct, a group of coarse punctures on the front at the upper border of each eye. Labrum fuscous. Thorax yellow, more than twice as wide as long, narrowed in front, sides feebly arcuate, margin narrow, disc regularly convex, usually shining, sometimes slightly alutaceous, sparsely indistinctly punctate, a small piceous spot on each .side of middle, placed more distantly from each other than from the apical border. Scutellum black. Elytra wider at base than the thorax, humeri obtuse, callus not prominent, surface very distinctly, but not closely punctate; color yellow, a narrow sutural black vitta joining the marginal, which does not include the extreme edge or epipleuræ; a median vitta wider than the sutural, but narrower than the yellow space on either side. Epipleuræ pale, at most slightly fuscous internally. Body beneath yellow or testaceous, legs somewhat more reddish, the tibiæ at tip and tarsi piceous. Abdomen slightly alutaceous, shining, punctures very sparse, pubescence short and sparse. Length .22–.26 inch.; 5.5—6.5 mm.

From either of the species with comparatively smooth abdomen this may be known by the narrow median vitta, pale epipleuræ and entirely pale head. Superficially it bears a close resemblance to *caroliniana*, in which, however, the abdomen is closely punctate and very distinctly pubescent.

Occurs in southern Arizona.

6. **D. marítima** Mann.—Oval, slightly narrower in front. Antennæ half the length of body, black, the underside of three basal joints paler. Head black, front yellow, the frontal carina and tubercles well marked, some very coarse punctures placed across the vertex. Labrum piceous. Thorax yellow, without spots, more than twice as wide as long, narrowed in front, sides arcuate, margin narrow, disc regularly convex, distinctly punctate, the punctures rather coarse, not close. Scutellum black. Elytra very little wider at base than the thorax, humeri rounded, callus not prominent, suture and entire margin including the epipleuræ, a rather broad median vitta black, the intervening space yellow, surface finely, sparsely and indistinctly punctate. Prothorax beneath yellow. Body and abdomen black, the last segment yellow; surface of abdomen shining, finely, transversely strigose with few scattered, coarse punctures and very few short hairs. Legs black, the outer side of the tibiæ yellow. Length .16—.20 inch.; 4—5 mm.

This species is about as little variable as any in the genus. It may be readily known by the distinctly punctate thorax and black underside.

Occurs in California and Nevada.

7. **D. glabrata** Fab.—Oblong oval, surface very shining as if varnished. Antennæ half the length of the body, black, three basal joints testaceous posteriorly. Head variable color, often entirely black, except the front, sometimes nearly entirely yellow, but always with the posterior portion of the occiput fuscous, frontal carina and tubercles well marked, surface smooth. Labrum brown. Thorax yellow, usually with a narrow median spot, sometimes an indistinct spot each side, rarely immaculate, surface smooth, shining, more than twice as wide as long, narrowed in front, sides feebly arcuate, margin narrow. Scutellum black. Elytra a little wider at base than the thorax, humeri rounded, umbone not prominent, surface smooth, shining, the punctures extremely fine and sparse ; color yellow, the suture and margin, involving the epipleuræ, a median vitta black. Body beneath yellow, the posterior portion of metasternum rarely piceous. Abdomen very finely alutaceous, sparsely punctate, hairs short and sparse. Legs usually yellow, sometimes the femora are infuscate, tips of tibiæ and tarsi piceous. Length .20—.22 inch. ; 5—5.5 mm.

In this species specimens rarely occur with the extreme lateral margin of the elytra and epipleuræ pale, in this case the broad median vitta, the more or less dark head, the thoracic ornamentation will distinguish it from *arizonæ*. From *maritima* it may at once be known by the pale underside and smooth thorax.

Occurs from Georgia to Arizona.

8. **D. abbreviata** Mels.—Oval, slightly oblong. Antennæ as long as half the body, piceous, the underside of three basal joints pale. Head (and labrum) yellow, the frontal carina obtuse, tubercles distinct, surface smooth, a rounded punctured fovea at the upper and inner border of the eye. Thorax twice as wide as long, narrowed in front, sides arcuate, margin narrow, surface regularly convex, smooth, entirely yellow, without spots. Scutellum yellow. Elytra slightly wider at base than the thorax, humeri obtuse, umbone distinct, a slight depression within it, surface sparsely, indistinctly punctulate, color yellow, a sutural black vitta, another median, both moderately wide, black. Body beneath and epipleuræ entirely yellow. Abdomen very sparsely punctate, rather shining, the pubescence short, sparse and inconspicuous. Legs yellow, the outer side of the tibiæ and the tarsi black. Length .24—.34 inch. ; 6—8.5 mm.

This species is one of the least variable of our vittate species. When recent the yellow color is slightly tinged with red. By the absence of the submarginal vitta and the immaculate thorax this species is easily known.

Occurs from the Middle States to Florida and Texas, extending into Mexico.

9. **D. tenuicornis** n. sp.—Oval slightly oblong, facies rather robust, pale yellow, surface very shining as if varnished, elytra with a single, slender, median vitta; thorax with two piceous spots. Antennæ nearly two-thirds the length of body and slender, piceous, the three basal joints nearly entirely yellow. Head smooth, a very few large punctures near each eye, frontal carina obtuse, tubercles feeble. Thorax twice as wide as long, narrowed in front, sides feebly arcuate, margin narrow, disc regularly convex, surface polished and with two small black spots in front. Elytra wider at base than the thorax, humeri distinct, but obtuse; umbone distinct, surface shining, very obsoletely punctate, a single, slender, median vitta on each elytron, suture very narrowly piceous posteriorly. Body beneath entirely yellow. Abdomen rather densely punctulate, pubescence very distinct. Legs yellow, tarsi brown. Length .26—.30 inch.; 6.5—7.5 mm.

The four specimens before me agree perfectly with the above description. The lateral margin is slightly reddish in color, and would lead one to suspect a marginal vitta, but the same appears in *alternata*. It is a little more robust than *quinquevittata*, and may be readily known by the long, slender antennæ.

Occurs in southern Arizona (Morrison).

10. **D. discoidea** Fab.—Oval, slightly depressed. Antennæ half the length of the body, black, the lower side of basal joint piceous. Head (and labrum) yellow, surface smooth, a small fovea at the upper inner border of the eye, frontal carina very obtuse, the tubercles indistinct. Thorax more than twice as wide as long, narrowed in front, sides slightly arcuate, margin narrow, a little wider in front, disc regularly convex, smooth, shining, yellow and immaculate. Scutellum yellow. Elytra scarcely wider than the thorax, humeri almost entirely obliterated, umbone moderate, surface distinctly and moderately closely punctate, color yellow, with a large, oval, discal black spot not reaching the apex and usually having a very narrow pale basal border. Body beneath entirely yellow. Abdomen rather closely punctate, the pubescence distinct, but not conspicuous. Legs yellow, the outer side of the tibiæ and the tarsi black. Length .22—.30 inch.; 5.5—7.5 mm.

This species varies but little; the black discal space rarely reaches the basal margin, in which case the scutellum is black. The space varies in width, and at times the yellow border of the elytra is rather narrow. When recent the yellow is tinged with red as observed in nearly all the species.

Occurs from North Carolina to Texas.

11. **D. funerea** Rand.—Oval, entirely black, with a velvety, subopaque surface, last segment of abdomen and sides of the fourth yellow. Antennæ scarcely half as long as the body, rather stout, the outer joints short. Front smooth, one large puncture and several smaller near each eye, the frontal carina very flat, the tubercles indistinct. Thorax barely twice as wide as long, narrowed in front, the sides feebly arcuate, margin very narrow, disc regularly convex, impunctate, surface minutely alutaceous. Elytra not wider at base than the thorax, humeri rounded, umbone indistinct, surface minutely, obsoletely punc-

tate, finely alutaceous. Body beneath more shining than above. Abdomen alutaceous, the punctures very sparse and indistinct, the pubescence very short. Legs entirely black. Length .20—.26 inch.; 5—6.5 mm.

There need be no difficulty in the identification of this species; the antennæ are much stouter than in any other and rather shorter. The male is narrower than the female, and the oblique truncation of the base near the hind angles is very feeble.

Occurs in Georgia.

12. **D. triangularis** Say.—Form oval, rather depressed, feebly shining, entirely black, thorax reddish yellow with three black spots arranged in triangle, the anterior pair round, the posterior linear and median. Antennæ slender, half the length of the body, piceous, the three basal joints pale beneath. Head entirely black, frontal carina obtuse, the tubercles indistinct, vertex and occiput coarsely and rather closely punctate. Thorax more than twice as wide as long, narrowed in front, sides feebly arcuate, the margin very narrow, surface alutaceous rather finely, not closely punctate. Elytra a little wider at base than the thorax, humeri obtuse, umbone not prominent, surface moderately closely, distinctly punctate; color black, with a slight bluish tinge. Prothorax beneath yellow. Abdomen rather coarsely, not closely punctate, pubescence short and indistinct. Legs entirely black. Length .20—.25 inch.; 5—6.5 mm.

This species is remarkably constant in all its characters, and but little variable in size. It is readily known by the entirely black color beneath and the three spots on the thorax.

Occurs in the entire region east of the Rocky Mountains, including Canada.

13. **D. xanthomelæna** Dalm.—Oval, slightly depressed, feebly shining, thorax yellow, elytra dark blue. Antennæ slender, a little longer than half the body, piceous, the three basal joints pale beneath and in front. Head black, front piceous, frontal carina moderately prominent, tubercles distinct, occiput with a few coarse and deep punctures irregularly placed. Thorax yellow, immaculate, not twice as wide as long, narrowed in front, sides very slightly arcuate, margin narrow, surface almost entirely smooth, the punctures very minute and sparse. Elytra wider at base than the thorax, humeri rounded, umbone not prominent, surface finely alutaceous, obsoletely punctulate. Prothorax beneath yellow, metasternum black. Abdomen entirely yellow, rather densely punctate and subopaque, with distinct pubescence. Femora yellow at basal half (sometimes entirely black), the apical piceous, also the tibiæ and tarsi. Length .22 inch.; 5.5 mm.

This species has heretofore been known in our cabinets, and is the one everywhere quoted as *collaris* Fab., but I am unable to adopt this name for the following reason—the description does not apply—" *Statura et magnitudine præcedentium*" (*Œd. fasciata*, about .35 inch.; 9 mm.) ; " *thorax rufus, macula una alterare dorsali, nigra*" (certainly not so); "*abdomen nigrum ano rufo*" (abdomen entirely yellow); "*pedes nigri*" (bicolored here).

While there are these essential differences it will be observed that
Fabricius describes it in association with species with inflated claw
joint, the two species immediately preceding belonging to Lithonoma
and Œdionychis, the two following to Œdionychis and Asphæra.
It is probable that the name should be used rather for some of the
larger Œdionyches from one of the West India islands or Cayenne.
The error in the interpretation of Fabricius' species is due to Illiger.
It seems to me that I am justified in rejecting the name from our
fauna.

The remarks by Suffrian (Wiegm. Archiv. 1868, i, p. 180) are so
unsatisfactory that it is impossible to say whether he had the true
Fabrician species before him or not. It is more than likely that he
did not see either the present species or *collata*.

Occurs from the New England States to Kansas and Texas and
Florida.

14. **D. cervicalis** Lec.—Closely resembling *xanthomelæna*, and differing
only as follows: Antennæ entirely piceous Legs entirely black, the coxæ yellow, underside of body entirely yellow. Abdomen coarsely, moderately closely
punctate, pubescence feeble. Length .20 inch.; 5 mm.

Of this species I have seen but one specimen from Georgia. Le-
Conte says (Ins. Kans. p. 25) that it occurs also in Kansas. This is
the only species with blue elytra with the underside entirely pale,
and, with the exception of *triangularis*, the only one with entirely
black legs.

15. **D. varicornis** n. sp.—Oval, slightly oblong, moderately convex; head,
thorax and entire underside yellow, elytra brilliant violaceous blue. Antennæ
nearly half half as long as the body, piceous, the four basal and one or two terminal yellow. Head entirely yellow, smooth, except a fovea of coarse punctures
near each eye, frontal carina broad and obtuse, tubercles small. Thorax twice
as wide as long, sides feebly arcuately narrowed to the front, anterior angles very
obtuse in front, a slight sinuation of the margin behind them, surface smooth,
entirely yellow. Scutellum black. Elytra a little wider at base than the thorax,
humeri rounded, umbone distinct, smooth, disc finely sparsely punctate at base,
smooth at apex. Body beneath entirely yellow. Abdomen smooth, sparsely
punctate. Anterior and middle femora yellow, the posterior tipped with piceous,
tibiæ and tarsi all black. Length .24 inch.; 6 mm.

This insect bears such a close resemblance to *Asphæra lustrans* as
to be readily mixed, except by careful examination. The generic
characters which separate them are also quite feeble, the claw joint
not being very different in the two. There is, however, a distinct
sinuation of the apex of the hind tibia above the tarsus in *Asphæra*
not seen in the present genus.

The species is remarkable in the color of the antennæ, the four basal joints are pale, also the two terminal in specimens from Texas, and but one in a specimen from Lower California in Mr. Ulke's cabinet.

Occurs in Texas and the Peninsula of California.

16. **D. politula** n. sp.—Oblong oval, slightly depressed, surface very shining. Antennæ slender, half the length of body, piceous, underside of three basal joints paler. Head shining, occiput blue-black, front yellow, labrum black, frontal carina very obtuse, tubercles distinct, a few coarse and deep punctures near each eye. Thorax pale yellow, immaculate, twice as wide as long, narrower in front, sides feebly arcuate, margin narrow, disc finely, sparsely and indistinctly punctulate. Elytra a little wider at base than the thorax, humeri distinct, umbone moderate, a slight depression within it, surface bright cobalt-blue, shining, distinctly, but rather densely not coarsely punctate. Prothorax beneath yellow, metasternum black. Abdomen piceous at middle, widely bordered with yellow, the surface shining, coarsely, not closely punctate, the pubescence scarcely evident. Anterior and middle femora yellow, the upper side more or less piceous, the tibiæ and base piceous. Posterior femora yellow at base, piceous at apex, the colors diagonally separated, the tibiæ and tarsi piceous. Length .20 inch.; 5 mm.

Among the species in the series with elytra more or less blue this may be known by the very distinctly punctate elytra. The colors are very constant; the posterior femora have the colors separated diagonally, so that the underside is more yellow, while the upper is more black.

Occurs in New Mexico and Arizona.

17. **D. mellicollis** Say.—Oval, similar in form and color to *xanthomelæna*. Antennæ half as long as the body, piceous, the three basal joints pale in front, the joints very gradually shorter from the fourth to tenth, eleventh longer. Head blue black between the eyes and posteriorly, front yellow (labrum piceous), a few coarse, deep punctures near each eye. Thorax pale yellow, twice as wide as long, narrowed in front, sides feebly arcuate, margin very narrow, disc regularly convex, extremely finely alutaceous, impunctate. Elytra a little wider at base than the thorax, humeri distinct, but obtuse, umbone not prominent, surface dull blue, very finely alutaceous, and with very indistinct, fine, sparse punctures. Prothorax yellow beneath, metathorax piceous, abdomen piceous at middle, with the apical segment and wide lateral border yellowish, the surface moderately closely punctate, pubescence indistinct. Femora entirely yellow, tibiæ piceous, paler at base, tarsi piceous. Length .18—.20 inch.; 4.5—5 mm.

This species is doubtless mixed with *xanthomelæna* in most collections, due to the hasty aggregation of a number of well defined species under one name. It is remarkable that the description by Say seems to have been lost sight of in our literature, as the same species has been redescribed by LeConte as *semicarbonata*.

From all the preceding species *mellicollis* may be known by the entirely yellow femora. From *politula*, which has a similarly colored head and abdomen, it may, in addition, be known by the almost entire absence of punctuation on the elytra. From *xanthomelæna* and *cervicalis* the color of the head, abdomen and legs will separate it. Occurs in Louisiana, Texas and Colorado.

18. **D. collata** Fab.—Oval, slightly oblong, subdepressed. Antennæ half as long as the body, piceous, the three basal joints pale beneath. Vertex and occiput black, with faint greenish tinge, front yellow, labrum piceous, a few very coarse punctures close to the eye, others finer, scattered on the vertex. Thorax yellow, immaculate, twice as wide as long, narrowed in front, sides feebly arcuate, margin narrow, surface polished, and, with high power, minutely sparsely punctulate. Elytra not wider at base than the thorax, humeri rounded, umbone not distinct, greenish blue, shining, when seen with high power minutely alutaceous, and with fine, distinct, sparsely placed punctures. Prothorax beneath yellow, metasternum black, abdomen piceous with the last segment and sides broadly yellowish, the surface moderately densely punctured and with quite distinct pubescence. Femora pale yellow, tibiae at tips and tarsi piceons. Length .16--.18 inch.; 4—4.5 mm.

This is the smallest species at present known in our fauna. The same remarks as under *mellicollis* will separate this species from all which precede. It is not so easily separated from that species, however, by description. It is smaller, more elongate, the elytra are shining blue-green and the punctuation, although very fine, more distinct. This species is, I believe, correctly determined in most cabinets.

Occurs in Georgia and Florida.

HEMIPHRYNUS n. g.

Head oval, inserted as far as the eyes, front nearly vertical, carina and tubercles distinct, clypeus truncate, labrum transverse, arcuate in front. Maxillary palpi not stout, second joint slightly clavate, third as long, obconical, fourth shorter, narrower, conical and acute at tip. Mandibles tridentate at apex, the middle tooth longer. Eyes oval, moderately prominent. Antennæ longer than half the body, filiform, first joint slightly clavate, second nearly half as long, third longer than second, fourth and fifth still longer, joints 6–10 gradually shorter, eleventh as long as fourth. Prothorax transverse, narrowed in front, apex truncate, base broadly arcuate; disc convex, with a vague depression each side close to basal margin. Elytra a little wider at base than the thorax, oblong oval, widest at middle, disc confusedly punctate. Prosternum very narrow between the coxæ, these oval, prominent and nearly contiguous at their apices, coxal cavities open behind. Mesosternum moderate in length, nearly horizontal. Ventral segments free, the first very little longer than the second. Legs moderate in length. Tibiæ slender, scarcely broader toward apex, the posterior not sulcate but with a very indistinct carina, the terminal spur small; tarsi moderate, the first joint longer, second short, oval, third broadly oval and bilobed, fourth not dilated, the claws broadly appendiculate at base.

The only genus of Halticites as constituted by Chapuis to which this is at all related is Disonycha, and the characters in the preceding table will enable it to be separated. The name above used is in the second half merely commemorative of the genus in which the species has been placed.

It is probable that *Phrynocepha elongata* Jacoby, should be referred to this genus.

H. intermedius Jacoby.—Oval, slightly oblong, rather depressed, body beneath piceous; head, antennæ, thorax and legs reddish yellow, elytra dull green. Head rather coarsely and closely punctate, except at middle. Thorax nearly twice as wide as long, narrowed in front, sides arcuate, anterior angles very obtusely dentiform, disc not very convex, somewhat irregular, a vague, shallow depression at base each side of middle, sometimes a transverse, vague, depression uniting them, surface alutaceous, subopaque, the punctures moderate in size and rather closely placed, less distinct in front. Elytra dull green, surface alutaceous, the punctuation fine and very indistinct. Abdomen shining, slightly pubescent, coarsely sparsely punctate. Length .16—.20 inch.; 4–5 mm.

The male has the first joint of the anterior tarsus moderately dilated. The last ventral segment is broadly emarginate at middle, the pygidium convex, inflexed and filling the emargination. The last ventral of the female is truncate at apex.

This insect has a certain amount of resemblance to the Disonychæ with unicolored elytra.

Occurs in southern Arizona.

Group VII.—MNIOPHILÆ.

Form orbicular or hemispherical. Head deeply inserted. Anterior coxal cavities open behind. Mesosternum very short, or almost entirely concealed by the close approximation of the pro- and metasterna. Antennæ 11-jointed. Posterior tibiæ with a short spur. Claws broadly appendiculate at base. Prothorax without ante-basal impression and usually without the lateral longitudinal impression.

The genera of this group are not numerous, and two only have representation in our fauna, separated as follows:

Antennæ gradually clavate ; epipleural fold of elytra vertical....**Argopistes.**
Antennæ slender, but slightly thickened externally; epipleural fold horizontal.
                  Sphæroderma.

ARGOPISTES Motsch.

Head rather deeply inserted, the front oblique, inflexed, distinctly carinate, the callosities distinct, but oblique. Clypeus truncate, labrum moderately prominent, truncate. Maxillary palpi moderate in length, the second joint elongate, clavate, third half as long, obconical, fourth slender and longer, acuminate. Antennæ but little longer than half the body, first joint moderately long, 2–3–4 more slender, together as long as the first, the following joints forming a club with the joints broader than the preceding, and of nearly equal length among themselves. Eyes large, slightly reniform, rather narrowly separated on the vertex. Thorax transverse, deeply emarginate in front, anterior angles obtuse, the posterior well defined. Scutellum small, narrowly triangular. Elytra slightly wider at base than the thorax, humeri obtusely rounded, no distinct umbone, punctuation confused, epipleural border vertical. Legs rather short, posterior femora rather widely dilated ; the tibiæ broader toward apex, the posterior tibiæ grooved on the outer edge, the borders of the groove finely spinulose, the apex with a small spur. Tarsi moderate, the first joint of posterior pair rather longer than the others combined. Claws rather broadly appendiculate. Pl. VII, fig. 15.

In this genus the eyes occupy a large part of the head and so closely placed that the antennæ are inserted close to their border in a slight emargination, the granulation is rather fine and the surface smooth.

But one species is known in our fauna.

A. scyrtoides Lec.—Orbicular, convex, piceous, black, shining, a broad, arcuate, transverse band on the thorax, a large triangular spot on each elytron, also the apex, red. Head reddish, obsoletely punctate. Antennæ pale rufotestaceous. Thorax more than twice as wide as long, very much narrowed to the front, sides feebly, base very broadly arcuate, surface distinctly alutaceous, finely and rather closely punctate. Elytra rather more finely punctate than the thorax. Body beneath and legs pale rufotestaceous. Length .12–.14 inch.; 3–3.5 mm. Pl. VII, fig. 4.

The male has the last ventral sinuate each side, the median lobe moderately prominent and with a small, moderately deep fovea near the margin.

At first sight this insect is very like an Exochomus. The arcuate red band on the thorax is absent in some specimens; the red spot on each elytron is in the form of a right angled triangle, the base slightly behind the middle, the perpendicular is toward the sides, while the hypothenuse is to the front. The spots meet at the suture. The apex is also bordered with red as in some Scymnus. Occurs in Biscayne Bay, Florida. It is remarkable that the other species of the genus occur in the Amur region and Japan.

SPHÆRODERMA Steph.

Head triangular, deeply inserted in the thorax, front obtusely carinate, the callosities small, clypeus truncate, labrum feebly emarginate at middle. Maxillary palpi with second joint slender, third short, obconical, fourth a little longer, acute. Eyes moderately prominent, round. Antennæ half as long as the body, slightly thicker toward tip, first joint slightly clavate, second and third equal, together as long as the first, 4–10 nearly equal, gradually wider, eleventh longer, acuminate at tip. Thorax transverse, anterior angles rounded, the posterior obtuse, margin narrowly explanate. Elytra not wider at base than the thorax, punctuation generally confused, substriate in places, epipleuræ horizontal. Legs moderate, hind thighs broadly oval. The tibiæ broader at apex, the posterior grooved on the outer face near the apex and with a small terminal spur, and distinctly prolonged on the inner side beyond the insertion of the tarsus. First joint of hind tarsi as long as the following together, the claws broadly appendiculate at base. Pl. VII, fig. 10.

The form of the posterior tibia partake of the characters of Chætocnema and Psylliodes, i. e., there is a slight sinuation near the apex limited above by an indistinct angulation, and the tibia is prolonged on the inner side beyond the insertion of the tarsus. The latter character is not mentioned by Chapuis, and may probably differentiate our species generally from the old world forms.

One species is known in our fauna.

S. opima Lec.—Orbicular, convex, piceous black, shining, front of head a little paler. Antennæ slender, pale rufotestaceous. Head closely punctate. Thorax more than twice as wide as long, rapidly narrowed in front, the sides nearly straight, rounded at the front angles, finely, moderately, closely punctate. Elytra not wider at base than the thorax, humeri broadly rounded, umbone feeble, the disc with coarse not close punctures forming rather irregular striæ at middle, but quite regular at the sides, intervals more finely punctulate. Epipleuræ paler. Body beneath piceous, tibiæ and tarsi reddish brown. Length .10 inch.; 2.5 mm.

The males of this genus are said to have the first joint of all the tarsi broader than in the female and the front tibia also broader.

This insect is very like *Scirtes tibialis* in form and color. It varies in color to piceous brown with the underside and legs pale; this is due probably to immaturity.

Occurs in Illinois, North Carolina and Texas.

Group VIII.--HALTICÆ.

Antennæ 11-jointed. Thorax regularly arcuate at base, with distinct ante-basal line variable in distinctness, not limited at its extremities by a longitudinal plica. Posterior tibiæ with, at most, a very slight sulcus on the posterior edge near the apex. Anterior coxal cavities open behind. Claw joint of posterior tarsi slender, claws appendiculate.

This group is nearly parallel with the Halticites as defined by Chapuis, and in our fauna is represented by Haltica alone. Several species had been referred to Cæporis by LeConte, which, however, do not possess the essential character of that genus.

HALTICA Geoffr.

Head short, usually deeply inserted, front regularly declivous, the interocular carina never very prominent, the tubercles usually feebly marked. Antennæ half as long as the body, joints 2–3–4 gradually longer, except in *rufa*. Labrum small. Maxillary palpi short, rather stout, the terminal joint short and conical. Thorax usually one-half wider than long and broadest at base, and with a more or less distinct ante-basal impressed line, base arcuate, lateral margin more or less thickened at the front angles. Elytra usually a little wider at base than the thorax, the punctuation of surface confused. Prosternum rather narrow between the coxæ, the coxal cavities open behind, angulate externally. Legs moderately long, tibiæ of posterior legs not or feebly sulcate, terminated by a small spur. Tarsi moderate in length, claws with a broad dilatation at base.

From the above description it will be observed that the differences between Haltica and Disonycha are very feeble and may be narrowed down to the form of the base of the thorax and the presence of a line more or less impressed in Haltica.

The character of the impressed line affords a means of grouping the species, but must be used with care and not too strictly interpreted. In other words, very little can be done with the species from a very few specimens. In *carinata*, for instance, the impression is usually deep and ends very abruptly, but specimens occur with the line as entire as in *chalybea*. One of our species has the line terminating in a fovea at each end. Color has scarcely any value in the separation of species and can only be used in the most general way as in *ignita* the color runs from bright golden to deep blue.

The sexual characters afford useful means for separating a certain number of very closely allied species of rather slender form placed at the end of the genus.

Among the species included in Haltica are two—*nana* and *Burgessi*—which form the genus Micraltica of the Class. Col. N. A. 1883, p. 352. This genus made part of the group Crepidoderæ, but as both of the species have open anterior coxal cavities they cannot remain in that group, and no course remains but to place them in Haltica, where Crotch placed one of them.

The genus is a difficult one, and the species can never be determined with any degree of certainty without a fair number of specimens, some of which must be males. Unfortunately, this sex is much less abundant than the females.

To assist students in the determination of species the following table has been prepared, but it must never be relied upon to the exclusion of the descriptions, or at least the tabular determination must be verified by reference to the description :

Body above blue, bronze, green, or cupreous, more or less metallic (head and thorax reddish yellow in two species)..2.
Body above reddish yellow, broadly oval,..13.
2.--Elytra longitudinally plicate at the sides.................1. **bimarginata.**
    Elytra not plicate..3.
3.—Antennæ and legs in great part yellow, in striking contrast with the color
    of the upper surface,...12.
. Antennæ and legs piceous, more or less metallic...4.
4.--Thorax with a deep ante-basal groove which extends *completely* across the
    thorax..5.
    Thorax with a moderate, sometimes obsolete ante-basal groove which is
    never entire ....6.
5.--Large species (5.5 mm.), usually blue, form robust, thorax very distinctly
    wider at base..2. **chalybea.**
    Smaller species (2—3 mm.), of more elongate form, thorax scarcely wider
    at base.
    Surface metallic blue, humeri scarcely evident, elytra rather coarsely and
    closely punctate; legs brown ; species quite small.............3. **nana.**
    Surface distinctly metallic, brassy, green, blue or bronze, elytral punctuation distinct...4. **ignita.**

Surface not metallic, brownish testaceous, antennæ pale, legs colored as
upper surface; elytra less distinctly punctate.................. **ignita** var.

6 —Transverse impression of thorax deep, humeral angles of elytra well marked,
a depression within the umbone................... ....7.

Transverse impression feeble or nearly absent; humeral angles of elytra
rounded ....10.

7.—Transverse impression terminating at either end in a fovea; form rather
short, as in *ignita*......... ....9. **evicta**.

Transverse impression gradually evanescent at its extremities................8.

8.—Larger species, thorax barely wider at base than apex ; last ventral ♂ with
a deep longitudinal impressed line.

Brilliant cupreous, with violet or purplish reflections.......6. **carinata**.

Blue, head more prominent, form more robust ....5. **vicaria**.

Smaller species of the form of *ignita*, thorax distinctly wider at base ; last
ventral of ♂ with at most a slight concavity...................................9.

9.—Thorax not visibly punctate, elytra relatively coarsely punctate ; cupreo-
æneous ....12 **amœna**.

Thorax alutaceous and finely punctulate, elytra alutaceous and finely punc
tulate, with a scabrous aspect ; greenish bronze.........10. **æruginosa**.

Thorax quite coarsely punctate, elytra with coarse punctures and finer intermixed ; cupreo-æneous.......... ....11. **obolina**.

10.—Species of robust facies and rather large size.

Moderately shining, punctuation indistinct, frontal carina and tubercles
feeble............... ....7. **californica**.

Subopaque, punctuation evident, frontal tubercles and carina well marked.
                                                                                     8. **obliterata**.

Species oblong, not very convex, the form recalling that of many *Luperus*..11.

11.—Antennæ slightly compressed, apparently thicker externally, the fourth
joint obviously longer than third.

Brownish bronze, last ventral ♂ with a long, but shallow median impressed line ; elytra very distinctly punctate......... 14. **tombacina**.

Blue, last ventral ♂ with a very deep impression extending half the
length of segment ; elytra finely moderately punctate.

                                                                                     13. **marevagans**.

Antennæ slender, not thicker externally, the fourth joint equal to or
scarcely perceptibly longer than third.

Last ventral ♂ with a deep longitudinal impression extending from apex
half to base ; elytra indistinctly punctulate......16. **punctipennis**.

Last ventral ♂ flattened near apex, a feeble longitudinal impression,
sometimes merely a smooth line ; elytra scarcely visibly punctate.

                                                                                     18. **foliacea**.

Last ventral ♂ as in *foliacea*, elytra relatively coarsely punctate.

                                                                                     15. **tincta**.

Last ventral ♂ not flattened, a feeble impression near the apex ; elytra
scarcely visibly punctate.................................17. **lazulina**.

12   Entire upper surface uniform in color and with metallic lustre.

Thoracic impression fine, but well marked.

Thorax not wider at base than apex ; abdomen and hind femora piceous.

                                                                                     20. **fuscoænea**.

Thorax distinctly wider at base; abdomen rufotestaceous, legs entirely
pale...19. **polita.**
Thoracic impression almost entirely obliterated, thorax wider at base,
elytra sparsely punctate, color violaceous,.............21. **opulenta.**
Head and thorax reddish yellow; elytra blue.
Thoracic impression rather feeble; elytra not shining...22. **floridana.**
Thoracic impression deep and entire; elytra rather brilliantly metallic.
23. **Burgessi.**
13.—Form rather broadly oval: thoracic impression almost obliterated; body
beneath brown; legs, except at base, black; elytra smooth...24. **rufa.**

1. **H. bimarginata** Say.--Oblong, subparallel, above blue, or slightly
bronzed, usually moderately shining, sometimes subopaque. Antennæ half as
long as the body, piceous, joints 2-3-4 gradually increasing in length. Head
feebly shining, frontal carina obtuse, tubercles usually well marked, a few punctures extending across the head above the tubercles and near the eyes. Thorax
one-half wider than long, slightly narrower in front, sides feebly arcuate, the
margin very narrow, disc moderately convex, the ante-basal transverse depression rather deep, slightly sinuous at middle, reaching the sides and joining the
marginal depression, surface distinctly alutaceous, sparsely punctate, punctures
more distinct near the apex and front angles. Elytra distinctly wider at base
than the thorax, humeri distinct, umbone moderately prominent and with a
slight depression within it, a prominent lateral plica begins at the umbone extends parallel with the margin, curves toward the suture near the apex, surface
alutaceous, the punctures fine and indistinct, not closely placed. Body beneath
and legs blue-black, shining, abdomen sparsely, indistinctly punctate. Length
.20--.24 inch.; 5--6 mm.

As might be expected, an insect distributed over such a wide extent of country exhibits some variation. The color is usually a
moderately bright cobalt-blue, but in the mountainous regions of
California specimens with a bronzed surface are quite common.
While the surface is usually shining, specimens are occasionally seen,
especially from Texas, with the surface subopaque. The ante-basal
thoracic groove may vary in depth, but is always entire. The lateral
plica, while usually prominent, is sometimes feebly so, in the former
case reaching, by incurving, nearly to the suture, and in the latter
scarcely curved at all. In some feebly developed individuals from
the vicinity of San Francisco the plica is almost entirely obliterated
and without the abundance of other specimens would be difficult to
identify. The lateral plica will enable this species to be separated
from all the others in our fauna.

Mr. D. W. Coquillett, of Los Angeles, informs me that this species
in all stages feeds on the leaves of Alder (*Alnus*).

Occurs in the entire northern portion of the continent as far south as Pennsylvania, thence westwardly extending in the western plains to Texas and Arizona, and on the Pacific slope from Alaska to Mexico.

2. **H. chalybea** Illig.—Oval, of moderately robust facies, color usually metallic shining blue, rarely cupreous or greenish. Antennæ half as long as the body, piceous, the basal half with metallic lustre, joints 2-3-4 gradually longer. Head smooth, slightly roughened near the eyes, frontal carina rather acute, the tubercles small, oblique. Thorax a little more than half wider than long, narrowed in front, sides arcuate, margin narrow, slightly thickened in front, disc convex, the ante-basal impressed line rather deep and extending from margin to margin, surface with extremely minute scattered punctures. Elytra scarcely wider at base than the thorax, humeri rounded, umbone moderately prominent, smooth, limited within by a slight depression, surface sparsely punctate, nearly smooth near apex. Body beneath and legs blue-black, moderately shining, abdomen sparsely punctate. Length .16—.20 inch.; 4—5 mm.

The variations from the usual blue color in this species seem very rare; for a cupreous specimen from Florida and a greenish one from Detroit I am indebted to Mr. E. A. Schwarz.

The thoracic impressed line is quite constant in its depth and extent, consequently there will be no great difficulty in distinguishing this from the other robust species, *californica*, *obliterata* and *vicaria*, all of which have the impression feeble, although in some of *carinata* it is moderately deep and nearly entire. The latter species has the thorax distinctly narrower than the elytra and a more prominent head.

The next species is the only other one with the impression entire, but this is smaller, more depressed and more evidently punctate.

Occurs from New England States and Michigan to Florida and Texas.

3. **H. nana** Crotch.—Oblong oval, convex, metallic blue or bluish green, shining. Antennæ as long as half the body, slender, joints 2-4 equal in length, outer joints piceous, basal four joints pale. Head smooth, frontal carina moderately prominent, acute, tubercles feeble and flat. Thorax one-third wider than long, narrowed at apex, sides arcuate, disc convex, sparsely indistinctly punctate, the ante-basal impression deep, sharply impressed and extending from side to side. Elytra scarcely wider at base than the thorax, humeri rounded, umbone scarcely prominent, a distinct depression at base within it, disc convex, the punctuation relatively very coarse, deep and close, but smoother toward the apex. Body beneath piceous, shining; abdomen sparsely punctate. Legs brownish testaceous, posterior femora piceous. Length .08 inch.; 2 mm.

The last ventral of the male has a deep semi-oval impression, which extends nearly half the length of the segment.

It is difficult to place this species in any tabular arrangement. The legs being in great part pale it might be associated with *polita* et al., but the short, robust form and the deep and entire ante-basal impression indicate its relationship with *ignita* and *chalybea*. It is the smallest species in our fauna, smaller than many Phyllotreta. It was described as a Crepidodera by Crotch, but the open anterior coxal cavities forbid such a reference. Later on we supposed it related to Cæporis, but the absence of tibial spurs to the front and middle legs forbids this reference. It is evidently merely a small Haltica.

Occurs from South Carolina to Florida.

4. **H. ignita** Illig.—Oval, slightly oblong, subdepressed, surface shining, variable in color from a coppery golden lustre through greenish to blue. Antenne half as long as the body, piceous, joints 2-3-4 gradually longer. Head smooth, an arcuate depression within each eye, frontal carina acute, tubercles distinct, but small. Thorax one-half wider than long, very little narrowed in front, sides feebly arcuate, disc convex, the ante-basal impression deep, extending entirely across the thorax from side to side, surface very minutely sparsely punctate. Elytra distinctly wider at base than the thorax, humeri prominent, but obtuse, umbone also moderately prominent, smooth, distinctly limited within by a depression, surface distinctly sparsely punctate near the base, gradually smoother to apex. Body beneath and legs colored as above ; abdomen alutaceous, sparsely punctate. Length .12—.16 inch. ; 3—4 mm.

In the males the last ventral segment is sinuate each side, the middle forming a short semi-circular lobe, which is flat, with the extreme edge often slightly reflexed.

The variations in color in this species are very striking. As a general rule the more northern habitats—Hudson's Bay to Pennsylvania—furnish the more brilliant golden specimens, the further south these become rarer, and the green, and finally the deep blue, become the characteristic colors in the Gulf States.

As a general rule the northern specimens are larger than the southern. The ante-basal groove varies in depth, although in the great majority it is deep and entire ; the sculpture of the elytra also varies in distinctness.

A form has been collected at Crescent City, Florida, in which the general color is brownish with scarcely any trace of metallic lustre and with the antennæ and legs of correspondingly pale color ; the sculpture is generally fainter than in the northern forms, yet preserving the intermixed character which seems peculiar to the species.

That the species here described is that intended by Illiger can hardly be doubted from the greater part of the description as well as from the Melsheimer tradition, but in the Illiger description he concludes : "*plica submarginali*," a character possessed by no species in our fauna, except *bimarginata*. Without attempting to explain the disagreement, the fact is noted to show that it has not been overlooked. I have no doubt that the insect which has, for more than fifty years, borne this name is the true species.

Occurs from the Hudson's Bay region to New England States south to Texas and Florida.

5. **H. vicaria** n. sp.—Elongate oval, much narrowed in front, not very convex, deep blue, moderately shining. Antennæ longer than half the body, piceous, basal joints bluish, joints 2-3-4 gradually longer. Head coarsely punctured near the eyes, frontal carina prominent, tubercles rather feeble. Thorax about one-third wider than long, scarcely narrowed in front, sides arcuate, margin narrow, slightly thickened at the front angles, disc convex, ante-basal impression moderately deep, but not sharply impressed, usually gradually evanescent at its ends, surface finely alutaceous, finely punctate, punctures a little coarser near the sides and front angles. Elytra distinctly wider at base than the thorax, humeri obtuse, umbone moderate, a slight impression within it, surface very finely alutaceous, moderately closely punctate, but smoother near the apex. Body beneath and legs colored as above ; abdomen indistinctly punctate. Length .18—.24 inch.; 4.5—6 mm.

The male has a sinuation each side of the middle of the last ventral, the median lobe semi-circular, flattened, with a deep longitudinal impression extending the entire length of the segment, finer in front.

From the fact that the thorax has the base and apex nearly equal, the species has the facies of having a relatively smaller thorax than any other and the humeri are consequently more prominent. The punctuation is as close as in *carinata*, but less coarse. By the well defined, but not entire ante-basal impressed line this species may be distinguished from any of the large blue forms.

Occurs from Massachusetts (Blanchard) to Florida, westward to Colorado and Arizona.

6. **H. carinata** Germ.—Oblong oval, subdepressed, bright coppery red with bluish or purplish reflections, shining. Antennæ half as long as the body, piceous, the basal half somewhat æneous, joints 2-3-4 gradually longer. Head nearly smooth, a transverse row of punctures between the eyes, carina feeble tubercles small. Thorax about one third wider than long, scarcely narrowed in front, sides slightly arcuate, margin narrow, thickened at the front angles, disc convex, ante-basal impression moderately deep at middle, gradually evanescent toward the sides, surface relatively coarsely, but not closely punctate. Elytra a little wider at base than the thorax, humeri obtuse, feebly prominent, a slight

impression within it, surface more coarsely and closely punctate than the thorax. Body beneath colored as above, slightly greenish at the sides; abdomen moderately, coarsely and closely punctate. Length .14--.18 inch.; 3.5- 4.5 mm.

This is one of the most easily known species in our fauna by the striking colors and the relatively coarse punctuation, which is, however, variable in degree. The thoracic impression also varies in depth, although at all times sharply defined and usually gradually evanescent at its extremities.

The male has a sinuation of the last ventral on each side, the intermediate lobe is semi-circular and has a sharply defined, impressed, median line, which extends half the length of the segment.

In the forms which occur in the Middle States region the color is more decidedly blue, but there can always be seen the tendency to cupreous or violaceous bicoloration.

One of our most widely distributed species, and consequently showing a tendency to vary locally. The form described by LeConte as *torquata*, from two individuals, has the thoracic impression rather less impressed, but otherwise shows no important difference from the large series examined.

Occurs from Bennington County, Vt., (Roberts) southward to Pennsylvania, thence west to the entire Pacific region and Arizona.

From Los Angeles Mr. D. W. Coquillett writes that it injures the grape vines by eating the leaves.

7. **H. californica** Mann.—Short oval, convex, facies robust, shining blue. Antennæ half as long as the body, piceous, basal joints bluish, joints 2-3-4 gradually longer. Head shining, with a few scattered punctures, frontal carina obtuse, tubercles small and indistinct. Thorax one-half wider than long, narrowed in front, sides regularly arcuate, margin very narrow, disc convex, ante-basal groove obliterated at middle, faintly visible at sides only, surface sparsely, finely punctate with an oblique series of coarser punctures beginning at the front angles. Elytra not wider at the base than the thorax, humeri rounded, umbone feeble, smooth, surface with very indistinct, sparse punctuation, smooth at apex and sides. Body beneath and legs bluish; abdomen sparsely punctate. Length .18 inch.; 4.5 mm.

This species has much the form, color and general appearance of *Gastrophysa cyanea*. From the other robust blue species it is best distinguished by the characters of the table. It is very closely related to *obliterata*, but the shining surface and shorter form will readily distinguish it.

One female (from Mannerheim), California.

8. **H. obliterata** Lec.—Oblong oval, convex and moderately robust, color subopaque, blue. Antennæ piceous, with slight metallic lustre, a little longer than half the body, joints 2-3-4 gradually longer. Head finely alutaceous, a group of coarse deep punctures near each eye, frontal carina obtuse, tubercles small. Thorax one half longer than wide, narrowed in front, sides arcuate, more strongly anteriorly, margin very narrow, slightly thickened at the front angles, disc convex, ante-basal impression almost entirely obliterated, visible at times only near the sides, surface subopaque, finely alutaceous, minutely and rather closely punctulate, an oblique series of slightly larger punctures beginning at the front angles. Elytra not wider at base than the thorax, humeri obliterated, umbone scarcely distinct, a slight flattening within it, surface subopaque, finely and rather closely punctulate, a little more coarsely near the base. Body beneath and legs colored as above : abdomen moderately closely punctate. Length .18—.26 inch. ; 4.5—6.5 mm.

The male has the last ventral sinuate each side, the median semicircular lobe short, flattened, smoother, the apical edge slightly reflexed.

This species is one of the largest in our fauna. It is especially known by the opaque blue color, convex and robust form, and almost entire obliteration of the ante-basal impression.

Occurs in Arizona and New Mexico.

9. **H. evicta** Lec.—Oblong oval, subdepressed, brassy bronze, shining. Antennæ a little longer than half the body, piceous, bronzed near the base, joints 2-3-4 gradually longer. Head smooth posteriorly, rugulose near the eyes, frontal carina moderately prominent, the tubercles not separated by the usual line. Thorax one-half wider than long, narrowed in front, sides arcuate, margin narrow, distinctly thickened at the front angles, disc moderately convex, the ante-basal impression fine, but well impressed, terminating at each end in a fovea extending toward the base, surface distinctly alutaceous, finely sparsely punctate, a little more coarsely near the sides and base. Elytra distinctly wider at base than the thorax, humeri obtuse, umbone moderately prominent, a distinct depression within it, surface shining, finely punctate, more closely at base and along the suture, smoother at sides and apex. Body beneath and legs colored as above ; abdomen rather coarsely sparsely punctate. Length .18 inch. ; 4.5 mm.

The last ventral of male is very slightly sinuate each side, at middle subtruncate, a vague, longitudinal, smoother impression.

At first glance this species is very like *Phyllodecta vulgatissima* in form and color. It is the only species at present known in our fauna with the ante-basal groove terminating in a fovea at each end.

Occurs in Oregon.

10. **H. æruginosa** Lec.—Oval, slightly oblong, feebly convex, greenish bronze, feebly shining. Antennæ a little longer than half the body, piceous, slightly bronzed at base, joints 2-3-4 gradually longer. Head subopaque, alutaceous, a few large punctures near the eyes, frontal carina very obtuse, tubercles small. Thorax a little more than half wider than long, narrower in front, sides

arcuate, margin narrow, slightly thickened at the front angles, disc convex, ante-basal impression broad, shallow and indistinct at middle, a little deeper near the sides, then gradually evanescent, surface alutaceous, subopaque, sparsely punctulate, punctures a little coarser near the front angles. Elytra wider than the thorax, humeri rounded, umbone moderate, a slight impression within it, surface subopaque, alutaceous, finely and moderately closely punctate, so as to appear somewhat scabrous. Body beneath more shining than above, very sparsely punctate. Length .12—.14 inch.; 3—3.5 mm.

The last ventral of male has a slight sinuation each side, the middle lobe short, flat and with a median smooth space.

This species is also similar in form to *ignita*, but differs in the ante-basal groove of the thorax and the style of surface sculpture.

Occurs in California and Oregon.

11. **H. obolina** Lec.—Oval, slightly oblong, narrower in front, not very convex, brilliant cupreo-æneous. Antennæ brownish, half as long as the body, joints 2-3-4 gradually longer. Head smooth, a few coarse punctures in a depression near the eyes, frontal carina moderate, the tubercles not separated by the usual median line. Thorax more than half wider than long, narrowed in front, sides regularly arcuate, margin narrow, a little thickened at the front angle; disc convex, ante-basal line broadly impressed and shallow, gradually evanescent, surface shining, sparsely finely punctate. Elytra a little wider at base than the thorax, humeri obliquely rounded, umbone scarcely prominent, surface shining, punctuation moderately coarse, but not close, with finer punctures intermixed. Body beneath colored as above; abdomen with coarse, sparse punctures. Length .12—.14 inch.; 3—3.5 mm.

The six specimens before me are all females. This species has quite the form and facies of the more brilliant forms of *ignita*, and the elytral punctuation is similar, except that in *ignita* the intermediate finer punctures have not been observed. The entire form of *obolina* is broader than in *amœna*, although not very different from *æruginosa*, which has a different color and surface sculpture.

Occurs in northern California and Nevada.

12. **H. amœna** n. sp.—Oblong oval, moderately convex, cupreo-æneous, shining. Antennæ slightly longer than the body, fuscous, joints 2-3-4 gradually longer. Head smooth, frontal carina moderately prominent, tubercles distinct, oblong. Thorax one third wider than long, distinctly narrowed in front, sides arcuate, margin narrow, distinctly thickened near the front angles, disc convex, ante-basal impression sharply defined, but gradually evanescent at its extremities, surface shining, not visibly punctulate, except with very high power. Elytra a little wider than the thorax, humeri obliquely rounded, umbone feeble, surface very finely alutaceous, relatively coarsely, but not closely punctate, the punctures at apex nearly as coarse as at base. Body beneath colored as above; abdomen moderately closely punctate. Length .12 inch.; 3 mm.

The last ventral of the male is slightly sinuate each side, the middle lobe flattened and with a smooth line along the middle, which, by reflected light, gives the appearance of a depression.

A small, inconspicuous species of the form nearly of *polita*. The characters in the analytical table give its distinctive points more clearly than can be done by comparison.

One male specimen, Georgia.

13. **H. marevagans** n sp.—Oval, slightly oblong, moderately convex, deep blue, rarely slightly greenish, shining. Antennae half as long as the body, obviously thicker externally, piceous, bluish at base, joint four distinctly longer than third and equal to fifth. Head smooth, frontal carina scarcely prominent, the tubercles flat and indistinct. Thorax more than half wider than long, sides arcuately narrowed to the front, margin very narrow, slightly thickened at front angles, disc convex, ante-basal impression extremely indistinct, often entirely obliterated, surface sparsely, finely punctate near the base, an oblique series of coarser punctures beginning at the front angles. Elytra a little wider at base than the thorax, humeri rounded, umbone feeble, a slight flattening within it, surface finely, but very distinctly punctate, not closely, smoother near the apex. Body beneath and legs colored as above; abdomen coarsely, not closely punctate. Length .16—.18 inch.; 4—4.5 mm.

The last ventral of the male has a very distinct sinuation each side, the middle lobe flat, with a deep longitudinal impression extending half the segment and ending abruptly.

In most of the collections examined this species is labelled *foliacea*, from which it differs in form, sculpture and male characters.

Occurs along the sea-coast region from Florida to New Jersey, and probably farther north.

14. **H. tombacina** Mann.—Oval, slightly oblong, moderately convex, brownish cupreo æneous, moderately shining. Antennae half as long as the body, slightly thicker toward the tip, piceous, æneous at base, joints 2-3-4 gradually longer. Head smooth behind, a group of very coarse punctures near each eye, frontal carina feeble, tubercles distinct, flat, separated by an impressed line. Thorax one-half longer than wide, slightly narrowed in front, sides feebly arcuate, margin very narrow, slightly thickened at apical angles, disc convex, ante basal line finely impressed, gradually evanescent at the sides, surface extremely finely sparsely punctate, an oblique series of slightly coarser punctures near the front angles. Elytra slightly wider at base than the thorax, humeri rounded, umbone feeble, a slight impression within it. surface finely sparsely punctate, smoother near the apex. Body beneath piceous, faintly metallic; abdomen very sparsely punctate. Length .16—.20 inch.; 4—5 mm.

The last ventral of the male is sinuate each side, the median lobe moderately prominent, slightly concave and smooth with a longitudinal, not deep, impression extending three-fourths the length of the segment.

While this species corresponds very well with the insufficient description by Mannerheim, there may be some doubt as to whether the name should be applied to this or to *ericta*. For a number of years it has had the unpublished name *cupreolus* in the LeConte cabinet and may have been distributed under that name.

This species and *marevagans* are a little stouter than the following species, the antennæ thicker toward the tip, although not greatly so, and the fourth antennal joint very plainly longer than the third, but the entire series is so difficult to separate by description that the sexual characters of the male, together with the elytral sculpture must be especially depended upon. In all the species none approach it in color in any of their variations, except *erieta*, which is easily known by the foveate ante-basal line.

Occurs in California and Montana, also in Alaska (Mannerheim).

15. **H. tincta** Lec.—Elongate oval, feebly convex, nearly of the form of *carinata*, deep blue to nearly black, moderately shining. Antennæ slender, a little longer than half the body, piceous, bluish at base, third and fourth joints equal in length. Head distinctly transversely impressed above the tubercles, these small, distinctly separated, carina not prominent. Thorax more than half wider than long, distinctly narrower in front, sides arcuate, more broadly anteriorly, margin very narrow, distinctly thickened at the front angles, disc convex, ante basal line moderately deeply impressed, ending rather abruptly near the sides, surface sparsely, finely punctate, a little more coarsely at base, a few coarse punctures near the front angles. Elytra a little wider at base than the thorax, humeri rounded, umbone feeble, a slight impression within it, surface moderately, coarsely and closely punctate, smoother near the apex. Body beneath and legs colored as above; abdomen sparsely, coarsely punctate. Length .16—.18 inch.; 4—4.5 mm.

The last ventral of the male is slightly sinuate each side, the middle lobe moderately prominent, with a concavity of triangular form.

Among the species of slender Luperoid form this one is sufficiently well marked by the relatively coarse punctuation of the elytra.

Occurs in California, Oregon, Nevada and Montana.

16. **H. punctipennis** Lec.—Elongate oval, of rather slender form, feebly convex, bright greenish, moderately shining. Antennæ slender, a little longer than half the body, piceous, greenish at base, fourth joint scarcely longer than the third. Head smooth, a group of coarse punctures near each eye, tubercles feeble, carina moderately prominent, but obtuse. Thorax one-half wider than long, narrowed in front, sides regularly arcuate, margin narrow, slightly thickened in front, disc convex, ante-basal impression very feebly indicated or almost entirely obsolete, surface very finely alutaceous, very minutely, sparsely punctulate, punctures a little larger near the sides. Elytra scarcely wider at base than the thorax, humeri rounded, umbone scarcely distinct, surface alutaceous, minutely sparsely punctate, smoother near apex. Body beneath colored as above; abdomen distinctly punctate. Length .14—.18 inch.; 3.5—4.5 mm.

The last ventral of male is sinuate each side, the middle lobe short, semi-circular, the margin reflexed; surface flat, with a short, deep, longitudinal impression near apex.

This species closely resembles *foliacea*, but has the elytra a little more distinctly punctate. The male characters afford the only sure means of separating them.

Occurs in Missouri, Kansas, Colorado and California.

17. **H. lazulina** Lec.—Elongate oval, feebly convex, bright blue or bluish green, shining. Antennæ a little longer than half the body, piceous, bluish at base, third and fourth joints equal. Head smooth posteriorly, a few coarse punctures near the eyes, a transverse impression above the tubercles, which are small, the carina obtuse. Thorax one half longer than wide, narrower in front, sides arcuate, margin narrow, distinctly thicker at apex, disc convex, ante-basal impression fine, feebly impressed, evanescent at the sides, surface alutaceous, distinctly and moderately closely punctulate, an oblique series of coarse punctures near the front angles. Elytra scarcely wider at base than the thorax, humeri rounded, umbone not distinct, surface sparsely finely punctate, smoother at apex. Body beneath as above; abdomen with few punctures. Length .14—.18 inch.; 3.5—4.5 mm.

Last ventral of male sinuate each side, median lobe not prominent, flat, smooth at middle, an extremely short and shallow impression near apex.

Closely resembling *tincta*, but less distinctly punctured and with different male characters; *punctipennis* and *foliacea* are less punctate.

Occurs in Colorado, Montana and Washington Territory.

18. **H. foliacea** Lec.—Elongate oval, feebly convex, color variable from bright green to dark blue, shining. Antennæ half as long as the body, slender, piceous, greenish near base, joints three and four equal. Head smooth behind, a group of coarse punctures near the eyes, a feeble transverse impression above the small tubercles, frontal carina obtuse. Thorax more than half wider than long, narrowed in front, the sides feebly arcuate, margin narrow, very slightly thickened at the front angles, disc convex, the ante-basal line almost entirely obliterated, surface alutaceous, distinctly, sparsely punctulate, a little more coarsely near the front angles. Elytra a little wider at base than the thorax, humeri rounded, umbone not prominent, surface alutaceous, sparsely indistinctly punctate, with a finely scabrous aspect. Body beneath as above; abdomen coarsely, not closely punctate. Length .14—.18 inch.; 3.5—4.5 mm.

The last ventral of male is slightly sinuate each side, the middle lobe short, the apical margin reflexed, a slight longitudinal impression near the apex which is often replaced by a smooth space.

The sexual characters are not very unlike those of *lazulina*, but that has the entire surface more distinctly punctate. Injures the grape vine.

Occurs in Texas, New Mexico and Arizona, those from the first two regions are generally of the green color, those from Arizona more generally blue.

19. **H. polita** Oliv.—Elongate oval, scarcely narrower in front, convex, æneous bronze, shining; legs and antennæ rufotestaceous. Antennæ half as long as the body, slender, joints 2-3-4 gradually longer. Head alutaceous, slightly roughened near the eyes, frontal carina moderately prominent, the tubercles distinct. Thorax one-fourth wider than long, narrowed in front, sides regularly arcuate, margin narrow, distinctly thickened at the front angles, disc convex, a feebly impressed ante-basal line extending very nearly across the disc, surface very finely alutaceous. Elytra not wider at base than the thorax, humeri not distinct, umbone scarcely prominent, surface alutaceous, very minutely, sparsely punctulate. Body beneath reddish brown, a faint bronze surface lustre, abdomen alutaceous, distinctly not closely punctulate. Length .16—.18 inch.; 4—4.5 mm.

The male has the last ventral sinuate each side, the middle forming a short, semi-circular lobe, which is triangularly impressed, with a short longitudinal impression near the apex.

The form of this insect is somewhat that of our Psylliodes, there being but a slight angle formed by the sides of the thorax and elytra. This form, together with the pale antennæ and legs, will enable the insect to be recognized.

This is erroneously placed as a synonym of *Systena frontalis* in the "Catalogus."

Occurs in Georgia and the Carolinas.

20. **H. fuscocnea** Mels.—Oblong oval, moderately shining, olivaceous green, antennæ and legs rufotestaceous. Antennæ a little longer than half the body, joints 2-3-4 gradually increasing in length. Head finely alutaceous, a faint transverse groove between the eyes in which are a few indistinct punctures, frontal carina broad and obtuse, the tubercles small. Thorax transversely subquadrate, very little wider than long, not narrower at apex than base, sides very feebly arcuate, margin very narrow, slightly thickened at the front angles, disc convex, the ante-basal impression fine, but moderately deep, extending nearly from side to side, surface finely alutaceous and with very minute, sparse punctures. Elytra not wider at base than the thorax, humeri broadly rounded, umbone not distinct, surface distinctly sparsely punctate near the base, smoother at apex. Body beneath piceous with æneous surface lustre; abdomen sparsely punctate. Legs rufotestaceous, the posterior femora piceous with æneous surface lustre. Length .12—.14 inch.; 3—3.5 mm.

In the male the last ventral is truncate at middle, a slight sinuation each side, the middle at apex flattened, the edge slightly reflexed.

This species has rather the habitus of a Chætocnema than Haltica in general. The nearly square thorax, together with the pale antennæ and legs will enable it to be distinguished from *polita* and all the others of the genus.

Occurs from Massachusetts to Georgia.

21. **H. opulenta** n. sp.—Oval, slightly oblong, moderately robust, cupreo-violaceous, antennæ and legs rufotestaceous. Antennæ half as long as the body, joints 2-3-4 gradually increasing. Head shining, a few scattered, very fine punctures, others coarser near the eyes, frontal carina moderately prominent, tubercles small. Thorax nearly twice as wide at base as long, narrowed in front, sides regularly arcuate, margin extremely narrow, slightly thickened at the front angles, disc convex, ante-basal impression almost entirely obliterated, surface very finely, sparsely punctulate. Elytra not wider at base than the thorax, humeri very broadly rounded, umbone feebly distinct, surface shining, finely, not closely punctulate　Body beneath piceous, without metallic lustre; abdomen sparsely punctate. Legs entirely rufotestaceous. Length .16 inch.; 4 mm.

Two female specimens only have been seen. The form is somewhat that of *obliterata*, but a little shorter, while the surface color is that of some of the darker forms of *carinata*.

The very feeble transverse impression of the thorax as well as the form will serve to distinguish this species from any of those with pale antennæ and legs in our fauna.

Occurs in southern Arizona.

22. **H. floridana** n. sp.—Oval, depressed, moderately shining, head, thorax, body beneath and legs reddish yellow, abdomen brown, elytra bluish green. Antennæ half as long as the body, rufotestaceous, the outer joints darker, joints 2-3-4 about equal in length. Head finely alutaceous, a few coarse punctures near the eyes, frontal carina very obtuse, tubercles indistinct. Thorax one-half wider than long, not narrower in front, sides feebly arcuate, anterior angles obliquely truncate, disc feebly convex, ante basal impression very feeble, surface finely alutaceous, sparsely, finely punctate, an oblique series of coarser punctures near the front angles. Elytra not wider at base than the thorax, humeri obliquely rounded, umbone scarcely prominent, smooth; surface alutaceous, sparsely, indistinctly, but relatively coarsely punctate, smoother near the apex. Body beneath reddish yellow, metasternum rather coarsely punctate; abdomen brownish, sparsely punctate. Length .12 inch.; 3 mm.

A small species resembling at first sight some of the smaller forms of *Dison. collata*. It is easily known among our species by its color. The front angles of the thorax are more distinctly obliquely truncate than in any other in our fauna.

Collected at Biscayne, Florida, by E. A. Schwarz, to whom I am indebted for the female in my possession.

23. **H. Burgessi** Crotch.—Oval, moderately convex, head and thorax reddish yellow, elytra metallic bluish green, shining, abdomen piceous, legs pale reddish yellow. Antennæ pale at base, joints five to eleven brown. Head smooth, frontal carina distinct, but obtuse, tubercles small, but well marked, distinctly limited above by a deep groove. Thorax one-half wider than long, sides arcuately narrowing to the front, ante-basal impression deep, arcuate, extending entirely across the thorax from angle to angle, disc convex, surface smooth, shining. Elytra a little wider at base than the thorax, humeri obtusely rounded, umbone moderately prominent, surface with coarse, deep, moderately closely placed punctures which become fainter toward apex; abdomen piceous, sparsely punctate, each puncture with a very short hair. Length .06—.07 inch.; 1.5—1.75 mm.

The male has the apex of the last ventral flattened and slightly upturned toward the pygidium.

Without an examination of the type it would have been impossible to have determined this insect. It was described by Crotch as a Haltica and placed in the series with closed front coxal cavities; the length was given as .16 inch., while the description, otherwise, is very unsatisfactory. While it is widely separated from nana, by the table, it is more closely related to it than any other species by the form of the ante-basal impression and the coarse punctures of the elytra. It is not at all a Cæporis, as we have recently placed it.

Occurs at Key West, Florida.

24. **H. rufa** Illiger.—Oval, broader behind, moderately convex, orange yellow, moderately shining. Antennæ half as long as the body, piceous, third joint distinctly longer than the fourth. Head yellow, labrum black, frontal carina broad and obtuse, tubercles very flat, a few coarse punctures in an arcuate series parallel with the border of the eyes. Thorax nearly twice as wide at base as long, narrowed to the front, sides arcuate, margin very narrow, anterior angles obtuse, a slight sinuation or notch in the margin behind them, posterior angles acute, sometimes slightly prominent, disc convex, ante-basal impression broad and shallow, not entire, surface sparsely, indistinctly punctate. Scutellum black. Elytra a little wider at base than the thorax, humeri rounded, umbone feeble, surface indistinctly, sparsely punctate. Body beneath, except prothorax, piceous; abdomen reddish, varying to piceous, sparsely punctate. Legs piceous, the posterior femora pale beneath and at base. Length .16—.20 inch.; 4—5 mm.

This insect seems to have some trouble in finding a permanent generic resting place. Following the "Catalogus" it is a Disonycha, while a species completely congeneric (and I think also specifically identical) has been described in the "Biologia" as *Lactica scutellaris*. That it cannot be referred to Lactica is evident from the character of the basal impression of the thorax, and the choice is plainly between Disonycha and Haltica. The latter genus has been chosen, because there is a well marked ante-basal depression of the thorax, which is, however, said to occur in Disonycha, but is not present in any of our species. The posterior edge of the hind tibiæ is scarcely at all sulcate as in the majority of our Halticæ. The genera are, however, so lacking in sharpness of definition in Halticini that in certain cases the position of species is purely opinionative, and this is one of them.

Occurs from Massachusetts to Illinois, Florida and Texas, extending through Mexico to South America.

Group IX. –LACTICÆ.

Antennæ 11-jointed. Thorax with a deep ante-basal groove distinctly limited at its ends usually by being bent abruptly toward the base. Anterior coxal cavities open behind.

These few characters define the tribe, while it otherwise shows considerable variation in its generic membership. The following genera are known in our fauna:

Elytra nearly smooth, the punctuation when present extremely fine and scattered..**Lactica.**
Elytra coarsely striato punctate.
  Form oval; without erect hairs...................................**Diphaulaca.**
  Form oblong, parallel: elytra with short hairs arising from interstitial punctures..**Trichaltica.**

These genera belong to the Asiatic region of our fauna.

LACTICA Erichs.

Head subtriangular, inserted in the thorax as far as the eyes, these oval, slightly emarginate in front, coarsely granulate. Front broadly, obtusely carinate, the tubercles feeble. Labrum transverse, slightly arcuate in front. Maxillary palpi stout, terminal joint acutely conical, shorter than the preceding, which is as broad at apex as long. Antennæ longer than half the body, slender, third joint shorter than fourth, joints 4–10 equal, eleventh very little longer. Thorax transverse, with a deep, transverse, ante-basal impression bent at each end rectangularly to the base, apical margin truncate, base arcuate. Elytra oval, scarcely wider at base than the thorax, the punctuation in our species extremely fine and confused. Prosternum separating the coxæ and slightly prolonged, the cavities open posteriorly. Metasternum oblique. Legs rather slender, the anterior and middle tibiæ bisulcate externally, posterior tibiæ with a short sulcus at apex and a row of ciliæ on the outer side extending nearly half to base, terminated by a small curved spur. Tarsi more than half the length of the tibiæ, the claws appendiculate.

As represented in our fauna Lactica is certainly very closely related to Haltica, but readily known by the deep basal impression rectangularly recurved at either end.

Two species are known, separable as follows:

Entirely lemon-yellow, tibiæ and tarsi black ....**tibialis.**
Head and thorax yellow, elytra deep violet blue............................... **Iris.**

L. tibialis Oliv.—Oblong oval, moderately convex, entirely pale yellow, surface shining. Antennæ piceous, two basal joints yellow. Head very sparsely punctulate. Thorax nearly twice as wide at base as long, distinctly narrowed in front, sides arcuate, margin narrowly explanate, front angles very obliquely truncate, disc convex, sparsely, finely punctate. Elytra scarcely wider at base than the thorax, humeri rounded, umbone not prominent, disc moderately convex, not gibbous near the base, punctuation fine, indistinct and moderately close. Body beneath entirely yellow; abdomen moderately closely punctate and sparsely pubescent. Femora yellow, except the upper side of knees, tibiæ and tarsi piceous. Length .14–.16 inch ; 3.5–4.5 mm.

The last ventral of male is broadly emarginate at middle, the first joint of anterior tarsus broader than in the female.

This species is often mistaken for *Haltica rufa*, but independently of the deep basal impression, the form is more elongate and the color always paler.

Occurs from North Carolina to Florida and Louisiana.

L. Iris Oliv.—Oval, slightly oblong, moderately convex, shining, head and thorax yellow, elytra deep violet blue. Antennæ piceous, three basal joints pale. Head sparsely, finely punctate, a large foveate puncture near each eye. Thorax twice as wide at base as at apex, narrower in front, sides arcuate, margin very narrow, front angles not obliquely truncate, disc convex, not visibly punctate. Elytra not wider at base than the thorax, humeri rounded, umbone moderately prominent, limited within by a slight depression, disc convex, very slightly gibbous at base, color deep violet-blue, surface shining, scarcely visibly punctate. Prothorax beneath, front and middle legs pale yellow; metasternum, abdomen and hind legs piceous. Abdomen moderately closely punctate on the intermediate segments, sparsely pubescent. Length .14–.16 inch.; 3.5–4 mm.

Males have not been observed.

The contrast in color between the front of body and the elytra make this one of our prettiest Halticides. It seems rather rare.

Occurs in Maryland (Lugger) and Georgia.

DIPHAULACA Clark.

Head inserted in the thorax as far as the eyes, the front obtusely carinate and with distinct tubercles, clypeus slightly emarginate, labrum slightly arcuate in front, maxillary palpi rather slender, the terminal joint as long as the preceding, acute. Antennæ slender, at least half as long as the body Thorax broader than long, narrower in front, the sides arcuate, anterior angles obliquely truncate (in our species), the ante-basal impression deep, slightly sinuous, limited each side by a short longitudinal impression. Elytra oval, wider at base than the thorax, disc coarsely striato-punctate. Prosternum moderate, slightly dilated at apex, the coxal cavities widely open behind. Legs moderate, tibiæ slightly broader to apex, the outer face slightly grooved near the apex, the posterior pair alone with a small spur. Tarsi moderate in length, the first joint of the posterior pair nearly one-third the length of the tibia. Claws appendiculate.

It is not without some doubt that I refer the small species before me to the present genus, having but one species at hand for comparison (*D. nitida* Jacoby), which is itself abnormal in several respects. The open front coxal cavities, the deep ante-basal impression limited each side by a (very short, it is true) longitudinal impression, the striato-punctate elytra cause me to place it in the Lacticæ and Diphaulaca is the only genus to which it can be referred, unless a new one be made, and this could not be accurately defined.

D. bicolorata n. sp.—Oval, moderately convex, head, thorax and legs reddish yellow, elytra and abdomen piceous black with faint purple lustre. Antennæ rufotestaceous, slightly darker externally. Head smooth. Thorax nearly twice as wide at base as long, narrowed in front, sides arcuate, anterior angles obliquely truncate, disc convex, very sparsely punctate. Elytra wider at base than the thorax, humeri rounded, umbone small, smooth, disc moderately convex, coarsely striato-punctate, punctures closely placed and deep, those near the suture very irregular, although variable in the specimens, intervals smooth, metasternum and abdomen piceous black, shining, the latter sparsely punctate. Legs pale rufotestaceous, the posterior femora slightly darker. Length .08 inch.; 2 mm.

The elytral punctuation is distinctly variable in the four specimens before me, but in all there is a very evident irregularity of the striæ near the suture.

Mr. Jacoby has suggested ("Biologia" vi, i. p. 263) that the genus is not sharply defined as to the species included by Clark, although a species is added (*nitida*) which rather adds to the confusion. While it must be admitted that the species above described differs somewhat generically from the species which Mr. Jacoby thinks should alone remain (those with anterior angles prominent externally) I feel unwilling to suggest a new name until the already known species are more carefully placed.

Occurs in Michigan and Louisiana (Schwarz), in Georgia (Morrison), Kansas (cabinet LeConte).

TRICHALTICA Harold.

Head inserted as far as the eyes, these oval, entire and coarsely granulated. Front obtusely carinate, the tubercles distinct, separated by a line and limited above by a moderately deep transverse groove. Antennæ slender, very slightly thicker externally, joints 1–4–5–11 longer than the others, which are equal. Labrum transverse, arcuate in front. Maxillary palpi rather short, the last joint elongate, conical, longer than the preceding, which is as broad at apex as long. Thorax broader than long, the base regularly arcuate, a deep antebasal groove which turns backward toward the base at its ends. Elytra a little wider at base than the thorax, the sculpture consisting of coarse punctures arranged in ten very regular striæ and on short scutellar stria. Prosternum separating the coxæ, the cavities rather widely open behind. Mesosternum oblique. Ventral segments 1–4 gradually shorter, the fifth longer than fourth. Legs moderate. Posterior tibiæ not sulcate, with a single, small terminal spur. Claws appendiculate.

This genus was erected by Baron Harold for some Columbian species, to which he added our *Crepidodera scabricula* Cr. In his description he compares it with Diphaulaca and Plectrotetra, the latter rather unnecessarily. The only representative of the former genus known to me is *nitida*, which, unfortunately, seems to be one of the irregular members. From what can be gathered from descriptions the differences between Trichaltica and Diphaulaca consist in the presence of erect hairs on the elytra of the former (very indistinct in our species) and the oval, convex elytra of the latter. In our fauna the only allied genus, in tribal relationship, is Lactica where the elytra are scarcely at all punctate and confusedly.

T. scabricula Crotch.--Oblong, nearly parallel, moderately convex, reddish yellow, elytra blue. Antennæ a little longer than half the body, piceous or brown. Head impunctate. Thorax more than one-half wider than long, not narrowed in front, sides regularly arcuate, hind angles distinct, base arcuate, disc convex, shining, a few scattered, coarse punctures. Elytra wider at base than the thorax, humeri obtuse, umbone scarcely distinct, disc slightly flattened at middle and with ten striæ of coarse, deep and closely placed punctures, a short scutellar row, intervals narrower than the striæ and with distantly placed, short, semi-erect hairs. Body beneath and legs reddish yellow; abdomen sparsely punctate. Length .10--.14 inch.; 2.5--3.5 mm.

In the male the last ventral segment is slightly sinuate each side, the middle lobe slightly bent upward. The first joint of anterior tarsus is also broader than in the female.

This insect is similar in color and style of sculpture to *Crepidodera rufipes*, but is more elongate and less convex, and the elytral punctures much deeper. The two differ radically, in the fact that the anterior coxal cavities are here open, and in Crepidodera closed.

Occurs from Ohio to Texas

Group X.—CREPIDODERÆ.

Antennæ 11-jointed, filiform. Prothorax with a well marked antebasal transverse impression, usually limited at each end. Anterior coxal cavities closed behind. Ventral segments all free. Posterior tibiæ usually feebly sulcate near the apex. Tarsi of moderate length, the claw joint simple. Claws appendiculate.

This group consists of a portion only of the genera placed there by Chapuis. For the same reasons which have induced me to separate those genera without distinct ante-basal groove from the Halticæ, similar genera have been removed to constitute the group Systenæ. There is, however, an additional reason here. All the Crepidoderæ have the elytra striato-punctate, while in the Systenæ the punctuation is confused.

The following genera occur in our fauna:

All the tibiæ with a terminal spur...................................**Hemiglyptus.**
Posterior tibiæ alone with a spur.
  Body above glabrous.
    Form more or less ovate; ante-basal groove limited each side; antennæ not
      unusually long..**Crepidodera.**
    Form elongate, parallel; ante-basal groove not limited; antennæ as long as
      or longer than body...**Orthaltica.**
  Elytra with rows of setæ on the interstices.
    Form short, ovate; anterior angles obliquely truncate; antennæ moderate.
                                                       Epitrix.
    Form elongate, parallel; anterior angles not obliquely truncate; antennæ
      long...**Leptotrix.**

Hemiglyptus occurs in California. Epitrix is represented on both sides of the continent; the other genera belong to the Atlantic region.

From the group as constituted in the Classification of Col. N. A. 1883, p. 352, in addition to Systena the following are removed:

Micraltica has open anterior coxal cavities and the species placed in Haltica.

Cerataltica has open cavities also, and is placed in Aphthona. *Luperaltica* is a composite genus, one species being a Systena, the other a Galerucidæ. It should be entirely dropped from the literature.

HEMIGLYPTUS n. g.

Head inserted on the thorax as far as the eyes, the front obtusely carinate and with two tubercles separated at middle. Eyes oval, rather coarsely granulated. Antennæ a little longer than half the body, gradually thicker externally, joints 2–10 gradually longer, eleventh longer. Clypeus truncate, labrum entire. Mandibles bidentate at apex, the lower tooth shorter. Maxillary palpi moderate in length, the terminal joint fusiform, acute, longer than the preceding joint. Thorax truncate in front, base arcuate, a moderately deep ante-basal transverse impression, limited at each end by a rather deeper longitudinal impression. Prosternum separating the coxæ, dilated behind them, the coxal cavities rather widely closed behind. Mesosternum oblique, metasternum moderate in length. Ventral segments 2–4 equal, fifth a little longer, first as long as the next two. Elytra with indistinct humeri, punctuation confused, rarely with a substriate arrangement. Legs moderate in length, tibiæ gradually broader to apex, outer edge rounded, the anterior and middle tibiæ each with a slender spur ; posterior tibiæ obliquely truncate at apex and with a terminal spur. Tarsi two-thirds as long as the tibiæ, claw joint slender, the claws appendiculate.

This genus has been erected for a species of elongate, parallel form, recalling Prasocuris, which must be referred to the Crepidodera series and differing from all the genera known to me in the Halticini by the presence of a spur to each of the tibiæ. The tibiæ themselves are rather stouter, *i. e.*, more dilated at tip than usual in the Crepidoderides, and the oblique truncation of the posterior pair is margined by a row of short, stiff ciliæ.

H. basalis Crotch.--Oblong, parallel, moderately convex, piceous, surface with brown bronze lustre. Antennæ half as long as the body, piceous, five basal joints rufotestaceous. Head smooth, frontal carina broad and flat, having a rhomboid area, tubercles very flat, separated from the front by a finely impressed line, a group of very coarse punctures near each eye. Thorax transversely quadrate, not narrowed in front, sides feebly arcuate, disc convex, the punctures coarse, deep and close, except near the apex, ante-basal impression moderately deep, the longitudinal impressions deeper and extend in front of as well as behind the transverse impression. Elytra distinctly wider at base than the thorax, the humeri obtusely rounded, umbone distinct, with a slight impression within it, sides parallel, disc convex, the punctuation less coarse than that of the thorax, very irregularly placed, but in some specimens showing the tendency to irregular striae. Body beneath piceous, slightly bronzed. Abdomen punctate, the first (and last ♀) segment sparsely, the others more closely, surface sparsely pubescent. Legs pale brown to rufotestaceous, the posterior femora usually darker. Length .12- .14 inch. : 3--3.5 mm   Plate VII, fig. 2.

In the male the last ventral segment is slightly sinuate each side, the middle lobe broadly, but feebly concave. The first joint of the anterior tarsus is broader than in the female. The antennæ are also longer and more slender. The last ventral segment is also more closely punctate.

In the female there is sometimes a transverse impression of the last segment near the apex.

This species does not show much variation. The elytral sculpture is faintly striate, but usually much confused and irregular. It is very rarely slightly bluish or greenish in color.

As specimens are usually seen in the cabinet the upper surface is glabrous, but in well preserved examples the surface is sparsely clothed with nearly erect short hairs arising from the punctures, usually evident near the sides of the thorax and elytra. There are a few also near the sides of the head.

Occurs in California, especially in the lower portion of the State.

CREPIDODERA Chev.

Front more or less triangular, inserted as far as the eyes, frontal carina more or less distinct, the tubercles often feeble. Eyes round, convex. Antennæ as long as half the body, gradually slightly broader to tip, first joint oblong oval, second half as long, 3–10 subequal, a little longer than second, eleventh longer, acute at tip. Maxillary palpi short, the fourth joint conical, as long as or a little longer than the preceding. Thorax broader than long, an ante-basal impressed line variable in depth, limited at each end by a longitudinal impression. Prosternum distinctly separating the coxæ, dilated behind them and with the epimera closing the coxal cavities. Mesosternum usually distinct, the middle coxæ either moderately or rather widely separated. Metasternum oval or acute in front, and in *robusta* prolonged over the mesosternum. First ventral segment as long as the next three, which are nearly equal in length, fifth a little longer. Legs moderate, the tibiæ rounded on the outer face, the posterior tibiæ obliquely truncate and with a small spur.

The above genus is identical with that defined by Chapuis in the "Genera." In his admirable monograph Foudras has divided the genus into six, to which Weise has added another for the German fauna (Ins. Deutschl. vi, p. 686). From the species before me which represent three of the genera,* while the three native species would form three more, I am heartily in accord with Chapuis and Harold in considering the differences totally insufficient for generic separation.

From those formerly enrolled in Crepidodera in our lists *C. scabricula* has been removed to form a genus Trichaltica in the Lacticites, while *C. basalis* Crotch forms a distinct new genus.

The following have been described by Boheman (Eugenies Resa), and the localities are given so that others may draw their inferences:

C. rufra Boh., loc. cit. p. 194. St. Francisco.

C. suturella Boh., p. 194. California (St. Francisco), Insula Puna.

C. bicolor Boh., p. 195. California (St. Francisco), Taiti.

This is a very small insect, but .05 inch. long.

C. puberula Boh., p. 196. Montevideo, California, Insula Puna, Taiti et Oahu.

This is doubtless an Epitrix.

The localities of the Eugenies Resa material are notoriously badly mixed, and no reliance can be placed upon them. As I have been unable to identify them, notwithstanding all the collecting that has been done in California I think it best to omit them from our lists.

The species known to me may be separated in the following manner:

Form oblong oval.
  Head and thorax yellow, elytra bright blue; prosternum smooth; thorax
    smooth..**rufipes.**
  Head and thorax similar in color to the elytra.
    Elytra uniform in coloration.
      Prothorax with very distinct and rather coarse punctuation.
        Form narrow, elongate; rufotestaceous, with greenish surface lustre;
          prosternum smooth...............................**longula.**
        Form oval; surface decidedly metallic; thoracic punctuation abundant
          and intermixed; prosternum sparsely punctate.........**Helxines.**
      Prothorax extremely finely punctate and very convex; color piceous
        brown without metallic lustre; prosternum densely and coarsely
        punctured; ninth stria rather distant from margin.......**robusta.**

* *C. helxines* is a Chalcoides; *C. modeeri* a Hippuriphila, and *C. rufipes* a Derocrepis.

Elytra at apical third indefinitely testaceous.
Prothorax very distinctly punctate; prosternum densely punctate.
                                                         Modeeri.
Form broadly oval and convex; color rufotestaceous, without metallic lustre;
    abdomen piceous.
Prothorax not distinctly punctured; prosternum punctate......**atriventris.**
Form ovate, a slight gibbosity at the middle of base of each elytron.
Prothorax coarsely and moderately closely punctate; color piceous black,
    shining..**nitens.**

C. rufipes Linn.—Oblong oval, nearly parallel, moderately convex; head,
thorax and legs reddish yellow, elytra blue, shining. Antennae as long as half
the body, gradually thicker externally. Head smooth, frontal carina obtuse,
tubercles distinct, well separated, distinctly limited above by a broadly V-shaped
line. Thorax nearly twice as wide as long, sides behind nearly parallel, in front
arcuately narrowed to the apex, disc convex, almost absolutely smooth, a deep
transverse ante-basal impression, limited at each end by a deep longitudinal impression which does not extend anterior to the transverse one. Elytra a little
wider at base than the thorax, obtuse, umbone moderately prominent and smooth,
a slight impression within it, disc moderately convex, a long scutellar stria of
punctures and nine discal striæ of coarse, closely placed punctures, the outer not
more distant from the margin than from the eighth, intervals narrower than the
striæ, slightly convex, and with a few minute punctures. Prothorax beneath
entirely smooth. Metasternum and abdomen piceous, the latter sparsely punctate and with short, sparse pubescence. Length .10 inch.; 2.5 mm.

The male has a slight impression at the middle of the apical margin of the last ventral segment and the first joint of the anterior
tarsus dilated.

This common European species has probably been introduced
into our fauna, and is now widely scattered over the Atlantic region
as far west as Iowa.

C. longula n. sp.—Elongate oval, nearly parallel, moderately convex, pale
rufotestaceous, surface with distinct greenish lustre. Antennæ half as long as
the body, very slightly thicker externally. Head smooth, frontal carina distinct, tubercles small, but indistinct. Thorax nearly twice as wide as long, very
little narrowed in front, sides feebly arcuate, anterior angles slightly oblique, a
feeble sinuation behind them, disc convex, ante-basal impression moderately
deep, abruptly bent toward the base at each end, surface with moderately coarse
and unequal punctures, irregularly scattered over the thorax. Elytra very little
wider than the thorax, humeri rounded, umbone not prominent, disc moderately
long, scutellar and nine discal striæ of coarse and rather closely placed punctures
which are finer near apex, the ninth not distant from margin, intervals narrower
than the striæ and with a single row of fine punctures. Prosternum and pleuræ
smooth. Abdomen sparsely punctate, not pubescent. Length .10 inch.; 2.5 mm.

The last ventral of the male has a feeble impression at apex and
the first joint of anterior and middle tarsi dilated.

While the color is entirely pale, there is a distinct greenish surface lustre. The suture is very narrowly piceous, the color becoming broader, but more indefinite near the base. In form this species is similar to Orthaltica. Collected near McPherson, Kansas, by Mr. William Knaus on willows.

C. Helxines Linn.—Oval, slightly oblong, moderately convex, piceous, surface metallic, varying from brown bronze to blue or green, antennae and legs pale. Antennae half as long as the body, very slightly thicker to tip, pale rufo-testaceous, often darker toward tip. Head smooth, frontal carina distinct, tubercles not evident, but replaced by an oblique ridge. Thorax more than half wider than long, not narrowed in front, sides very feebly arcuate, anterior angles obliquely truncate, disc moderately convex, ante-basal impression deep and at each end suddenly flexed to the base, the surface coarsely, but unequally punctate. Elytra distinctly wider at base than the thorax, obliquely rounded, umbone moderately prominent, a slight depression within it, disc with a scutellar and nine discal striae of moderate punctures, not closely placed, becoming gradually finer to apex, intervals broader than the striae, very minutely punctate or smooth. Prosternum punctate, but not densely. Abdomen sparsely, finely punctate, with few hairs. Legs rufotestaceous, the posterior femur usually darker. Length .09—.13 inch.; 2.2—3.3 mm.

In the male the last ventral segment has a slight impression at apex.

This species seems to vary in a manner similar to that observed in Europe, and the reddish or brownish bronze forms seem the most abundant. There is a decided variation in the sculpture of the elytra. In the specimens from the more northern regions of our country the elytra are distinctly striate, while those from the warmer regions and California have simply the rows of punctures. Consequently, those with the elytra simply striato-punctate, the intervals are flat, while those punctato-striate have convex intervals. The interstitial punctuation is always fine, but in some specimens before me cannot be observed.

Specimens have been observed from nearly every part of the United States.

C. robusta Lec. - Oval, slightly oblong, convex, facies robust, piceous brown, shining, legs and antennae brownish testaceous. Head smooth, frontal carina obtuse, tubercles flat, transverse, not separated, limited above by a fine sinuous line. Antennae half as long as the body, joints 3-10 very slightly increasing in length and width, eleventh a little longer and acute at tip. Thorax very nearly twice as wide as long, slightly narrowed in front, sides rather irregularly arcuate, obliquely rounded near the front angles, disc rather strongly convex, sparsely, very finely punctate, ante-basal transverse impression moderately deep, the lon-

gitudinal impressions deep, slightly oblique and extending one-third the length
of the thorax. Elytra not wider at base than the thorax, humeri obliquely
rounded, umbone moderate and smooth, disc convex, with nine striae of moderately coarse punctures, rather closely placed near the base, more distant and finer
at apex, the ninth distant from the margin, a scutellar stria extending one-third
from base, intervals flat, very minutely, sparsely punctulate. Prosternum
coarsely and closely punctate, the pleurae smooth. Abdomen rather closely punctate, scabrous, first segment smoother. Length .12 inch.; 3 mm.

In this species the metasternum is prolonged in front in an acutely
oval process, almost meeting the prosternum, and the mesosternum
is consequently practically invisible. In all the species of Crepidodera (sensu Chapuis) the metasternum varies in form in such a manner as to render it impracticable to use it for the separation of genera.
By the Chapuis table *robusta* would, in all probability, be supposed
to be a Mniophilite, but these have the anterior coxal cavities open
and the thorax without transverse impression.

With the general form of *Modeeri* the present species has the thorax
more convex than usual, so that the head is scarcely visible from
above. The ninth discal stria is rather distant from the marginal,
a character unknown in our other species. It is probable that *robusta* should be separated generically, and with other species having
similar characters such a course would be advisable.

By a clerical error Dr. LeConte describes the thorax as twice as
long as wide.

This species is rare at present; the only two known to me, except
the type, are in the collections of Mr. Blanchard and Mr. Ulke, who
have kindly given me the use of all their material.

Collected in the White Mountains, N. H.

C. Modeeri Linn.—Oval, narrowed in front, moderately robust, piceous,
with slight aeneous lustre, apical third of elytra indeterminately testaceous.
Antennae half as long as the body, gradually broader externally, brownish or
piceous, the four basal joints pale. Head alutaceous, sparsely punctate, frontal
carina distinct, but obtuse, the tubercles not well defined. Thorax one-half
wider than long, sides nearly parallel behind, arcuately narrowed in front, disc
convex, a moderate ante-basal transverse impression, limited at each end by a
deep longitudinal impression which extends slightly in front of the transverse
one, disc convex, surface alutaceous, the punctures coarse, moderately close, but
not deep, behind the impression smoother. Elytra distinctly wider at base than
the thorax, humeri obtusely rounded, umbone moderate, slightly impressed
within, disc moderately convex, scutellar stria long, disc with nine striae of
coarse punctures, moderately closely placed near the base, becoming finer and
more distant near the apex, the ninth stria not distant from the margin. Prosternum coarsely and closely punctured, the pleurae smooth. Abdomen finely,
indistinctly punctate, with fine pubescence. Legs brown, the anterior and middle pair usually paler. Length .08—.10 inch.; 2—2.5 mm.

The male has a slight impression at the apex of the last ventral and the first joint of anterior and middle tarsi dilated.

The specimens taken in our fauna are of the color described above, but varieties occur in Europe bluish or green. It is usually found on aquatic plants in the manner of Donacia. Occurs in Canada, at Detroit, also in Oregon.

C. atriventris Mels.—Form rather broadly oval and convex, rufotestaceous, without metallic lustre. Antennæ half as long as the body, pale rufotestaceous, very slightly thicker externally. Thorax twice as wide as long, sides posteriorly feebly arcuate, anteriorly obliquely truncate, a slight angulation one-third from apex, disc convex, impunctate, ante-basal transverse impression moderately deep, rectangularly bent at each end to the base. Elytra wider at base than the thorax, humeri rounded, umbone scarcely prominent, disc convex, scutellar stria long, nine discal striæ all with coarse, moderately closely placed punctures, which become rapidly finer to apex, ninth not distant from the margin, intervals a little broader than the striæ, slightly convex and smooth. Prosternum indistinctly coarse punctate, pleuræ smooth. Metasternum and abdomen piceous, the latter sparsely, indistinctly punctate. Legs pale rufotestaceous. Length .06—.07 inch.; 1.5—1.75 mm.

The specimens before me are all females. The male characters are probably as in *Modeeri*.

This is the smallest species in our fauna. It is known by its rather broadly oval and convex form and the very oblique truncation near the front angles.

Occurs from Massachusetts to Maryland.

C. nitens n. sp.—Ovate, robust, black, shining. Antennæ pale rufotestaceous; front smooth. Thorax rather more than twice as wide as long, distinctly narrowed in front, sides slightly arcuate, obliquely truncate at the front angles, disc convex, the punctures rather coarse and deep, but not crowded, intervals smooth, ante-basal impression feeble, but slightly arcuate toward the base. Elytra scarcely wider at base than the thorax, humeri rounded, umbone rather feeble, disc convex, with a vague transverse depression one-third from base and along the suture, giving the aspect of a feeble gibbosity on each elytron, striæ not impressed, the punctures relatively small, not closely placed, intervals flat, much wider than the striæ, smooth and shining. Prosternum and pleuræ coarsely punctate. Abdomen sparsely punctate. Femora piceous black, tibiæ brown, tarsi paler. Length .08 inch.; 2 mm.

This species has been found rather troublesome to place generically. The form and facies suggest Epitrix, but there is no pubescence, nor are there any fine punctures in the intervals to suggest their probable presence; the metasternum in front is rather broad, as in *Modeeri*, and suggests a relationship with that species, although quite different in form and appearance. With a predilection for placing it in Epitrix, a strict interpretation of characters, as at present used, makes it necessary to place it for the time in Crepidodera. Three specimens, Illinois.

EPITRIX Foudras.

The differences between this genus and Crepidodera are very feeble, and in fact there is but one constant. While in that genus the upper surface is entirely glabrous, in this the upper surface has short, semi-erect hairs, sparsely placed over the thorax and at the sides, and on the elytra arranged in a single row on each interval. The frontal carina is feeble and the tubercles are absent ; there is, however, an oblique ridge each side extending from the end of the frontal carina to the eye, limited above by a well impressed line, the two forming together a broad V. The anterior angles of the thorax are conspicuously obliquely truncate, the truncation posteriorly limited by a dentiform process. The ante-basal impressions are variable according to the species, well marked in some or feeble, and almost obliterated in others. The elytra are punctato-striate with punctures of variable size according to species, the intervals rarely wider than the striæ and with a single row of finer punctures from which the seriate hairs arise.

The sexual characters are rather feeble ; the male has the first joint of the anterior tarsus broader than in the female, the last ventral segment shorter and subtruncate, while the surface of the abdomen is less distinctly punctate than in the female.

The species are not numerous ; those of Europe live on plants of the order Solanaceæ. Harris states that cucumeris injures cucumber vines. It is probable that the natural food plants of our species are of the same order as those of Europe.

The following table will assist in the recognition of the species :

Species of piceous surface.
  Thorax very densely and coarsely punctate ; ante-basal impression feeble
                                          fuscula.
  Thorax not densely punctate, the punctures well separated.
    Ante-basal impression well marked.
      Elytral striæ rather deep, the punctures coarse, close and quadrate ; punctures of thorax close, though separated ....**lobata.**
      Elytral striæ, especially those nearest the suture, very feeble ; the punctures round and not crowded..................... ....**cucumeris.**
    Ante-basal impression very feeble.
      Species quite small ; thoracic punctures close, but not crowded...**brevis.**

Species with distinct æneous surface lustre.
Thorax closely punctate; impression distinct. ....**suberinita.**
Species rufotestaceous; legs always pale.
Thorax moderately closely punctate, the ante-basal impressions scarcely
visible ....**parvula.**

E. fuscula Crotch.—Form ovate, rather robust, piceous, feebly shining.
Antennæ rufotestaceous, sometimes darker toward the apex. Front with a few
coarse and deep punctures. Thorax twice as wide as long, slightly narrowed in
front, sides moderately arcuate, anterior angles obliquely truncate, disc convex,
punctuation coarse, dense and deep, the ante-basal impressions feeble, being
almost obliterated by the punctuation. Elytra scarcely wider at base than the
thorax, humeri obtuse, umbone moderately prominent, disc regularly convex,
the striæ of the middle slightly impressed and acute, round, not crowded punctures, those at the sides deeper, with deep and closely placed punctures, intervals
near the suture distinctly wider than the striæ and all with a single series of
minute punctures. Prosternum coarsely, not closely punctured. Abdomen
piceous, sparsely punctate and pubescent. Femora of all the legs piceous, tibiæ
and tarsi rufotestaceous. Length .08 inch.; 2 mm.

This species is, as a rule, larger and more robust than *cucumeris*,
the thoracic punctuation so close, coarse and deep that it would be
called cribrate if in the same proportion on a larger insect and the
ante-basal impressions very feeble.

Seems to be a widely distributed species over the entire country
east of the Mississippi, also in Missouri.

E. lobata Crotch.—Ovate, of robust facies, piceous, feebly shining. Antennæ rufotestaceous. Front smooth, a few coarse punctures near the eye.
Thorax twice as wide as long, slightly narrowed in front, sides nearly straight,
obliquely truncate at anterior angles, disc convex, the punctures coarse and deep,
round, not densely crowded, the intervals shining, the ante-basal impression
moderately deep, arcuate at middle toward the base, the longitudinal impressions
distinct. Elytra distinctly wider at base than the thorax, humeri rounded,
umbone distinct, disc rather deeply striate, the punctures coarse, deep, quadrate
and closely placed, the intervals very narrow and at the sides almost like acute
costæ, each with a row of fine punctures. Prosternum coarsely, not closely
punctate. Abdomen brownish, sparsely punctate and pubescent. Legs rufotestaceous, the posterior femora piceous. Length .06 –.08 inch.; 1.5 –2 mm.

The species with *fuscula* and *cucumeris* are closely related. *E.
lobata* has a more closely punctate thorax than *cucumeris*, but much
less so than in *fuscula*. The latter has the ante-basal impression
almost entirely obliterated. In *lobata* the elytral punctures are
denser, coarser and deeper than in either of the others.

Occurs in North Carolina and Florida, N. Smyrna (Schwarz).

E. cucumeris Harris. -Ovate, slightly oblong, piceous, shining. Antennæ
rufotestaceous. Head smooth, rarely with a few punctures near the eye. Thorax
nearly twice as wide as long, slightly narrowed in front, anterior angles obliquely

truncate, sides moderately arcuate, disc convex, the ante-basal impression deep and slightly arcuate toward the base, the longitudinal impressions well marked, the punctures moderately coarse, not closely placed, the intervals well marked and shining. Elytra slightly wider at base than the thorax, humeri distinct, umbone moderately prominent, disc regularly convex, striæ very feebly impressed punctures large and closely placed, but distinctly separated, intervals narrow shining, with a single series of fine punctures. Prosternum coarsely and rather closely punctate, the pleuræ smooth. Abdomen piceous, shining, sparsely punctate and pubescent. Legs rufotestaceous, posterior femora piceous. Length .06—.08 inch.; 1.5—2 mm.

This species varies somewhat in the punctuation of the thorax, at times being rather sparser and again comparatively close, but never so dense as in *fuscula* or *lobata*. The anterior and middle femora are at times brownish.

Widely distributed from Massachusetts to Georgia and westward to California.

E. brevis Schwarz.—Form broadly ovate, piceous, shining. Antennæ rufo-testaceous. Head brownish, front smooth, a small group of punctures near each eye. Thorax fully twice as wide as long, slightly narrowed in front, sides distinctly arcuate, anterior angles obliquely truncate, disc convex, the punctuation moderate in size, not closely placed, distant from each other by their own diameters, ante-basal impression very feeble, the longitudinal impressions not evident. Elytra a little wider at base than the thorax, humeri distinct, umbone moderately prominent, striæ scarcely at all impressed on the disc, more deeper at the sides, the punctures of the former rounded and distinct, those at the sides more quadrate and closer, intervals very narrow, with a single series of fine punctures. Prosternum coarsely and rather closely punctate, pleuræ smooth. Abdomen piceous, shining, sparsely punctate and slightly pubescent. Legs pale rufotestaceous, posterior femora piceous. Length .06 inch.; 15 mm.

By its comparatively sparsely punctate thorax this species is related to *cucumeris*, but differs in its shorter form and the feeble ante-basal impressions.

Collected by Mr. E. A. Schwarz at Enterprise, Florida, and at Columbus, Texas.

E. subcrinita Lec.—Oblong ovate, moderately convex, surface with distinct æneous lustre. Antennæ rufotestaceous, slightly darker externally. Head smooth at middle, a group of coarse punctures near each eye. Thorax nearly twice as wide as long, not narrowed in front, except by the obliquely truncate front angles, sides very slightly arcuate, disc convex, punctuation moderately coarse and very close, but not densely crowded, the ante-basal transverse impression well defined and straight, the longitudinal impressions well marked. Elytra distinctly wider at base than the thorax, humeri distinct, umbone moderately prominent and smooth, disc evenly convex, striæ very feebly impressed, the punctures large, closely placed, intervals narrow, with a series of finer punctures. Prosternum coarsely sparsely punctate, the pleuræ smooth. Abdomen piceous, shining, sparsely punctate and very slightly pubescent. Legs rufotestaceous, the posterior femora piceous. Length .08 inch.; 2 mm.

This species is easily known by the submetallic surface lustre, and is of more oblong form than any other, except *parvula*. It represents in our fauna the *intermedia* Foudras of southern Europe. Occurs in Oregon, California, Nevada and Arizona.

E. parvula Fab.—Oblong ovate, moderately convex, rufotestaceous, abdomen brown, elytra often with a dark, transverse cloud at middle. Antennae pale rufotestaceous, the outer four joints usually darker Head smooth, with several large punctures near each eye. Thorax nearly twice as wide as long, not narrowed in front, sides arcuate, feebly obliquely truncate at the front angles, disc convex, the punctures moderate, rather closely placed, but not dense, the intervals shining, ante-basal groove almost entirely obliterated. Elytra very little wider than the thorax, humeri rounded, umbone feeble, striae feebly impressed on the disc, a little deeper at the sides, the punctures moderate and not crowded on the disc, closer and deeper at the sides, the inner intervals a little wider than the striae and flat those at the sides narrow and slightly convex, all with a row of finer punctures. Prosternum coarsely, but not closely punctate. Metasternum and abdomen brown, the latter sparsely punctate and feebly pubescent. Legs pale rufotestaceous. Length .06—.08 inch.; 1.5 -2 mm.

Very many of the specimens are entirely rufotestaceous above, but others have an indistinct transverse cloud at the middle of the elytra. In one specimen before me this forms a well marked band, which does not reach the suture, the latter narrowly bordered with brown. The legs are uniformly rufotestaceous.

Occurs throughout the entire United States, extending also to the West India islands.

ORTHALTICA Crotch.

Head oval, moderately deeply inserted, the eyes free, these round, moderately prominent. Frontal carina short, obtuse, the tubercles prominent and well separated. Labrum short, truncate. Maxillary palpi slender, but short ; the terminal joint elongate conical, as long as the preceding. Antennae three-fourths the length of body ♂ . shorter in ♀ , first joint stout, claviform, second half as long, the others dissimilar in the sexes, terminal joint acute at tip. Thorax broader than long, scarcely wider at base, apex truncate, base arcuate, sides arcuate, the margin not thickened in front, disc convex, a moderately deep ante-basal impressed line not limited externally by a longitudinal impression, the ends gradually approaching the base. Prosternum moderately separating the coxae, dilated behind them, and with the epimera closing the coxal cavities behind. Mesosternum not wide, nearly horizontal. First ventral segment as long as the next three, these gradually decreasing in length, fifth longer than

the fourth. Legs rather short, tibiæ slightly broader to tip, outer
edge rounded, posterior terminated by a short spur, tarsi stout, claws
appendiculate at base. Elytra striato-punctate; surface glabrous.
The antennæ are dissimilar in the sexes. In the male they are
more than three-fourths and in the female shorter and more slender.

This genus was instituted by Crotch for two species, one of which
cannot remain, in such a brief and unsatisfactory manner that it
would not be possible to refer it with certainty to any group, except
by inference from the position in which it was placed in the paper.
It is closely related to Crepidodera, and differs especially in the
form of the ante-basal groove and the very long antennæ dissimilar
in the sexes. The form is similar to Pseudepitrix, but more convex.

Two species are known to me which may be separated in the following manner :

Antennæ rather stout in both sexes; punctures of striæ confused on each side of
    scutellum; ante-basal impression moderately deep, but not sharply im-
    pressed; color usually piceous or brownish; front punctate......**copalina.**
Antennæ slender (in both sexes?); striæ entire, not confused near the scutellum;
    ante-basal impression deep and sharply defined; color pale rufotestaceous;
    front smooth ....**melina.**

O. copalina Fab.—Elongate parallel, moderately convex, shining, brownish
or piceous, in the latter case the head and thorax paler. Antennæ rufotestaceous. Head shining, coarsely punctate, front rather flat. Thorax one-half wider
than long, base scarcely broader than apex, sides arcuate, more distinctly in
front. margin finely serrate, disc convex, the punctuation coarse and deep, but
not dense, ante-basal sulcus moderately deep, feebly arcuate, joining the basal
margin near the hind angles. Elytra distinctly broader than the thorax, humeri rather prominent, umbone distinct, limited within by a slight depression,
disc convex, with nine striæ of coarse, closely placed punctures, the outer distant
from the margin, those of the inner series confused near the scutellum, intervals
narrower than the striæ and slightly convex. Body beneath colored as above.
Abdomen with very few punctures. Legs rufotestaceous. Length .08—.10 inch.;
2—2.5 mm.

In the male the antennæ are rather more than three-fourths the
length of the body, first joint stout, clavate, second conical, more
slender, half as long, third and fourth equal, a little longer than
second, fifth distinctly longer than either fourth or sixth, joints 6–10
very gradually shorter and slightly stouter, eleventh one half longer
than the tenth, acuminate at tip.

In the female the antennæ are about half the length of body,
rather more distinctly thickened toward tip; joints 1–2 as in male,
third as long as second, but more slender, joints 4–10 shorter than
third, equal in length, eleventh longer and acuminate.

In addition to the sexual characters already noted in the antennæ, the males have the first joint of the anterior tarsi more dilated and the last ventral has a small, but deep triangular impression near the apex.

Occurs from Massachusetts to Florida, westward to Missouri and Iowa.

O. melina n. sp.— Elongate, parallel, pale rufotestaceous, shining. Front convex, smooth, the carina obtuse, tubercles distinct. Thorax about one-half wider than long, widest in front of middle, sides arcuate, slightly oblique in front of base, margin entire, not crenate; disc convex, punctures rather coarse, sparsely irregularly placed, the ante-basal impression well defined and deep, extending from side to side. Elytra wider at base than the thorax, humeri rounded, umbone moderate, disc convex, with feebly impressed striæ of moderate punctures not closely placed, intervals flat, smooth. Prosternum and pleuræ smooth. Metasternum and abdomen brown or piceous, the latter sparsely punctate. Legs pale. Length .06–.08 inch.; 1.5–2 mm.

Unfortunately, the males before me are deprived of antennæ. Those of the female are more slender than in *copalina* and gradually stouter to tip. The males have the first joint of the anterior tarsi dilated and an impression at the apex of the last ventral segment. In some specimens the body beneath is entirely pale like the upper surface.

Occurs in Kansas and Texas.

LEPTOTRIX n. g.

Head triangularly oval, not deeply inserted in the thorax. Eyes free, slightly longer than wide, coarsely granulated. Antennæ slender, slightly thicker externally, third joint shorter than second. Front vertical, the carina short and obtuse, tubercles small and indistinct. Clypeus truncate, labrum small, arcuate in front. Maxillary palpi moderate in length, the terminal joint short, conical. Thorax truncate at apex and base, the angles distinct, the anterior slightly prominent externally, lateral margin distinctly crenate, disc with an ante-basal and moderately deep impression, which at each end bends abruptly toward the base. Elytra wider at base than the thorax, humeri distinct, disc striato-punctate, the intervals with short semi-erect hairs as in Epitrix. Prosternum rather wide between the coxæ, apex truncate, the coxal cavities closed. Legs moderate in length, the posterior thighs rather feebly dilated, tibiæ slender, not grooved externally, the posterior with a minute spur. Tarsi moderate in length, claws appendiculate at base.

The antennæ are slender, thickened externally, especially the last five joints, without, however, forming a distinct club. The first joint is stout, not as long as the next two, second as stout, but shorter; third more slender, a little shorter than second, four to six equal to third, seven to ten a little broader, although slightly decreasing in length, eleventh a little longer than the seventh.

This genus is rather unwillingly made for a small Californian species which cannot be placed in any genus of Crepidoderides, although related to Orthaltica and Pseudepitrix. While it resembles the first in its narrow and parallel form it differs in the shorter antennæ and presence of setæ on the elytral intervals. Pseudepitrix has still more slender antennæ, the third joint longer than second, the base of thorax on each side oblique and a very narrow prosternum.

As Epitrix is closely related to Crepidodera, but with interstitial setæ, so is the present genus to Orthaltica and Pseudepitrix to Sangaria.

L. recticollis Lec.--Elongate, parallel, moderately convex, pale reddish brown, shining, surface sparsely hairy. Antennæ a little longer than half the body, pale, the outer joints slightly darker. Head alutaceous, sparsely indistinctly punctate. Thorax distinctly broader than long, narrower at base than apex, sides arcuate, the margin distinctly crenate, anterior angles prominent externally, disc convex, coarsely and deeply, but not closely punctate. Elytra wider at base than the thorax, humeri obtusely prominent, umbone scarcely evident, disc slightly flattened at middle, striato punctate, the punctures rather coarse, close and quadrate, as wide as the intervals on the disc, the intervals wider at the sides, scutellar stria one fourth the length of suture; intervals flat, with a single series of fine punctures, each with a short semi-erect hair. Prosternum smooth. Abdomen brown or piceous, with very few punctures and short hairs. Legs rufotestaceous. Length .07--.09 inch.; 1.75--2.25 mm. Plate VI. fig. 11.

In the small number of specimens examined no sexual differences have been observed.

Occasionally the elytra are slightly clouded along the suture with fuscous, and then there is a faintly evident æneous lustre, otherwise there seems to be no variation.

Occurs in California and Oregon, and seems rather rare in collections.

Group XI.—ARSIPODES.

Antennæ 11-jointed. Pronotum without *transverse* impression at base. Anterior coxal cavities closed behind, ventral segments free. Fourth joint of hind tarsus simple. Posterior tibiæ with a small simple spur.

By these few characters it will be seen that the group forms the link between the Crepidoderæ on the one hand with the Chætocnemæ. But one genus is known in our fauna characterized by the well marked, short, longitudinal basal impression. In much of the European literature the name Balanomorpha is used, but Mantura should properly remain.

MANTURA Steph.

Head inserted as far as the eyes, front flat, without carina or tubercles. Eyes rounded, entire, rather coarsely granulated. Labrum narrow, slightly sinuate at middle. Antennæ slender, half as long as the body, the outer five joints abruptly slightly broader. Maxillary palpi cylindrical, last joint elongate conical, a little shorter than the preceding. Thorax much broader than long, narrower in front, a deep impression adjacent to the base, opposite the middle of each elytron extending nearly half way to apex, no transverse impression. Prosternum moderately separating the coxæ, the cavities closed behind. Middle coxæ more widely separated, the mesosternum declivous. First ventral segment nearly as long as all the others. Legs rather short, tibiæ gradually slightly broader to tip, each one with a small terminal spur, outer edge rounded, slightly flattened near the apex ; claws simple.

This genus is the only representative in our fauna of the group Arsipodites of Chapuis (Genera xi, p. 37), which is closely related to the Crepidoderites differing only in the absence of the transverse ante-basal impression. The longitudinal impressions are deeper than in any of our Crepidoderites and are triangular in form, broadest at the base of the thorax. Mantura is notable in being one of the few genera of Halticides with a spur on each tibia.

M. floridana Crotch.- Elongate oval, moderately convex, brownish, surface with faint bronze lustre, elytra indefinitely paler at apical third. Head alutaceous, coarsely, not closely punctate, a well marked, transverse groove between the eyes. Thorax nearly twice as wide as long, widest at base, gradually narrowed in front, sides feebly arcuate, apex truncate, base arcuate, a little more broadly at middle, disc convex, coarsely, deeply and moderately closely punctate, basal impressions deep, triangular, reaching nearly to middle. Elytra scarcely wider at base than the thorax, humeri obliquely rounded, umbone not prominent, disc with ten entire striæ of moderately coarse punctures, closely placed, but not serrate, the outer stria distant from the margin, a short scutellar stria of but few punctures, intervals broader than the striæ, smooth. Body beneath brown, the abdomen almost smooth. Legs rufotestaceous, the hind femora darker. Length .08 inch.; 2 mm.

The only sexual difference apparent in the specimens before me is in the broader first joint of the anterior tarsus of the male.

Specimens occur with the apical pale space quite sharply limited, while others have been seen in which the elytra are almost entirely piceous.

Occurs from Massachusetts (Blanchard) to Florida and Texas. I have seen one in the LeConte cabinet from California.

Group XII.—EUPLECTROSCELES.

Antennæ 11-jointed. Anterior coxal cavities closed behind. Thorax with a faint ante-basal impressed line. Middle and posterior tibiæ sinuate near the apex, the posterior grooved their entire length. Tarsal claws divaricate, not appendiculate. Ventral segments all free.

This group is suggested for the genus Euplectroscelis *Crotch*, which that author had associated with Chætocnema. From the group containing the latter it differs in the free ventral segments, the presence of a feeble ante-basal impression, the irregularly punctate elytra and the simple claws. The only other tribe to which the key of Chapuis directs is the Oxygonites, from which the form of the tibiæ and claws at once separates it.

As remarked by Crotch the facies of the only species known is rather that of a Eumolpide than a Halticide.

EUPLECTROSCELIS Crotch.

Head inserted in the thorax as far as the eyes, front not carinate. the tubercles distinct and widely separated, clypeus arcuate in front. Labrum transverse, slightly emarginate at apex. Maxillary palpi slender, second joint elongate conical, third cylindrical, fourth acutely oval, longer than the preceding and not narrower at base than it. Antennæ slender, a little longer than half the body, first joint elongate conical, second short, oval, third twice as long, joints 4–7 equal, a little longer than third, 8–10 slightly progressively shorter, eleventh longer, acute at tip. Thorax transverse, a very vague, arcuate, ante-basal impressed line. Scutellum triangular. Elytra a little wider at base than the thorax, punctuation coarse and confused. Prosternum rather narrow between the coxæ, dilated behind them joining the epimera, the coxal cavities closed behind. First ventral segment not much longer than the second, the articulation between them well marked, not connate. Legs moderately long. Tibiæ slightly broader at apex, the outer edge with a feeble groove extend-tending their entire length, limited on each side by a fine carina ; middle and posterior tibiæ sinuate near the apex, the sinuation limited above by a tooth, below which the margin is ciliate. Posterior tibia alone slightly arcuate and terminated by a spur. Tarsi moderately long, the first joint nearly as long as the others together. the last joint slender, the claws stout, divaricate and not appendiculate at base.

This genus was described by Crotch, and placed by him in association with Chætocnema, a position in which it cannot be allowed to remain for reasons already given.

One species is known :

E. Xanti Crotch.—Oblong oval, robust, pale ochreous, upper surface darker and with a slight purplish lustre. Antennæ longer than half the body, brownish, darker outwardly. Head with irregular surface, coarsely cribrately punctured between and above the eyes. Thorax twice as wide as long, scarcely narrower in front, sides arcuate, anterior angles acute outwardly, hind angles obtuse, sides feebly arcuate, disc moderately convex, a feeble, but distinct ante-basal impression, another post-apical, parallel with the margin, surface with very coarse, closely placed punctures which are cribrate near the sides, basal marginal line distinct, the edge slightly reflexed. Scutellum smooth. Elytra a little wider than the thorax, humeri rounded, umbone moderately prominent and smooth, disc coarsely and closely punctate, punctures confused, but with a vague tendency to a strial arrangement, in some specimens the intervals, by their regularity, vaguely resemble costæ. Abdomen sparsely punctate and shining at middle, more densely and finely punctate at the sides and finely pubescent. Femora pale rufotestaceous, the tips brownish, tibiæ and tarsi brown. Length .24—.26 inch. ; 6—6.5 mm. Plate VII. fig. 3.

In the male the first joint of the four front tarsi is rather broadly dilated, the last ventral broadly emarginate at the middle of the apex. In the female the last ventral is longer and oval at tip.

This insect has rather the facies of a Colaspis than a Halticide.

Occurs in the peninsula of Lower California.

Group XIII. CHÆTOCNEMÆ.

Antennæ 11-jointed. Thorax without trace of ante-basal impression. Elytra regularly striato-punctate. Anterior coxal cavities closed behind. Middle and posterior tibiæ distinctly sinuate on the outer edge near the apex, the sinuation limited above by an angulation. Tarsal claws appendiculate at base. Abdomen with first two segments closely united and immobile, the suture distinct.

This tribe is sufficiently well characterized among those with closed coxal cavities by the close union of the first two ventral segments. By this character alone it may be distinguished. In our fauna but one genus is known, the species having a facies that will enable it to be recognized without difficulty.

CHÆTOCNEMA Steph.

Head inserted in the thorax as far as the eyes, the front flat, not carinate (in our species). Clypeus broadly emarginate, labrum truncate. Maxillary palpi rather slender, the second and third joints obconical, the last joint more slender, elongate conical. Antennæ slender, at least half the length of the body, slightly thicker externally, first joint clavate, second elongate oval, third to sixth slender and longer, seven to eleven gradually broader and flattened, the terminal joint nearly as long as the two preceding, acute at tip. Thorax always broader than long, usually twice as wide, narrowed in front with but few exceptions, sides regularly arcuate, obliquely truncate at the front angles in some, base regularly arcuate. Scutellum transverse. Elytra at most but little wider than the thorax at base, humeri never prominent, surface striato-punctate. Prosternum moderately wide between the coxæ, usually coarsely punctate, the apex dilated behind and with the epimera closing the coxal cavities. Abdomen with the first two segments connate, the suture, however, distinct. Legs moderately long, the middle and posterior tibiæ broader below the middle and with a sinuation limited above by a more or less triangular tooth, the posterior tibiæ more or less grooved at apex on the outer edge, the margins of the groove ciliate with short hair, and above these more or less denticulate, terminated at apex by a moderately stout and long spur. Tarsi moderate in length, the claw joint simple. Claws appendiculate at base. Pl. VII, fig. 9.

Our species belong to the subdivision Chætocnema proper as defined by Foudras and Chapuis, having the flat front, while in Plectroscelis the carina is distinct.

It will be observed in all our species that the genæ are coarsely and closely punctate without any exception; for this reason no mention will be made in the separate descriptions.

In the greatest number of species the thorax has regularly arcuate sides, converging to the apex, but in a small number the anterior angles are obliquely truncate with a post-apical angulation, and in two of these species the thorax is not narrowed in front. In the former series the antennæ, with very few exceptions, have the outer joints piceous, while in those with the angles truncate the antennæ are entirely pale, or in no case decidedly piceous externally.

On comparison of our species with those of Europe it will be seen that the number of species in which the elytral striæ have confused punctuation is more than twice as great as those with regular striæ, while in our fauna only three of the twenty-three have irregular striæ. In number, as many species are known in our fauna as in Europe, including Plectroscelis and Chaetocnema under the one name. It is therefore hardly probable that our species will be greatly increased by future collections.

In the accompanying table it has been found necessary to modify the arrangement given by Dr. LeConte (Proc. Am. Philos. Soc. 1878, p. 419) and to remove species from the series with smooth head to the punctate series. By some accident or oversight two of Melsheimer's species had been omitted, but have been studied from the types now in the Museum of Comparative Zoology at Cambridge. My thanks are due to Dr. Hagen for his kind assistance in their discovery.

The following table will assist in the identification of the species, but care must be used in the determination of single examples:

Sides of thorax regularly arcuate from base to apex, without oblique truncation
    at the front angles..2.
Sides of thorax obliquely truncate at the front angles, with a post-apical angu-
    lation ....13.
2.--Head punctate, sometimes indistinctly..3.
    Head absolutely impunctate...10.
3.--Punctures of elytral striæ confused or irregular, at base,....................4.
    Punctures of elytra in regular striæ......................................5.
4.--Striæ 1-4 or beyond much confused as far as the middle or even beyond.
    The outer two striæ only regular, the confused punctures of disc extend-
      ing beyond the middle....................................1. **cribrata.**
    The outer three or four striæ regular, the confused punctures of disc ex-
      tending barely to middle; sides of elytra opaque....2. **perturbata.**
    Striæ 1-2 or 1-3 irregular, near the base only; punctures of thorax coarse.
    Form regularly oval....................................3. **irregularis.**
    Form elongate, subcylindrical...........................4. **subcylindrica.**

5.—Form elongate oval, more than twice as long as wide; punctuation of head
   well marked.
   Piceous, surface æneous; antennæ externally and all the femora piceous.
                                                      5. **protensa.**
   Pale reddish brown, with slight æneous lustre; antennæ and legs pale
   rufotestaceous ....6. **brunnescens.**
   Form oval, not twice as long as wide......................................6.
6.—Punctures of head distinct........... ....7.
   Punctures of head small, indistinct...... ....8.
7.—Punctures of clypeo-frontal region dense and rugulose, subopaque.
                                                      7. **denticulata.**
   Punctures of clypeo-frontal region coarse, well separated, surface shining.
                                                      8. **cribrifrons.**
8.—Punctures of elytral striæ feebly impressed, nearly obsolete at apex.
                                                      9. **pinguis.**
   Punctures of striæ well impressed and not obliterated at apex..............9.
9.—Thorax with distinct basal marginal line, without basal series of punctures;
   surface scarcely alutaceous................... ....10. **remula.**
   Thorax with distinct basal marginal row of punctures, or with coarser punctures than the discal close to the basal margin.
   Head and thorax very opaque, the latter distinctly widest at base; intervals scarcely wider than the striæ..... ....11. **opacula.**
   Head and thorax less opaque, the latter widest at middle; intervals wider
   than striæ.......... ....12. **minuta.**
10.—Thorax with an entire basal marginal line, which is not defined by punctures...................... ....11.
   Thorax with a basal marginal row of punctures, sometimes continued to
   middle as a line.............. ....12.
11.—Legs entirely piceous, surface very distinctly alutaceous and subopaque.
                                                      13. **alutacea.**
   Legs more or less testaceous or brown, surface shining.
   Thorax alutaceous, with median smooth space posteriorly; scutellar stria
   usually confused; color greenish bronze; tibiæ in part and tarsi piceous.................. ....14. **subviridis.**
   Thorax not distinctly alutaceous, without smooth space; scutellar stria
   regular; color golden bronze; tibiæ and tarsi testaceous.
                                                      15. **opulenta.**
12.—Thorax extremely indistinctly punctate.
   Thorax indistinctly alutaceous, the basal marginal row of rather coarse
   distant punctures ....16. **obesula.**
   Thorax alutaceous, basal punctures fine and close ....17. **ectypa.**
   Thorax finely and sparsely, but very distinctly punctate.
   Thorax shining, not alutaceous.....................18. **parcepunctata.**
   Thorax alutaceous, subopaque..... ....19. **pulicaria.**
   Thorax with coarse, moderately deep punctures, irregularly placed.
                                                      20. **crenulata.**
13.—Thorax arcuately narrowed from base to apex..........................14.
   Thorax transversely quadrate, not narrowed, except at the oblique trunca-
   tion.................. ....15.

14.—Thorax without distinct basal marginal line..................21. **confinis.**
Thorax with nearly entire basal marginal line.
Form oblong, elytral intervals on the disc flat and broader than the
striæ...22. **elongatula.**
Form oval, robust, elytral intervals convex and scarcely wider than the
striæ (small species)...........................23. **dispar.**
15.—Basal marginal line of thorax distinct ; antennæ and legs entirely yellow.
24. **quadricollis.**
Basal marginal line indistinct ; outer joints of antennæ and all the femora
piceous ....25. **decipiens.**

1. **C. cribrata** Lec. Oblong oval, convex, brassy bronzed, shining. Antennæ rufotestaceous, the outer five joints piceous Head alutaceous, the front
coarsely and deeply punctate, with a median smooth space, vertex more finely
and sparsely punctate. Thorax about one-half wider than long, scarcely narrowed in front, sides arcuate disc moderately convex, basal marginal line visible
only near the hind angles, the surface rather closely punctate, the punctures
moderate in size, a little coarser near the sides. Elytra not wider at base than
the thorax, humeri very obliquely rounded, sides regularly arcuate, widest at
middle, disc punctato-striate, the punctures rather coarse and deep, and moderately closely placed, the punctures of the striæ from the suture a little beyond
the umbone very much confused, extending thus beyond the middle, intervals
slightly convex, impunctate. Body beneath piceous, faintly bronzed. Prosternum and pleuræ coarsely punctate. Abdomen moderately, closely, but not
coarsely punctate. Anterior and middle femora brown, the posterior piceous,
bronzed, tibiæ and tarsi rufotestaceous. Length .08 inch ; 2 mm.

This species is best known by the greater extent of the confused
punctuation of the elytra, but two of the striæ reaching the humeri
at the sides and the irregular punctuation extending quite to the
declivity. The surface is shining everywhere, while in *cribratus* the
sides of the elytra are decidedly opaque.

The type is from Massachusetts, and I have another specimen from
Oregon (no special locality) kindly given me by Mr. H. Ulke.

2. **C. perturbata** n. sp.—Oblong oval, convex, piceous, surface distinctly
bronzed and shining, the sides of the elytra more opaque. Antennæ rufotestaceous at base, the outer six joints piceous. Head alutaceous, the punctures moderate in size, not dense. Thorax not much wider than long, sides arcuate, gradually narrowed in front of middle, basal marginal line distinct at the sides,
surface shining, not distinctly alutaceous, punctures moderate in size, closely,
not densely placed, a little coarser along the base. Elytra not wider at base than
the thorax, humeri oblique, umbone feeble, the punctures moderately coarse and
deep, much confused at base as far as the fifth or sixth stria and nearly to the
middle of the elytra, the striæ at apex and sides regular, the latter deeply impressed and more closely punctate, the intervals convex and without punctures.
Body beneath piceous, feebly bronzed, shining. Prosternum closely punctate,
the side pieces with few punctures. Abdomen rather coarsely and at the sides
closely punctate. Anterior and middle femora brown, posterior piceous bronzed,
tibiæ and tarsi rufotestaceous. Length .08 .09 inch. ; 2-2.25 mm.

This species has two characters which will enable it to be easily known. The punctures of the striae at base are truly confused and extend in this condition to the umbone, forming from this a triangle to the middle; the sides of the elytra are opaque, while the disc is shining. In general outline the form is not unlike *denticulata*.

Occurs in Minnesota and at Veta Pass, Colorado (cab. Schwarz).

3. **C. irregularis** Lec.– Oblong oval, convex, not twice as long as wide, piceous, surface distinctly bronzed, feebly shining. Head moderately closely punctate and distinctly alutaceous. Antennae piceous, three basal joints pale. Thorax very nearly twice as wide at base as long, sides regularly arcuately narrowed to apex, basal marginal line distinct at the sides, surface rather coarsely and closely punctate, a little finer near apex, distinctly alutaceous. Elytra wider than the thorax, humeri rounded, form regularly oval, disc with rows of coarse punctures closely placed, those of the scutellar and first three discal striae irregular from base one-third to apex, outer striae impressed and serrately punctate, intervals smooth, wider than the striae, the outer ones slightly convex, the inflexed border of the elytra with numerous punctures; surface not distinctly alutaceous. Body beneath piceous, slightly bronzed. Prosternum densely and coarsely punctate, the side pieces sparsely punctate. Abdomen sparsely, moderately, coarsely punctate. Femora piceous, tibiae and tarsi rufotestaceous. Length .08 inch.; 2 mm.

An easily known species and readily separated from all the others with irregular striae by the characters given in the table.

After an examination of the type of *rudis* Lec. it proves to be a variation with the striae a little less irregular. It has been unfortunately compared with *cribrata*.

A variety in Mr. Ulke's collection has the striae much more confused than the typical form, the irregularities extending to the humeri and even beyond the middle. By the table this form might be considered to be *cribrata*, but in this the sides of the elytra are opaque.

Occurs in California from San Jose northward to Oregon, Nevada and Michigan.

4. **C. subcylindrica** Lec.–Oblong, nearly parallel, more than twice as long as broad, piceous, surface with aeneous bronze lustre. Antennae piceous, three basal joints paler. Head alutaceous, punctures not coarse nor closely placed, a smooth median space, front not densely punctured. Thorax about one third wider than long, widest at middle, apex not narrow, sides rather strongly arcuate, disc convex, a slight depression along the middle, punctures moderately coarse and close, coarser along the sides and base, surface not distinctly alutaceous. Elytra a little wider at base than the thorax, humeri rounded, umbone scarcely prominent, disc with rows of moderately coarse punctures closely placed, but not serrate, the scutellar and first two discal striae irregular at base, outer striae not impressed, intervals not convex, wider than the striae and smooth, epipleural fold with numerous punctures, biseriate at base. Pros

ternum coarsely not densely punctate, side pieces with numerous coarse punctures. Body beneath piceous, shining. Abdomen sparsely punctate, more closely on last segment. Legs piceous, the tibiæ and tarsi dark brown. Length .08—.10 inch.; 2—2.5 mm.

This species is readily known by its very elongate subcylindrical form. At first described under the name *cylindrica*, the name was changed, two pages after, in the table, having been already used.

Occurs from Massachusetts to Pennsylvania, Michigan, Wyoming and British Columbia.

5. **C. protensa** Lec.—Very elongate oval, more than twice as long as wide, surface distinctly bronzed, but slightly variable. Antennæ rufotestaceous at base, the outer six joints piceous. Head faintly alutaceous, the punctures not coarse nor close, those of the front closer. Thorax one-third wider at base than long, sides regularly arcuate and narrowing to apex, basal marginal line distinct at the sides, surface not distinctly alutaceous, the punctures moderate in size, not closely placed, separated by at least their own diameters. Elytra a little wider at base than the thorax, humeri rounded, umbone not prominent, disc convex, the striæ regular, not impressed, composed of rather coarse and moderately closely placed punctures, the intervals all flat, wider than the striæ, without interstitial punctures, surface not alutaceous. Body beneath piceous, with slight brassy bronze. Prosternum closely punctate, the side pieces with few punctures. Abdomen moderately, coarsely, but not closely punctate. Femora piceous, bronzed, tibiæ and tarsi rufotestaceous. Length .10—.11 inch.; 2.5—2.8 mm.

This species varies in form, and in its narrowness approaches *subcylindrica*, while the usual form is obtusely fusiform. The color is usually coppery bronze and varies to brassy. A specimen from Garland, Colorado, has the thorax distinctly cupreous and the elytra greenish bronze.

Dr. LeConte describes the thorax as not narrowed in front, but the specimens are all narrower at apex than at base, but not very greatly.

Occurs in Colorado (Veta Pass and Garland), Detroit, and at Deer Park, Maryland.

6. **C. brunnescens** n. sp.—Oblong oval, moderately convex, pale reddish brown, the surface with faint æneous lustre. Antennæ pale rufotestaceous. Head alutaceous, with moderate punctures rather closely placed, the clypeofrontal region more coarsely punctate. Thorax rather more than twice as wide as long, narrowed in front, sides arcuate, basal marginal line entire, fine, containing fine punctures, surface alutaceous, the punctures coarse, close and very regularly placed. Elytra not wider at base than the thorax, humeri broadly rounded, umbone smooth, not prominent; the striæ slightly impressed on the disc, more deeply at the side, punctures moderate, closely placed, intervals lightly convex, scarcely wider than the striæ, the interstitial punctures distinct,

surface not distinctly alutaceous. Body beneath paler than above. Prosternum not densely punctate, side pieces smooth. Abdomen very sparsely punctate, smooth. Legs entirely pale rufotestaceous. Length .07 inch.; 1.75 mm.

The punctuation of the head in this species is as distinctly pronounced, if not relatively more so than in any species in our fauna. It is easily known by its rather unusual color, which is not, however, due to immaturity.

Occurs at Key West, Florida (Schwarz).

7. **C. denticulata** Illig.—Form irregularly oval, facies robust, surface brightly bronzed, slightly brassy. Antennae rufotestaceous at base, the outer five or six joints piceous. Head alutaceous, opaque, the punctures moderate, or even small, not closely placed, those of the clypeo-frontal region coarser and densely placed. Thorax very nearly twice as wide at base as long, the sides regularly arcuately narrowing to the apex, basal marginal line feeble at the sides, surface distinctly alutaceous, the punctures moderate, not closely placed. Elytra not wider at base than the thorax, very nearly continuing the curve, umbone not prominent, disc convex, the punctures coarse and deep, not densely placed, except in the lateral striae, scutellar stria usually irregular, intervals flat, wider than the striae, with a row of distant fine punctures, lateral intervals slightly convex. Body beneath piceous, slightly bronzed. Prosternum coarsely punctured, the side pieces slightly wrinkled near the margin, rarely with a few punctures. Abdomen moderately, coarsely, not closely punctate. Anterior and middle femora brown, posterior piceous bronzed, the tibiae and tarsi rufotestaceous. Length .08—.10 inch.; 2—2.5 mm.

Notwithstanding the wide distribution of this species it seems to vary but little. The punctuation of the head is never very coarse, nor is it ever indistinct. In some specimens the thorax has a narrow, smooth space along the median line near the base.

Occurs from the New England States to Florida, Texas and Montana, also in California.

8. **C. cribrifrons** Lec.—Form regularly oval, but more elongate than in *denticulata*, surface dark bronze, moderately shining. Antennae brownish at base, the outer joints piceous. Head faintly alutaceous, the punctures sharply impressed, not large nor closely placed, the clypeo-frontal region more shining, the punctures coarse, deep and well spaced. Thorax nearly twice as wide at base as long, sides feebly arcuately narrowed to front, basal marginal line distinct at the sides, surface saightly alutaceous, the punctures moderate in size, rather closely, but not densely placed, a little coarser toward the sides. Elytra not wider at base than the thorax, the curve nearly continuous, umbone not convex, punctures arranged in regular striae, which are not impressed, coarse, deep and closely placed, but not serrate, intervals all flat, wider than the striae, each with a series of fine punctures visible only near the base. Body beneath piceous, slightly bronzed. Prosternum coarsely punctured, the side pieces smooth. Abdomen coarsely, sparsely punctate, the last segment more closely. Anterior and middle femora brown, posterior piceous bronzed. Tibiae and tarsi rufotestaceous. Length .09—.11 inch.; 2.25—2.75 mm.

This species differs particularly from all those with punctate head by the punctures of the clypeo-frontal region being very coarse and deep, but well spaced. The only species with which it might be confounded is *denticulata*, which is, however, a broader species. Occurs in Colorado, Texas, Dakota, Georgia and California (Ulke).

9. **C. pinguis** Lec. - Oval, slightly oblong, nearly twice as long as wide, surface feebly shining, distinctly alutaceous and bronzed. Antennæ rufotestaceous at base, the outer joints piceous. Head subopaque, sparsely finely punctate, clypeo-frontal space more coarsely punctured. Thorax nearly twice as wide at base as long, sides regularly arcuately narrowed to the front, basal marginal line very feeble, surface distinctly alutaceous, punctures fine not close. Elytra not wider at base than the thorax, the margin very nearly continuous with that of the thorax, umbone not distinct, disc finely striato punctate, the punctures small, moderately close not deeply impressed, the intervals much broader than the striæ, flat on the disc, slightly convex at the sides, without distinct interstitial punctures, surface very distinctly alutaceous, inflexed margin with a row of closely placed punctures along the inner border. Body beneath piceous, shining, feebly bronzed. Prosternum closely punctate, side pieces smooth. Abdomen sparsely, indistinctly punctate, the last segment more coarsely and closely at the sides. Anterior and middle femora brown, posterior piceous, bronzed, tibiæ and tarsi rufotestaceous. Length .08 - .09 inch.; 2 - 2.5 mm.

This species is very like a small *denticulata*, but differs in having the entire punctuation of the surface finer and less deep, more especially in the elytral striæ. The feebly punctate head makes this species a natural intermediate between those with the head decidedly punctate or smooth.

Occurs in Florida, North Carolina and Texas.

10. **C. remula** n. sp. — Oval, rather robust, surface shining, slightly brassy. Antennæ rufotestaceous at base, piceous externally. Head alutaceous, sparsely, finely punctate, clypeo frontal region very distinctly, not densely punctate. Thorax one-half wider than long, widest a little in front of base, sides arcuately narrowing to the front, basal marginal line very indistinct at the sides, surface indistinctly alutaceous, the punctures rather fine, closely placed, but not dense. Elytra a little wider at base than the thorax, humeri broadly rounded, umbone not evident, striæ slightly impressed, the punctures moderately coarse, close and deep, the intervals very little wider, very slightly convex on the disc, more so at the sides, the interstrial punctures indistinct and very fine. Body beneath piceous black, slightly bronzed. Prosternum coarsely punctured, the side pieces smooth. Abdomen coarsely, but sparsely punctate. Femora piceous, tibiæ and tarsi rufotestaceous. Length .09 inch.; 2.25 mm.

This species presents nothing remarkable. The head is finely and indistinctly punctate as in *pinguis*, but the elytral striæ are comparatively coarsely punctured The regularity of the oval outline is interrupted at the humeri in this species, while in *cribrifrons* and *pinguis*, with which it is most closely related, the outline is continuous.

Occurs in Arizona, probably Fort Thomas ; represented by one specimen only.

11. **C. opacula** Lec.—Oval slightly oblong, moderately robust, dark greenish bronze, very feebly shining. Antennæ with basal joints brownish, the outer piceous. Head very opaque, sparsely, indistinctly punctate. Thorax about one-half wider than long, distinctly narrowed in front, sides regularly arcuate, widest at base, basal marginal line indistinct, but with punctures coarser than the discal, forming an irregular series, discal punctures rather fine, feebly impressed, moderately closely placed, the surface opaque. Elytra a little wider at base than the thorax, humeri distinct, umbone smooth, moderately prominent, striæ scarcely impressed, composed of moderately coarse, closely placed subtransverse punctures, the intervals scarcely wider, not convex, more shining than the thorax, indistinctly punctulate. Body beneath piceous, slightly bronzed. Prosternum coarsely punctate, side pieces smooth. Abdomen subopaque, coarsely, sparsely punctate at the sides, smoother at middle. Femora piceous, tibiæ and tarsi brown. Length .06 inch. ; 1.5 mm.

Although quite different in appearance from *minuta*, it is difficult to separate it by description. The characters given in the table, supplemented by the description, will enable separation to be made.

A specimen which I am at present unwilling to separate from this species, in Mr. Schwarz's collection from Alamosa, Colorado, has much more shining elytra and the basal punctures of the thorax less distinct.

Occurs in California (Gilroy) and Colorado?

12. **C. minuta** Mels.—Oval, facies very robust, piceous, surface distinctly bronzed, shining. Antennæ with four basal joints brownish testaceous, the outer piceous. Head distinctly alutaceous, sparsely, indistinctly punctate. Thorax twice as wide as long, evident at middle, scarcely narrower at apex than base, sides arcuate, disc very faintly alutaceous, the punctuation sparse and fine, basal row of punctures distinct and a little more in front of basal margin than usual, and coarser than those of the disc. Elytra distinctly wider at base than the thorax, humeri broadly rounded, umbone smooth, not prominent, striæ faintly impressed, the punctures moderate in size, rather closely placed, a little transverse, intervals feebly convex, very slightly alutaceous, not visibly punctulate, wider than the striæ. Body beneath piceous black, faintly bronzed. Prosternum closely punctate, the side pieces smooth. Abdomen sparsely punctate. Legs piceous, the tibiæ and tarsi sometimes paler. Length .08 inch. ; 2 mm.

This species escaped the notice of LeConte and Crotch. Fortunately, the type in the Museum at Cambridge is in good condition, and the above description has been taken from it in comparison with other specimens.

By its indistinctly punctate head it resembles *æmula*, which has no basal marginal row of punctures. *C. parcepunctata* also closely resembles it, but the head is entirely devoid of punctures, but it is possible that future collections may make it necessary to unite them. Specimens have been seen from Pennsylvania, Maryland, North Carolina, Florida and Arizona, and Garland, Colorado.

13. **C. alutacea** Crotch.- Oval, rather robust, surface subopaque, olive-green bronze, very distinctly alutaceous. Antennæ with basal and five outer joints piceous, the others pale. Head impunctate. Thorax one-half wider than long, very little narrowed in front, sides arcuate, base a little coarctate, basal marginal line distinct and entire, surface alutaceous, the punctures coarse, deep and close at the sides, less so at middle. Elytra not wider at base than the thorax, humeri obliquely rounded, umbone not prominent, but smooth ; striæ distinctly impressed, composed of coarse, deep and closely placed punctures, these, however, wider, slightly convex, each with a row of very fine punctures. Body beneath piceous, faintly bronzed. Prosternum closely punctate, the side pieces entirely smooth. Abdomen sparsely punctate. Legs entirely piceous. Length .06—.08 inch. ; 1.5—2 mm.

This species is one of the most readily known. Its quite opaque surface, coarse sculpture and entirely piceous legs separate it very easily from any other. In consequence of the thorax being slightly coarctate at base the marginal line of the body is not continuous from the thorax to the elytra.

Occurs from northern Georgia to Florida.

14. **C. subviridis** Lec.- Oval, robust, surface shining, bright green bronze or slightly bluish. Antennæ with basal joints rufotestaceous, tipped with brown, the outer seven joints piceous. Head finely alutaceous, a punctured fovea near each eye. Thorax fully twice as wide as long, narrower at apex, sides feebly arcuate, basal marginal line fine and entire, surface alutaceous, but not well marked, the punctures coarse, deep and close, a smoother median line near the base. Elytra not wider at base than the thorax, humeri obliquely rounded, umbone moderately prominent and smooth, striæ finely impressed, the punctures relatively free, not coarser than those of the thorax, closely placed, intervals slightly convex, wider than the striæ, distinctly punctulate, subbiseriately near the base. Body beneath piceous, with slight blue or greenish tinge. Prosternum punctate, the side pieces smooth. Abdomen not coarsely, but rather closely punctate, except at the middle of the last segment. Femora piceous, bronzed, tibiæ brown at apex, pale at base, tarsi brown. Length .08 .14 inch.; 2—3.5 mm.

This species is the largest at present known in our fauna, and by that and the usually bright green surface may be readily known.

Specimens do, however, occur with a bluish or slightly cupreous surface. Two specimens are before me from Colorado with the thorax not more coarsely punctate than in *denticulata*, but these are considered merely variations. In the majority of specimens the scutellar stria is slightly irregular. The posterior thighs are elongate oval, nearly twice as long as broad.

Occurs in Kansas, Colorado, Montana, Arizona and California (Owen's Valley).

15. **C. opulenta** n. sp.—Oval, moderately convex, surface not alutaceous, bright golden or brassy bronze. Antennæ rufotestaceous at base, gradually darker to tip. Head slightly alutaceous and feebly wrinkled. Thorax twice as wide as long, narrowed at apex, sides regularly arcuate, basal marginal line entire and well marked, the surface coarsely, deeply and closely punctate. Elytra a little wider at base than the thorax, humeri rounded, umbone smooth, not prominent, striæ feebly impressed, the punctures very coarse and deep, closely placed, the intervals slightly convex, more so at the sides, not wider than the striæ, distinctly punctulate. Body beneath distinctly æneous. Prosternum closely punctate, side pieces smooth. Abdomen sparsely punctate, last three segments smooth at middle. Femora piceous, the tibiæ and tarsi testaceous. Length .08–.10 inch.; 2—2 5 mm.

Closely resembles *subviridis*, but may be known by the color, the distinctly wrinkled head, the coarser elytral punctures with narrower intervals and by the very pale tibiæ and tarsi. The scutellar stria is always regular. The posterior thighs are strongly incrassate, the width being nearly three-fourths the length.

Occurs in California (Owen's Valley) and western Nevada, also New Mexico (Ulke).

16. **C. obesula** Lec.—Oval, moderately robust, black bronzed, rather shining. Antennæ reddish brown at base, piceous externally. Head extremely finely alutaceous, impunctate. Thorax nearly twice as wide at base as long, arcuately narrowed to apex, surface extremely finely alutaceous, not visibly punctate, the basal marginal line fine and entire, the punctures at the side relatively coarse and distant. Elytra wider at base than the thorax, humeri rounded, umbone distinct, disc convex, shining, not alutaceous, striæ finely impressed, the punctures relatively coarse, deep and close, the intervals wider than the striæ, very slightly convex with a row of distant, interstrial punctures. Body beneath black, shining. Abdomen very indistinctly punctate. Femora piceous, tibiæ and tarsi pale. Length .05 inch.; 1.25 mm.

This species is one of the smallest in our fauna, and is especially characterized by the impunctate thorax and almost truly black color.

Occurs at Enterprize and Lake Ashby, Florida.

17. C. cetypa n. sp.

This species resembles *obesula* so closely that the following differences only need be given :

Surface distinctly æneous. Antennæ rufotestaceous at base, the five outer joints piceous. Thorax distinctly alutaceous, the punctuation extremely fine, indistinct and sparse, the basal marginal line consists of fine, closely placed punctures. Anterior and middle femora brown, the posterior femora piceous, tibiæ and tarsi rufotestaceous. Length .06 inch.; 1.5 mm.

Occurs at Los Angeles, California, also in Arizona.

18. C. parcepunctata Crotch.—Oval, robust, surface æneous, shining. Antennæ rufotestaceous at base, piceous externally. Head finely alutaceous, impunctate. Thorax nearly twice as wide as long, scarcely narrowed in front, sides arcuate, basal marginal row of punctures distinct, but somewhat irregular, disc indistinctly alutaceous or even smooth, the punctures fine, sparse and indistinct. Elytra distinctly wider at base than the thorax, humeri rounded, umbone moderately prominent and smooth, the striæ not distinctly impressed, the punctures large, round and moderately closely placed, intervals scarcely wider than the striæ, shining, not punctulate. Body beneath distinctly æneous. Prosternum punctate between the coxæ, smooth in front and at the sides, side pieces smooth. Abdomen sparsely and indistinctly punctate. Femora piceous, the tibiæ and tarsi brownish or rufotestaceous. Length .06 inch.; 1.5 mm.

As already stated this species is closely related to *minuta* in form, size and color, the sculpture is also nearly identical, except that here the head is impunctate. As a rule the thorax here is more distinctly punctate.

Occurs in Massachusetts (Blanchard), Pennsylvania, Maryland, North Carolina, Florida and Texas.

19. C. pulicaria Mels.—Oval, slightly oblong, convex, surface shining, with faint greenish bronze lustre. Antennæ with three or four basal joints rufotestaceous, the outer piceous. Head alutaceous, impunctate. Thorax one-half wider at base than long, distinctly narrowed in front, sides very feebly arcuate, slightly obliquely truncate at the front angles, basal marginal line distinct, closely punctured from the sides nearly to middle, surface distinctly alutaceous and subopaque, the punctures fine, feebly impressed and sparsely placed. Elytra a little wider at base than the thorax, humeri rounded, umbone smooth, distinct, the striæ faintly impressed, the punctures relatively coarse, closely placed, not crenate, the intervals slightly convex, very little wider than the striæ, surface smooth, with an indistinct series of fine punctures. Body beneath piceous black, faintly bronzed. Prosternum punctate, side pieces smooth. Abdomen sparsely punctate. Femora piceous, tibiæ and tarsi brownish testaceous. Length .06 inch.; 1.5 mm.

In this species the legs vary a little in color, the anterior and middle femora being sometimes brown, in which case the tibiæ and tarsi are rufotestaceous. The thorax has a slight intimation of an oblique truncation in front, but there is no post-apical angulation. *C. æneola* Lee. does not differ specifically from *pulicaria.*

Specimens have been seen from Pennsylvania, Maryland, North Carolina, Texas and Colorado.

20. **C. crenulata** Crotch.—Form oval, convex, robust, the thoracic and elytral margins almost exactly continuous, piceous, faintly bronzed, shining. Antennæ rufotestaceous Head extremely finely alutaceous, impunctate. Thorax twice as wide at base as long, distinctly narrowed in front, sides feebly arcuate, the basal marginal line distinct, defined by a row of closely placed, fine punctures, the disc very distinctly alutaceous, the punctures coarse, deep, sparsely and rather irregularly placed. Elytra not wider than the thorax at base, humeri smooth, not prominent, striæ scarcely impressed, the punctures large, deep and moderately closely placed, intervals wider than the striæ, shining, slightly convex, very indistinctly uniseriately punctulate. Body beneath piceous black, faintly bronzed. Prosternum smooth, the side pieces smooth. Abdomen not distinctly punctate, except at the sides of the last segment. Femora piceous, bronzed, tibiæ and tarsi rufotestaceous. Length .06-.08 inch.; 1.5-2 mm.

This species is noteworthy in having the coarse punctures of the thorax rather unequally placed, and the prosternum smooth.

Occurs in North Carolina, Georgia and Florida.

21. **C. confinis** Crotch.—Rather broadly oval and of robust facies, piceous, slightly æneous. Antennæ rufotestaceous. Head faintly alutaceous, impunctate. Thorax twice as wide as long, distinctly narrowed in front, anterior angles obliquely truncate, a distinct post-apical angulation, behind which the sides are feebly arcuate, disc distinctly alutaceous, without basal marginal line, the punctures of moderate size, closely, but not densely placed, not deeply impressed. Elytra scarcely wider at base than the thorax, humeri rounded, umbone moderate, the striæ impressed on the disc, more deeply at the sides, the punctures relatively coarse, close and deep, but not serrate, intervals slightly convex, wider than the striæ on the disc, but not at sides, surface smooth, shining, with fine interstrial punctures. Body beneath piceous black, shining. Prosternum punctate, side pieces smooth. Abdomen sparsely indistinctly punctate. Anterior and middle legs and posterior tibiæ and tarsi rufotestaceous, posterior femora piceous. Length .06 inch. : 1.5 mm., a little larger and smaller.

This species varies a little in form and somewhat in the distinctness of the thoracic punctures.

After an examination of *flavicornis* I can find no reason to separate it from the present species. The basal puncture, of which Dr. Le-Conte wrote, is an optical deception, caused by a slight impression close to and along the basal margin, which looks punctiform when seen from above.

Occurs from Pennsylvania to Florida, Michigan, Colorado, Dakota and California (Mendocino).

22. **C. elongatula** Crotch.—Oval, slightly oblong, moderately convex, surface with slight æneous lustre. Antennæ rufotestaceous, very slightly darker to the tip. Head distinctly alutaceous, impunctate. Thorax nearly twice as wide at base as long, distinctly narrowed in front, the anterior angles obliquely truncate with a post-apical angulation, sides thence to base regularly arcuate, basal marginal line extremely fine, disc very distinctly alutaceous, the punctures rather coarse and deep, moderately close, but separated by their own diameters. Elytra very little wider at base than the thorax, the humeri rounded, umbone moderately prominent and smooth, disc with distinctly impressed striæ, the punctures relatively fine, seriately placed, the intervals broader than the striæ, slightly convex and with a row of extremely fine punctures. Body beneath piceous black, shining. Prosternum coarsely, closely punctate, the side pieces smooth. Abdomen very sparsely punctate, slightly wrinkled transversely. Anterior and middle femora brown, the posterior piceous, tibiæ and tarsi rufotestaceous. Length .06—.08 inch.; 1.5—2 mm.

This species is not unlike some of the smaller forms of *denticulata*. The small number of species in which the thorax is narrowed in front and the anterior angles obliquely truncate renders them easily separable.

Occurs in Kansas, Colorado and Dakota.

23. **C. dispar** n. sp.—Oval, slightly oblong, surface piceous, moderately shining, with scarcely a trace of bronze lustre. Antennæ entirely rufotestaceous. Head finely alutaceous, impunctate. Thorax twice as wide as long, distinctly narrowed in front, anterior angles obliquely truncate with a post apical angle, the sides thence to base arcuate, basal marginal line fine, but distinct, surface very distinctly alutaceous, the punctures moderately coarse, very closely placed, but not deeply impressed. Elytra not wider at base than the thorax, the margin nearly continuous, umbone feeble, disc deeply striate, the striæ relatively coarsely, crenately punctured, the intervals convex, narrower than the striæ, interstrial punctures not distinct. Body beneath piceous black, shining. Prosternum punctate, the side pieces entirely smooth. Anterior and middle femora brownish testaceous, posterior piceous, paler at tip ; tibiæ and tarsi all rufotestaceous. Length .06 inch.; 1.5 mm.

This is one of the smallest species in our fauna. It is readily known among those with truncate thoracic angles by the deep, crenately punctured striæ.

Occurs in northern Georgia (Morrison).

24. **C. quadricollis** Schwarz.—Form oval, not very convex, piceous black, with faint æneous lustre. Antennæ entirely rufotestaceous Head alutaceous, impunctate. Thorax nearly twice as wide as long, very obliquely truncate at the front angles, the sides behind the angulation nearly straight and slightly convergent to base, the basal marginal line distinct, entire, disc distinctly alutaceous, the punctures feebly impressed and not closely placed. Elytra wider at base than the thorax, humeri rounded, umbone moderately prominent and smooth, striæ slightly impressed, the punctures moderate in size and closely

placed, intervals wider than the striae, slightly convex, each with a series of distant fine punctures, surface not alutaceous. Body beneath piceous shining. Prosternum punctate, the side pieces smooth. Abdomen sparsely, indistinctly punctate. Legs usually entirely pale rufotestaceous, the posterior femora sometimes slightly darker. Length .06—.08 inch.; 1.5—2 mm.

Easily known by the transversely quadrate thorax, obliquely truncate front angles, the pale antennae and legs.

Occurs in Florida (Enterprise, New Smyrna, Biscayne Bay).

25. **C. decipiens** Lec. –Oval, less convex, surface dark greenish bronze, shining. Antennae rufotestaceous at base, the outer joints piceous. Head quite shining, impunctate, not distinctly alutaceous. Thorax twice as wide as long, anterior angles obliquely truncate, the sides behind the angulation feebly arcuate and slightly narrowed to base, basal marginal line feebly distinct near the sides only, surface rather shining at middle in front, alutaceous at the sides and base, the punctuation fine and indistinct on the smoother space closer and deeper near the sides and base. Elytra a little wider at base than the thorax, humeri rounded, umbone feeble, the striae moderately impressed, the punctures relatively coarse, closely placed and deep, the intervals slightly convex, rather narrower than the striae, smooth, not alutaceous. Body beneath black, shining. Prosternum shining, not distinctly punctate, side pieces smooth. Abdomen nearly smooth. Femora piceous, tibiae and tarsi rufotestaceous. Length .06 inch.; 1.5 mm.

This species resembles *quadricollis*, but has the sides of thorax more distinctly arcuate, the basal line feeble, abdomen smoother and the antennae and legs differently colored.

Occurs in Kansas.

Group XIV.- SYSTENÆ.

Antennae 11-jointed. Thorax without a distinctly impressed line. Anterior coxal cavities closed behind. Ventral segments free. Posterior tibiae faintly sulcate, these alone with a terminal spur. Claws appendiculate.

This group contains genera which have heretofore made part of the Crepidoderae. While it is already difficult to sharply define the groups into which the Halticini have been divided, part of the difficulty in several instances has resulted from the association of heterogeneous material. To define a group as possessing an ante-basal impression and include in it genera without it is unnatural, unscientific and confusing.

It is possible that Clamophora and Prasona should form part of this group. In our fauna we have Systena alone.

SYSTENA Clark.

Head inserted as far as the eyes, front with very feeble frontal carina and tubercles. Antennæ slender, half as long as the body, slightly thicker toward the tip, fourth joint longer than third or fifth. Maxillary palpi comparatively slender, the last joint acuminate and longer than the preceding. Prothorax transversely quadrangular, very little narrowed in front, margin very narrow, sides feebly arcuate, anterior angles usually obliquely truncate, hind angles acute, disc often broadly, but vaguely impressed in front of base; coxæ narrowly separated, the cavities closed behind, angulated externally, the trochantin visible. Elytra usually wider at base than the thorax, humeri obtuse. Legs rather slender, the posterior tibiæ grooved on the outer edge and carinate, terminated by a single spur. Claws appendiculate.

The base of the thorax is usually feebly, regularly arcuate, occasionally near the hind angles the base is slightly oblique as in Disonycha. The ante-basal impression is vague at best, but many specimens occur in every species in which it is entirely obliterated.

In his generic description Chapuis states that the posterior tibiæ are not grooved. Quite the contrary will be observed in our species. There is not only a groove from the apex upward, but the edge of the tibia forms a carina along the middle of this groove, especially observable in the larger species. In *marginalis*, however, the groove is short and apical and in *senilis* it is entirely absent. The latter is the only species in which there is an ante-basal impression, which is, however, shallow and vague.

The species occur in every part of our territory, each rather widely spread. They are not numerous and easily known by the characters of the following table:

Elytra uniformly piceous or dark brown, slightly bronzed, or bright blue........2.
Elytra vittate, or testaceous ....7.
2.—Legs piceous, or black..3.
    Legs rufotestaceous ; thorax reddish brown...6.
3.--Thorax black ....4.
    Thorax reddish yellow..5.
4.—Head entirely black..**hudsonias.**
    Head rufotestaceous..**frontalis.**
5.—Head black, elytra slightly bluish.......................................**collaris.**
6.—Elytra brown bronze.
    Elytral punctuation sharply defined and closely placed.........**subænea.**
    Elytral punctuation coarse and confused, not well defined......**pallipes.**
    Elytra bright blue; posterior tibiæ not at all grooved.............**senilis.**

7.—Genæ very coarsely punctate.. **elongata.**

Genæ smooth..8.

8.—Surface shining, the punctuation never very coarse; posterior tibiæ indistinctly grooved near apex.............. ....**arniata.**

Surface subopaque, the punctuation coarse, close and deep...**marginalis.**

S. hudsonias Forst.—Form elongate, subdepressed, piceous black, shining. Antennæ slender, as long as half the body, two basal joints piceous, 3-4-5 testaceous, the outer joints gradually darker. Head indistinctly alutaceous, sparsely punctate. Thorax about one-third wider than long, scarcely narrowed in front, sides feebly arcuate, margin narrowly reflexed, front angles obliquely truncate, disc moderately convex, slightly alutaceous, indistinctly punctate, somewhat scabrous. Elytra wider at base than the thorax, humeri obtuse, disc rather coarsely and closely punctate, surface shining. Body beneath more shining and smooth than above, abdomen very sparsely punctate. Legs black. Length .18 inch.; 4.5 mm.

The male has the last ventral segment notched each side, the middle lobe triangularly impressed with a deeply impressed short median line.

This species is so common and well known as to need no further comment. It is the only one in our fauna totally black.

Occurs over the entire region east of the Rocky Mountains.

S. frontalis Fab.—Similar in form to *hudsonias*, but a little broader, piceous black, less shining, head rufotestaceous. Antennæ as in *hudsonias*. Head sparsely, indistinctly punctate. Thorax one third wider than long, slightly narrowed in front, sides slightly arcuate, margin narrowly reflexed, anterior angles obliquely truncate, disc moderately convex, alutaceous, coarsely not closely punctate. Elytra wider at base than the thorax, humeri rounded, surface closely and moderately coarsely punctate. Body beneath more shining than above, abdomen very sparsely punctate. Legs piceous. Length .14—.20 inch.; 3.5—5 mm.

The male sexual characters are very like those of *hudsonias*.

While closely related to *hudsonias*, it is, apart from the color of the head, distinguished by its rather broader form; elytral punctuation less coarse, but rather more dense.

Occurs with *hudsonias*. As a rule the specimens from the Canadian region are smaller than those from the Southern States.

S. collaris Crotch.—Oblong, rather parallel, subdepressed, piceous, moderately shining, thorax yellowish red. Antennæ half as long as the body, piceous, joints 3 and 4 and the underside of first and second pale. Head piceous, front yellow, a few scattered, rather fine punctures on the sides of vertex. Thorax one half wider than long, very little wider at base than apex, widest one-third from the front angles, sides moderately arcuate, margin narrowly reflexed, front angles obtuse, disc moderately convex, smooth, with a few scattered fine punctures. Elytra wider at base than the thorax, humeri obtuse, disc finely and not closely punctate, smoother at sides and apex, surface with slight æneous lustre. Body beneath piceous black, shining; abdomen with a few scattered punctures with short hairs. Legs piceous, the bases of the anterior and middle femora usually paler. Length .14—.18 inch.; 3.5—4.5 mm.

The sexual characters of the male are similar to those of *hudsonias*, but the middle lobe is rather longer and the longitudinal impression extends the entire length of the segment.

A very easily known species, which shows no variation, except in size. The ante-basal impression is, however, in some specimens entirely obliterated.

Occurs in southwestern Texas.

S. senilis Say.—Moderately elongate and convex, occiput piceous, thorax fuscotestaceous, elytra bright blue. Antennæ slender, half as long as the body, brownish, the basal joints paler. Head smooth, occiput piceous, front and mouth pale. Thorax nearly twice as wide at middle as long, not narrowed in front, sides regularly arcuate, slightly sinuate posteriorly, the hind angles slightly prominent as in *tæniata*, disc convex, a vague ante-basal impression, surface minutely alutaceous, punctuation very minute and sparse, color pale brownish testaceous, a vague darker cloud each side. Elytra distinctly wider at base than the thorax, humeri obtuse, umbone distinct, limited within by a slight depression, color bright blue, shining, moderately closely punctate, epipleuræ pale. Prothorax beneath and legs rufotestaceous, posterior femora darker. Metasternum piceous. Abdomen brown, sparsely punctate and slightly pubescent. Length .14—.16 inch.; 3.5—4 mm.

The last ventral of the male is broadly truncate and flattened.

This insect with *Malacosoma fuscula* Lec. were made the representatives of a new genus—Luperaltica—by Crotch, which was defined in such a manner that it cannot contain either, and must therefore be dropped from our literature. As the form and coloration resemble *S. collaris* it is rather remarkable that the affinities of *senilis* should have escaped Crotch.

Occurs from Pennsylvania to Illinois.

S. subænea Lec.—Form oblong, rather more oval than *hudsonias*, moderately convex, piceous, with very distinct æneous surface lustre, head and thorax brownish. Antennæ half as long as the body, rufotestaceous, two basal joints darker. Head brownish, coarsely not closely punctate, front paler. Thorax one-third wider than long, not narrow at apex, widest one third from apex, sides moderately arcuate, margin very narrow, front angles obliquely truncate, disc moderately convex, ante-basal impression not evident, surface coarsely, deeply and moderately closely punctate. Elytra scarcely wider at base than the thorax, humeri obtusely rounded, disc more finely and densely punctured than the thorax. Body beneath piceous, abdomen alutaceous, sparsely punctate. Legs testaceous, posterior femora brown. Length .14—.16 inch.; 3.5—4 mm.

The last ventral of male is emarginate each side, the middle lobe moderately prominent, slightly concave, a moderately deep longitudinal impression extending nearly to the base.

By its pale legs and antennæ, and the distinct, sharp punctuation, this species is easily known. The genæ are slightly rugulose and punctate, but not so well marked as in *elongata*.

Occurs in California and Nevada.

S. pallipes Schwarz.—Similar in form and coloration to *subænea*, but rather more elongate and without the æneous surface lustre. Antennæ half as long as the body, rufotestaceous, the terminal four or five joints piceous. Head very sparsely and finely punctate. Thorax about one-fourth wider than long, not wider at base, sides nearly straight, margins very narrow, anterior angles obliquely truncate, disc moderately convex, indistinctly alutaceous, sparsely, obsoletely punctate. Elytra scarcely wider at base than the thorax, humeri obliquely rounded, surface slightly wrinkled, indistinctly coarsely punctate. Body beneath brownish, abdomen very sparsely punctate. Legs entirely yellowish testaceous. Length .12—.14 inch.; 3—3.5 mm.

The last ventral of the male is lobed at middle as usual, flat and with a longitudinal impressed line extending the entire length of the segment.

This species is related to *subænea*, but has no æneous lustre, and the punctuation of the surface very indistinct. The legs are entirely pale, the genæ smooth.

Occurs in Georgia and Florida.

S. elongata Fab.—Elongate oval, moderately convex, piceous, surface with slight æneous lustre, each elytron with a yellow vitta reaching nearly to the apex. Antennæ half as long as the body, brownish. Head dark brown, coarsely and closely punctate, the genæ coarsely and deeply punctate. Thorax one-fourth wider than long, slightly narrowed at apex, sides slightly arcuate, margin narrow, anterior angles slightly obliquely truncate, disc rather coarsely and closely punctate. Elytra distinctly wider at base than the thorax, humeri rounded, surface more finely and sparsely punctate than the thorax, the yellow vitta is nearly in the middle of each elytron, and extends nearly to apex. Body beneath piceous, abdomen sparsely, finely punctate. Anterior and middle legs and posterior tibiæ reddish, the posterior femora piceous. Length .12—.16 inch.; 3—4 mm.

The male characters are a repetition of those of *subænea*.

This species is the only one known to me in which the sides of the head beneath and in front of the eyes are coarsely punctate and rugulose. It is also remarkable for the constancy of its general characters, while our other vittate species varies excessively.

Occurs in Georgia and South Carolina.

S. teniata Say.-- Form of *elongata*, but narrower, surface shining. Color very variable, but even when entirely pale, the elytra show traces of the vittæ by the paler color of the yellowish white. Pl. VII, figs. 5--8, varieties.

This species is best described by giving a brief description of the varieties, or at least of certain forms which have been indicated as distinct, while it must be remembered that these intergrade so gradually as to be inseparable.

ligata Lec.--Head moderately, coarsely, sparsely punctured. Thorax more coarsely deeply and closely punctate. Elytra moderately closely and deeply punctate, the punctures finer than those of the thorax. Color piceous, antennæ and legs brown, elytra with a median yellow vitta reaching nearly to the apex. Length .12--.15 inch.; 3--4 mm.

Under this style of punctuation the color varies. The head and thorax become reddish brown, others have pale epipleuræ, the side margin becomes pale and finally the whole surface is pale yellowish white and form the variety *ochracea* Lec.

This variety occurs in California and Nevada, going as far south as San Bernardino.

Variety ³ Rather more elongate than the preceding form and with the punctuation as abundant, but less deep. Length .12--.16 inch.: 3--4 mm.

The feebly colored forms of this type resemble *elongata*, and from this it varies in the manner indicated for *ligata* until the specimens are entirely yellowish white above and beneath.

This form occurs in Dakota, Colorado and northern Arizona.

blanda Mels.--Punctuation of thorax fine and sparse, that of the elytra fine and moderately close, but not deep. Length .12--.18 inch.; 3--4.5 mm.

This variety is not often so dark as the preceding. It varies in color to entirely pale. Forms with the underside of body and sides of thorax narrowly piceous constitute the true *blanda* Mels.

This variation is common in Dakota, Kansas, Colorado and New Mexico, extending to Pennsylvania and New England States.

mitis Lec.--Of the same form as the preceding. Thorax almost absolutely smooth, elytral punctuation fine and feeble, sometimes the elytra are quite smooth. Length .12-.16 inch.; 3--4 mm.

This variety goes through all the forms from those colored like *elongata* to others entirely pale.

Occurs abundantly in Nevada, California and southern Arizona.

In the vast majority of the darker specimens the thorax has at base a broad paler band. The male has the last ventral of the usual trilobed form, the middle lobe flat or slightly concave, with a finely impressed median line.

This species has cost me a vast amount of study and trouble. It has been studied from every point and the conclusion has been reached that all the forms mentioned constitute one excessively variable species.

For convenience of study I have arranged the specimens in series in which the general punctuation has been taken as the initial point, beginning with those most coarsely punctured, arranging in a vertical series down to those almost absolutely smooth. In four or five arbitrary beginnings the first specimen chosen is fully colored. Then in a transverse line I have arranged the specimens by color, and in every case end with individuals of yellowish white color with the vittæ barely perceptible.

The name used for this species has generally been placed as a synonym of *Phyllotreta vittata*, but there can be no doubt as to what Say had before him from his mention of *S. elongata* in the description. The prominent or excurved hind angles of the thorax are especially mentioned, a character universal in Systena, but unknown in Phyllotreta.

In glancing over the localities for the various forms it will be observed that the species is an inhabitant of the northern half of our territory from the Atlantic to the Pacific, and from Oregon and Dakota to Arizona, extending to Mexico, where it has received several additional names.

In reviewing the species of Systena recorded from Mexico by Mr. Jacoby in Vol. VI, Part 1, of the "Biologia," it will be observed that *elongata* has been identified among the collections from Guatemala. From the known distribution of this species in our fauna it is highly probable that the species does not extend so far south.

On the other hand *discicollis*, *capitata* and *semivittata* seem to be varieties of the same and correspond with those indicated under *tæniata*. The latter species has long been known to me from many parts of Mexico.

S. marginalis Illig.—Elongate oval, rather depressed, yellowish testaceous, scarcely shining, sides of thorax and elytra narrowly brown or piceous. Antennæ half as long as the body, pale yellowish testaceous, the terminal half of the outer joints darker, the two basal joints brownish above. Head alutaceous, sparsely, regularly punctate, genæ smooth. Thorax one-third wider than long, not broader at base than the apex, sides regularly arcuate, margin very narrow, front angles obtuse, disc moderately convex, coarsely, not closely punctate, color pale yellow, the margin narrowly black or brown. Elytra distinctly wider at base than the thorax, humeri rounded, disc rather flat, a slight intraumbonal arcuate impression, moderately densely punctate, the punctures finer than those of the thorax, color pale yellowish white, sides piceous or brownish, which is gradually evanescent toward the apex. Body beneath and legs entirely pale yellow, abdomen sparsely, finely punctate. Length .14—.16 inch.; 3.5—4 mm.

The last ventral of male has the usual trilobed form, the middle lobe moderately produced, concave and with a smooth median line.

This species may be difficult to distinguish from the pale forms of *blanda*, but the surface is never shining and the elytral punctures denser. In the pale forms of *blanda* the vittate character of the species can always be distinguished.

Occurs from Massachusetts to Florida and westward to Missouri.

Group XV.—APHTHONÆ.

Form oval. Antennæ 11-jointed. Anterior coxal cavities open behind. Thorax without trace of basal impressions. Posterior tibiæ grooved at least near the apex and terminated by a moderately long spur. Mesosternum distinctly visible. Posterior tarsi with last joint not inflated, the claws simple.

These few characters are all which can be used to define the entire group. All the genera are represented in both our fauna and in Europe. They are as follows :

Posterior tibiæ with the apex entire, the spur placed in the middle in front of the tarsus.

First joint of hind tarsi nearly or quite as long as half the tibia; punctuation of elytra confused..**Longitarsus.**

First joint of hind tarsus not more than one-third the length of the tibia and scarcely as long as the three following joints united; punctuation of elytra disposed in regular striae.............................**Glyptina.**

Posterior tibiæ with the inner apex notched or bilobed, the spur placed on the inner lobe.

First joint of hind tarsus not longer than one-third the tibia; punctuation of elytra in great part or entirely confused.................**Aphthona.**

After a study of our species of Glyptina in comparison with Batophila there does not seem to be any tangible character for separating them, and, as the former name has priority, has been adopted.

Aphthona is confined to the Atlantic region, the other genera are represented on both sides of the continent.

LONGITARSUS Latr.

Head oblong, not inserted as far as the eyes, front distinctly carinate and with the usual two tubercles distinctly separated and limited above. Labrum truncate. Eyes oval, convex, entire. Maxillary palpi rather slender, second joint cylindrical, third obconical, fourth more slender, conical and acute at tip. Antennæ always longer than half the body, often nearly as long, slightly stouter at tip. Prothorax broader than long, not, or only apparently narrowed in front, sides arcuate, often oblique at the front angles, base arcuate, but sometimes feebly so. Elytra oval or oblong, usually convex, the humeri variable, sometimes entirely obliterated in the apterous species, surface variably punctate, but always in a confused manner. Prosternum narrow, slightly dilated behind, the coxal cavities broadly open. Legs moderately long. Posterior thighs robust and often attaining the apices of the elytra. Tibiæ as long as the femora, dilated toward the apex, the posterior broadly grooved on the outer edge and finely denticulate, terminated by a long curved spur. Tarsi slender, the first joint of the posterior pair nearly or fully half the length of the tibia and as long as all the following joints united (Pl. VII, fig. 14). Abdomen with five free ventral segments.

An important modification of the definition of the genus as given by Chapuis must be made in reference to the structure of the antennæ. The fourth joint is not always longer than the third, as a considerable number of our species have the joints 2–3–4 very nearly equal in length. This has afforded an important means of dividing the genus primarily as will be seen in the table. The other characters are sufficiently plain, and will not require special comment. It must, however, be observed that the colors are slightly variable, and the consequent determination of unique examples is attended with more or less uncertainty.

The sexual characters have been observed and recorded in several species. In nearly all the males have the first tarsal joint of the front and often the middle legs longer and broader than in the female. The last ventral of the male varies in its characters, and is sometimes sinuate each side with a median impressed lobe as in Systena, or again subtruncate with a slight longitudinal impression, or finally, simply more convex than in the female. The antennæ are often longer and stouter in the male; the sutural angle of the elytra in several species is more distinct in the male, broadly rounded in the female.

The genus is an extremely difficult one to deal with, certainly more so than any other Halticini of our fauna, and the attempts to reduce the species to some sort of tabular order has not been very satisfactory, and the present one may prove no better than its predecessors, but the structure of the antennæ and the presence of certain apterous forms enables several divisions to be made, so that the difficulties are somewhat reduced.

Of but few species are the food plants known, these have been recorded in the specific names of the species themselves.

With these preliminary remarks the following table is presented:

Antennæ with joints 2-3-4 successively longer; body always winged...............2.
Antennæ with joints 2-3-4 of equal length, or at least with the fourth not lon
   ger than the second; body winged, or apterous................ ....,.12.
2.--Species rufotestaceous, brown or piceous; form always convex, except in
   postremus ....…… …… 3.
   Species yellowish white, or pale yellowish testaceous; form usually de
   pressed ....8.
3.--Rufotestaceous, or pale castaneous species............ ....4.
   Brownish, or piceous species..................... ....5.
4.--Thorax nearly square; color bright rufotestaceous, each elytron with a
   small, darker cloud; surface very shining, punctuation very indis
   tinct...... ....1. **Heliophyti.**
   Thorax very plainly broader than long, dull rufotestaceous; punctuation
   distinct..................... ....2. **subrutus.**
5.--Thorax without basal marginal line: a faint æneous surface lustre..........6.
   Thorax with basal marginal line; without æneous lustre ....7.
6.--Thorax not twice as wide as long; punctuation of elytra vaguely substriate
   form more oblong......... ....3. **turbatus.**
   Thorax very nearly or fully twice as wide as long; form short, robust;
   elytral punctuation very much confused...............4. **oregonensis.**
7.--Form robust and convex, rufopiceous or brown; species large.
                                         5. **traductus.**
   Form oblong, rather depressed; piceous, umbones paler, species small.
                                         6. **postremus.**
8.--Body above not distinctly punctate, either on thorax or elytra; body be
   neath concolorous ....7. **repandus.**
   Body above distinctly punctate...................... ....9.
9.--Body beneath rufotestaceous......................... ....10.
   Body beneath piceous or brown ....11.
10.-Form depressed; surface shining, as if varnished; elytral punctuation fine,
   smooth at apex...................... ....8. **livens.**
   Form moderately convex; surface less shining; elytral punctuation very
   distinct, even at apex......... ....9. **vanus.**
11.-Thorax and elytra similar in color......... ....10. **occidentalis.**
   Thorax and head decidedly reddish, elytra yellowish..........11. **bicolor.**
12.--Body more or less fully winged; elytra wider at base than the thorax, um
   bone distinct.............. .. ..,..,............... ....13.
   Body apterous; elytra not wider than the thorax, humeri oblique, umbone
   wanting; lateral margin visible from above at humerus................17.

13.—Surface always more or less alutaceous, the thorax always so; form rather
   elongate; humeri not prominent..16.
   Surface entirely shining; form robust, the humeri well marked and rather
   prominent; elytral punctuation rather coarse in all the species......14.
14.—Color rufoferruginous; surface of thorax sparsely, finely and indistinctly
   punctate. ....12. **alternatus.**
   Color brownish, or nearly piceous; thorax rather coarsely punctate...... .15.
15.—Abdomen of similar color to the upper surface; posterior femora piceons
   brown and distinctly punctate..........................13. **montivagus.**
   Abdomen piceous, nearly black; legs entirely piceous................14. **erro.**
   Abdomen paler than the upper surface; posterior femora yellowish and not
   distinctly punctate......................................15. **pygmaeus.**
16.—Elytra not shining, the punctuation very indistinct; color yellowish testaceous..16. **testaceus.**
   Elytra shining, punctuation coarse and well marked; color from nearly
   piceous to dark rufotestaceous..........................17. **melanurus.**
17.—Elytra covering the entire abdomen, or at most with merely the tip of the
   pygidium exposed... ...... 18.
   Elytra broadly rotundato-truncate, leaving rather more than the pygidium
   exposed ....19.
18.—Testaceous, or brownish testaceous, without metallic lustre.
   Elytra not very coarsely punctate.
      Thorax distinctly punctate, the punctures nearly as coarse as those of
      the elytra..18. **rufescens.**
      Thorax indistinctly punctate, or nearly smooth; elytral punctures
      coarser than those of *rufescens*......................19. **insolens.**
   Elytra with coarse, deep, close punctures, with an apparent substriate
   arrangement.
      Thorax with scattered, coarse, deep punctures.........20. **perforatus.**
   Piceous, with or without metallic lustre; sutural angles rounded.
      Surface without metallic lustre; punctures of elytra nearly as coarse at
      apex as at base; species minute.....................21. **solidaginis.**
      Surface with distinct metallic lustre; punctures of elytra much less dis-
      tinct at apex; species larger.. ....22 **nitidellus.**
19.—Surface shining, slightly metallic; punctuation very sparse and feebly
   impressed...... ....23. **maneus.**

1. **L. Heliophyti** n. sp.—Oblong oval, convex, rufotestaceous, shining,
each elytron with a fuscous cloud at middle. Antennæ with four basal and three
apical joints rufotestaceous, the intermediate joints fuscous. Head smooth,
shining. Thorax one-fourth wider than long, not narrowed in front, sides
slightly sinuous, obliquely truncate at front angles with distinct post-apical an -
gulation, basal marginal line entire, distinctly impressed at middle, disc convex,
smooth. Elytra much wider at base than the thorax, humeri obtusely prominent, umbone moderately prominent, sutural angles distinct, but obtuse, disc
convex, sparsely, finely and indistinctly punctate, but absolutely smooth at apex.
Body beneath and posterior femora a little darker than above. Abdomen sparsely
punctate. Legs pale rufotestaceous. Length .08 inch.; 2 mm.

This species is readily known by its color and bright shining surface, the antennæ being of different colors at base, apex and middle, and by the small fuscous cloud on the middle of each elytron. The humeri is more prominent than in any other species in our fauna. Feeds on *Heliophytum indicum*, as I am informed by Mr. Schwarz. Occurs at Selma, Alabama, and Columbus, Texas.

2. **L. subrufus** Lec.--Oblong oval, convex, rufotestaceous, moderately shining. Antennæ pale, outer five joints fuscous. Head smooth, shining. Thorax one-third wider than long, not narrowed in front, sides arcuate, not distinctly oblique at the front angles, basal marginal line extremely fine, disc moderately convex, very sparsely and finely punctate and shining. Elytra wider at base than the thorax, humeri obtusely rounded, umbone moderately prominent, sutural angle obtuse ♂, or rounded ♀, disc convex, the punctures moderate, not closely placed, smoother at sides and apex. Body beneath a little darker than above. Abdomen sparsely punctate. Legs pale rufotestaceous, the posterior femora a little darker. Length .10—.12 inch. : 2.5—3 mm.

This is one of the larger and more conspicuous species in our fauna. It resembles *alternata*, but in addition to the structure of the antennæ, the present species is much more finely punctured.

The male has the last ventral segment sinuate each side, the median lobe moderately prominent and concave. The male is narrower than the female and the thorax less transverse.

Occurs in Kansas, collected in numbers by Prof. F. H. Snow. Lives on *Onosmodium*, Dr. Shimer.

3. **L. turbatus** n. sp.—Oblong oval, not very convex. piceous brown or castaneous, shining. surface with extremely faint bronze lustre. Antennæ with four basal joints pale, outer joints gradually piceous. Head smooth. Thorax nearly one-half wider than long, apparently slightly narrowed in front, sides feebly arcuate, slightly obliquely truncate at anterior angles, base arcuate, marginal line wanting. Elytra wider at base than the thorax, humeri rounded, umbone moderate, sutural angles well defined, disc moderately convex, the punctuation rather coarse and close, smoother at apex, the punctures vaguely in series. Body beneath as dark as above. Abdomen sparsely punctate. Anterior four legs and posterior tibiæ yellowish testaceous, posterior femora brown. Length .10 inch. ; 2.5 mm.

This species is more oblong and more coarsely punctate than *oregonensis*. It seems to be mixed in all collections with *melanurus*, but differs from that not only by the structure of the antennæ, but in the absence of the alutaceous surface seen in that species.

Occurs at Galesburg, Ill. (Strumberg), and Detroit, Mich., Selma, Ala., San Antonio, Texas (Schwarz).

4. **L. oregonensis** n. sp.—Oval, slightly oblong, facies robust, convex, castaneous brown, surface with a very faint bronze lustre. Antennæ with four basal joints pale, outer joints fuscous. Head impunctate. Thorax very nearly twice as wide as long, not narrowed in front, sides very feebly arcuate, slightly obliquely truncate at front angles, base arcuate, marginal line not distinct, disc moderately convex, sparsely and very finely punctate, almost smooth at sides and apex. Elytra wider at base than the thorax, humeri broadly obliquely rounded, umbone moderate, sutural angle obtuse, disc convex, the punctures moderately coarse and close near base, finer and sparser at apex and sides. Body beneath darker than above, nearly piceous. Abdomen sparsely punctate. Anterior and middle legs yellowish testaceous, posterior femora castaneous. Length .08—.10 inch.; 2—2.5 mm.

In the male the last ventral is faintly sinuate each side, the median lobe has a small foveiform impression.

This species is not conspicuously marked, except by the very transverse thorax, the slight bronze surface lustre, and very dark underside.

Occurs in Oregon.

5. **L. traductus** n. sp.—Oval, slightly oblong, moderately robust, brown or piceous, moderately shining. Antennæ rufotestaceous, the outer five joints gradually piceous. Head smooth. Thorax rather more than half wider than long, not narrowed in front, sides arcuate, distinctly obliquely truncate at front angles, base arcuate, the marginal line fine, but distinct, disc moderately convex, the punctures fine and rather close near the base, very sparse and indistinct at front and sides. Elytra wider than the thorax at base, humeri rounded, umbone moderately prominent, sutural angle obtuse, disc convex, the punctures moderate in size, not close, gradually finer and smoother at apex and sides, a vague indication of a sutural stria is seen near the apex. Body beneath and posterior femora similar in color to the upper surface. Abdomen rather coarsely and closely punctate at middle. Legs pale rufotestaceous. Length .12—.14 inch.; 3—3.5 mm.

The male has the last ventral segment distinctly sinuate each side, the middle lobe moderately prominent and with a short, but vague longitudinal impression.

This is the largest and most robust species at present known in our fauna.

Occurs in southwestern Virginia; collected by Prof. E. D. Cope (see Trans. Am. Ent. Soc. 1868, p. 125).

6. **L. postremus** n. sp.—Elongate oval, rather depressed, piceous, moderately shining, umbones paler. Antennæ pale rufotestaceous, gradually infuscate externally, joints 2-3-4 progressively longer. Head smooth. Thorax one-third wider than long. Apparently narrowed in front, sides feebly arcuate, slightly subangulate at middle, the oblique truncation scarcely evident, disc feebly convex, finely, sparsely punctate, basal marginal line fine, but distinct Elytra a

little wider at base than the thorax, humeri rounded, umbone not prominent. apical angle distinct, but obtuse, disc not very convex, the punctuation fine, but very distinct, rather close about the scutellum, thence gradually sparser to apex and sides. Body beneath piceous. Abdomen sparsely punctate. Legs uniform rufotestaceous. Length .08 inch.; 2 mm.

This species is readily known in the present series by its very dark color and rather elongate form, resembling in this respect a diminutive *Systena elongata*. In the two specimens before me the umbones are a little paler than the rest of the surface.

Occurs in western Nevada (Morrison).

7. **L. repandus** Lec.—Oblong oval, moderately convex, pale yellowish testaceous, shining. Antennæ slightly darker externally, joints 2-3-4 gradually longer. Head smooth, slightly rufescent. Thorax about one half wider than long, not narrowed in front, sides feebly arcuate, the oblique truncation of the anterior angles scarcely evident, base with extremely fine, but entire marginal line, disc moderately convex, the surface not punctate, but slightly irregular near the base. Elytra wider at base than the thorax, humeri rounded, umbone moderately prominent and smooth, sutural angle distinct, but obtuse, disc feebly convex, the surface rather shining, the punctuation extremely fine, sparse and obsolete, faintly visible near the base only. Body beneath and legs similar in color to the upper surface, the posterior femora very slightly darker and nearly smooth. Abdomen with extremely few, scattered, fine punctures. Length .065—.08 inch.; 1.5—2 mm.

A very inconspicuous species, which, however, could only be confounded with *livens* or *vanus*, both of which have the underside entirely pale, but the surface very distinctly punctate.

Occurs at Los Angeles and San Diego, California.

8. **L. livens** Lec.—Oblong oval, subdepressed, yellowish testaceous, or yellowish white, surface very shining. Antennæ faintly infuscate, the three basal joints pale, joints 2-3-4 progressively longer. Head faintly rufescent, smooth. Thorax about one-third wider than long, not narrowed in front, sides arcuate, the anterior angles feebly obliquely truncate, a basal marginal line very feeble and often indistinct, disc moderately convex, surface sparsely punctate, punctures finer in front. Elytra wider at base than the thorax, humeri rounded, umbone not prominent, sutural angle distinct, but obtuse, disc sparsely, finely punctured at basal half, smooth at apex and sides. Body beneath and posterior femora slightly darker than the upperside. Abdomen distinctly, but sparsely punctate, the first two segments smooth at the sides. Anterior and middle legs and posterior tibiæ pale yellowish testaceous. Length .10 inch.; 2.5 mm.

This species is known by its pale underside and legs, punctate abdomen, very shining and finely punctate surface.

Occurs in California from Los Angeles to Fort Yuma.

9. **L. vanus** n. sp.—Oblong oval, moderately convex, pale yellowish testaceous, shining, the suture very narrowly infuscate behind the middle. Antennæ pale, the outer five joints slightly darker. Head decidedly darker than the thorax, smooth. Thorax about one-third wider than long, not narrowed in front, sides very distinctly arcuate, at anterior angles obliquely truncate, basal marginal line entirely wanting, disc moderately convex, surface slightly wrinkled, the punctures relatively coarse, but not close. Elytra distinctly wider at base than the thorax, humeri rounded, umbone moderate, sutural angle distinct, but obtuse, disc moderately convex, the punctures moderate, rather closely placed, a little finer at apex, but distinctly impressed throughout. Body beneath and legs similar in color to the upper surface. Abdomen very indistinctly punctate. Length .08 inch. ; 2 mm.

This species is the most distinctly punctate of the present series of pale species, and while a little variable in degree, it is never so finely punctate as in *lirens* or *repandus*.

Occurs in western Texas and at Seligman, Ariz. (Wickham).

10. **L. occidentalis** n. sp.—Oblong oval, feebly convex, yellowish testaceous, moderately shining. Antennæ pale at basal half, darker externally. Head slightly rufescent, smooth, shining. Thorax one-half wider than long, apparently slightly narrowed in front, broadest a little behind the middle, sides arcuate, slightly obliquely truncate at front angles, hind angles very broadly rounded, base truncate at middle and with an extremely indistinct marginal line, disc moderately convex, the surface very distinctly and moderately closely punctate at base, sparser and fine in front. Elytra distinctly wider at base than the thorax, humeri rounded, umbone not prominent, sutural angle obtusely rounded, disc moderately convex, the punctuation fine and sparse, nearly smooth at apex. Body beneath and posterior femora brownish testaceous, abdomen sometimes piceous, the legs otherwise pale yellowish testaceous. Abdomen very distinctly, but not closely punctate. Length .08—.10 inch. ; 2–2.5 mm.

Resembles *repandus*, but very distinctly punctate, and with the underside darker, in fully mature specimens nearly black.

This species has been heretofore considered and determined for several correspondents as *nigripalpis* Lec., but an examination of the type of the latter shows it to be at least congeneric with (Malacosoma) fuscula Lec. (Lyperaltica *Crotch*) and probably not specifically different.

Occurs in Colorado, Utah and Arizona.

11. **L. bicolor** n. sp.—Oblong oval, moderately convex, beneath piceous, head and thorax rufotestaceous, elytra and legs yellowish testaceous, surface moderately shining. Antennæ pale, slightly darker externally. Head rufotestaceous, smooth. Thorax one third wider than long, not narrowed in front, sides arcuate, distinctly obliquely truncate in front, base truncate at middle, with distinct marginal line, disc convex, sparsely, but distinctly punctate. Elytra distinctly wider at base than the thorax, humeri rounded, umbone moderate,

sutural angle obtusely rounded, disc moderately convex, the punctuation distinct, moderately close at base and coarser than that of the thorax, finer at apex. Abdomen very distinctly punctate. Anterior and middle legs pale yellowish testaceous, the punctuation slightly darker. Length .08 inch.; 2 mm.

In the male the last ventral segment is sinuate each side, the middle produced in a slight lobe, which has a triangular impression which extends to the base of the segment.

The color at first sight will readily distinguish this species. The thorax is more nearly square than in the others of this series.

Occurs in New Mexico.

12. **L. alternata** Ziegl. —Oblong oval, moderately convex, rufocastaneous, shining. Antennæ three-fourths the length of the body, piceous, four basal joints pale, joints 2–3 4 equal in length. Head smooth, impunctate. Thorax one-third wider than long, apparently slightly narrowed in front, sides arcuate, the oblique truncation scarcely evident, disc convex, nearly smooth, a few sparsely placed, fine punctures along the base. Elytra wider at base than the thorax, humeri rounded, umbone feeble, form regularly oval, sutural angle rounded, disc convex, the punctuation moderate, not deep nor closely placed, very confused, finer near the sides. Body beneath similar in color to the upper surface. Abdomen smooth, sparsely punctate. Legs rufotestaceous, the anterior and middle paler. Length .10 inch.; 2.5 mm.

This is the largest species in the series with the joints 2–3–4 of the antennæ of equal length, and has the thorax much less punctate than in any other. The suture is sometimes narrowly infuscate.

I have examined the types of Ziegler, Melsheimer and LeConte, and find *alternata* (Psylliodes), *rubicunda* (Aphthona) and *rubidus* identical. The types of the latter are in bad state.

Occurs in Pennsylvania, near Denver, Colorado, and at Fort Laramie (LeConte).

13. **L. montivagus** n. sp.—Oval, convex, moderately robust, brownish, shining. Antennæ slender, rufotestaceous at base, the outer five joints piceous, joints 2–3–4 equal in length. Head shining, impunctate. Thorax one-fourth wider than long, not narrowed in front, sides feebly arcuate, anterior angles indistinctly obliquely truncate, disc convex, shining, not alutaceous, the punctuation coarse and close, but not deep, finer toward the sides and nearly as coarse as that of the elytra. Elytra distinctly wider at base than the thorax, humeri obtusely rounded, umbone moderately distinct, form regularly oval, widest at middle, sutural angle distinct, very little obtuse, disc convex, shining, punctuation moderately coarse, close and deep, finer toward apex, confused. Body beneath as dark, or darker than above. Abdomen coarsely, sparsely punctate. Anterior and middle legs rufotestaceous, posterior femora piceous, alutaceous and distinctly punctate, tibiæ paler. Length .07—.08 inch.; 2 mm.

This species resembles *melanurus*, but is more robust, the humeri more distinct, and the surface not alutaceous. It is larger and more elongate than *pygmæus*, and with the elytral punctuation confused. Occurs in California, in the Calaveras region, also in western Nevada.

14. **L. erro** n. sp. —Oval, convex, facies robust, piceous, shining. Antennæ piceous, nearly black. Head shining, impunctate. Thorax one half wider than long, not narrowed in front, sides nearly straight, anterior angles obliquely truncate, disc convex, the punctuation fine and sparse, the apical region and a rather broad median space impunctate. Elytra wider at base than the thorax, humeri obliquely rounded, umbone moderately prominent, sutural angles well defined, disc convex, the punctuation rather coarse and close, but finer and sparser toward apex and sides. Body beneath entirely black. Abdomen sparsely punctate. Legs entirely piceous. Length .07 inch.; 2 mm, nearly.

This species is nearly related to *montivagus*, but is more shortly oval. It differs notably from every species in our fauna by the very dark legs.

Occurs at White Fish Point, Lake Superior region (Schwarz).

15. **L. pygmæus** n. sp. -Oval, robust, convex, piceous, shining. Antennæ slender, brown, three basal joints paler. Head impunctate, feebly shining. Thorax one-half wider than long, not narrowed in front, sides feebly arcuate, vaguely subangulate at middle, anterior angles obliquely truncate, disc moderately convex and shining, the punctuation moderately coarse and deep, closely placed at base, sparser in front. Elytra very obviously wider at base than the thorax, humeri obtuse, umbone moderately prominent, form regularly oval, widest at middle, scarcely more than a fourth longer than wide, sutural angle well defined, disc convex, punctuation coarse, deep and closely placed, substriately arranged at base, less deep at apex. Body beneath paler than above. Abdomen very indistinctly punctate. Legs entirely yellowish testaceous, the posterior femora not distinctly punctate. Length .06 inch.; 1.5 mm.

The sides of the elytra at and near the apex are paler in color than the disc, the epipleuræ also paler. The posterior femora are much darker on the upperside than on the lower. The characters given in the table will enable this small species to be known.

Occurs in Georgia (Morrison).

16. **L. testaceus** Mels.—Oblong oval, moderately convex, yellowish testaceous, head slightly darker, surface finely alutaceous and with a greasy aspect. Antennæ slender, yellowish testaceous, joints 2-3-4 equal in length. Head impunctate. Thorax one-third wider than long, not narrowed in front, sides irregularly arcuate, the anterior angles slightly obliquely truncate, disc moderately convex, very distinctly alutaceous, the punctuation sparse, rather fine and indistinct. Elytra very little wider at base than the thorax, humeri rounded, umbone distinct, but not prominent, form regularly oval, widest at middle, sutural

angle obtusely rounded, disc moderately convex, surface distinctly alutaceous, punctuation sparse, fine and obsolete. Body beneath a little darker than above. Abdomen shining, sparsely indistinctly punctate. Legs yellowish testaceous, posterior femora sparsely obsoletely punctate. Length .07 - .08 inch. ; 2 mm.

This species makes the nearest approach in form to the apterous forms by the rather narrow elytral base and rounded humeri, but the umbone is quite distinct and the body winged. The base of the thorax is without marginal line. The distinctive characters of this species are in form of the antennæ, the color and the character of the surface and punctuation.

Occurs from Pennsylvania to Georgia.

17. **L. melanurus** Mels.—Oblong oval, moderately convex, brownish, moderately shining. Antennæ slender, rufotestaceous, outer five joints darker. Head minutely alutaceous, impunctate. Thorax slightly wider than long, not narrowed in front, sides feebly arcuate with a slight angulation at middle, apical angles obliquely truncate, with distinct post apical angulation, disc moderately convex, very distinctly alutaceous and slightly wrinkled near base, punctuation moderately coarse, but very indistinct, especially near apex. Elytra a little wider at base than thorax, humeri rounded, umbone distinct, form regularly oval, widest at middle, sutural angle obtusely rounded, disc convex, very faintly alutaceous, the punctuation coarse, deep and close, less so at apex. Body beneath similar in color to the upper surface. Abdomen shining, sparsely, indistinctly punctate. Anterior and middle legs yellowish testaceous, posterior femora brown, sparsely, indistinctly punctate, posterior tibiæ rufotestaceous. Length .08 inch. ; 2 mm.

In this species the thorax is probably more rugulose than in any other of our fauna. It has the coarsest elytral punctuation of all those with the joints 2-3-4 of antennæ equal.

Occurs from Canada and Dakota to North Carolina, Kansas, Illinois and Missouri.

18. **L. rufescens** n. sp.— Oblong oval, rufotestaceous, moderately shining. Antennæ longer than half the body, pale rufotestaceous, slightly darker externally, joints 2-3-4 equal in length. Head smooth, a distinct fovea near the top of each eye. Thorax one-half wider than long, not narrowed in front, base moderately arcuate, without marginal line, sides nearly straight, anterior angles feebly obliquely truncate, disc convex, the punctures moderate, sparsely placed, smaller at apex. Elytra not wider at base than the thorax, form regularly oval, humeri oblique, umbone wanting, sutural angles distinct, but obtuse, pygidium concealed, disc convex, the punctuation moderately coarse, not close, finer and sparser at apex and sides. Body beneath a little darker than above. Abdomen very indistinctly punctate. Legs pale rufotestaceous. Length .05 inch. ; 1.25 mm.

Also a small species, entirely apterous, and distinguished from those at present known in this series by the pale color. The apices of the elytra are not rounded, the sutural angle quite distinct, and the pygidium covered.

Occurs in Mendocino County, California.

19. **L. insolens** n. sp.—Oblong oval, pale rufotestaceous, moderately convex and shining. Antennæ longer than half the body, pale rufotestaceous, joints 2-3-4 equal in length. Head smooth, a few coarse punctures near each eye. Thorax one-third wider than long, not narrowed in front, sides obliquely truncate in front, then feebly arcuate, base arcuate, without marginal line; disc moderately convex, sparsely, finely and indistinctly punctate. Elytra not wider at base than the thorax, oval, humeri and umbone indistinct, sutural angle obtuse, disc moderately coarsely, not closely punctate, punctures very little finer to apex. Body beneath and legs colored as above. Abdomen coarsely punctate. Length .08 inch.; 2 mm.

This species is considerably larger than either of those with which it is associated. It resembles some of the paler forms of *melanurus*, and also *alternatus*, but is readily known by the rounded humeri and absent umbones.

Occurs in Virginia and New Jersey.

20. **L. perforatus** n. sp.—Elongate oval, very convex, rufotestaceous, shining. Antennæ with four basal joints pale, the outer brown. Head smooth, shining. Thorax one-third wider than long, not narrowed in front, sides straight, anterior angles obliquely truncate, base broadly arcuate, disc convex, slightly alutaceous, the punctuation rather coarse, but indistinct and sparse. Elytra not wider at base than the thorax, form regularly oval, umbones not evident, sutural angle well defined, pygidium entirely concealed, disc convex, the punctuation relatively very coarse, deep and rather close, well marked at sides and apex. Body beneath concolorous. Abdomen indistinctly punctate. Legs pale yellowish. Length .05 inch.; 1.25 mm.

This minute species may be known in the apterous series by its color and the coarse elytral punctuation. The elytra meet fairly at apex and conceal the pygidium completely.

Occurs at Tampa, Florida (Schwarz).

21. **L. solidaginis** n. sp.—Oblong oval, convex, piceous black, without metallic lustre. Antennæ longer than half the body, rufotestaceous, slightly darker at tip, joints 2-3-4 equal in length. Head smooth, impunctate. Thorax one-fourth wider than long, not narrowed in front, base moderately arcuate, hind angles distinct, but obtuse, sides nearly straight, anterior angles obliquely truncate, with slight post-apical angulation, disc convex, without basal marginal line, surface not very shining, punctuation moderate, not closely, but very regularly placed. Elytra not wider at base than the thorax, humeri oblique, umbone wanting, form regularly oval, gradually narrowed at apical third, the apices separately rounded, leaving the tip of the pygidium exposed, disc convex, moderately, coarsely, deeply and closely punctate, not smoother at apex. Body beneath piceous. Abdomen indistinctly punctate. Legs rufotestaceous, the posterior femora brown. Length .04—.05 inch.; 1—1.25 mm.

This species may be readily known by its small size, almost true black color and very coarsely punctate elytra, the entire surface without metallic lustre.

Occurs in Sumter Co., Fla., on a species of *Solidago* (Schwarz).

22. **L. nitidellus** Cockerell.—Oblong oval, convex, piceous, surface distinctly bronzed, shining. Antennae longer than half the body, slender, rufotestaceous at base, piceous externally. Head impunctate. Thorax a little wider than long, not narrowed in front, base broadly arcuate, hind angles rounded, sides feebly arcuate, anterior angles obliquely truncate, with distinct post apical angulation, disc convex, distinctly alutaceous, the punctures moderate, neither deep nor closely placed, finer in front. Elytra not wider at base than the thorax, humeri oblique, umbone wanting, form regularly oval, broadest at middle, apices separately rounded, tip of pygidium exposed, disc convex, the punctuation rather coarse and close at base, gradually finer toward apex and sides. Body beneath piceous, less shining. Abdomen alutaceous, rugose, the punctures coarse and close, but shallow. Legs rufotestaceous, the posterior femora much darker. Length .08 inch.; 2 mm.

In the male the last ventral segment is truncate at apex and with a small, smooth tubercle at middle of disc

As the bronze surface is not a common character among our species there need be no difficulty in distinguishing this by its apterous form, obliterated humeri and rounded tips of elytra.

This species was rather imperfectly described by Mr. Cockerell in a little sheet which may not fall in the hands of many students. Through his kindness I possess the specimen described, and am able to fix its specific relationships with greater certainty.

Occurs in Arizona, New Mexico and Colorado.

23. **L. maucus** Lec.—Oblong oval, convex, piceous, surface distinctly bronzed and shining. Antennae longer than half the body, piceous, the outer six joints distinctly stouter, joints 2-3-4 equal in length. Thorax very little wider than long, not narrowed in front, base broadly arcuate, hind angles very obtuse, sides feebly arcuate, front angles slightly obliquely truncate, disc moderately convex, punctuation sparse and indistinct, at apex smoother, base without marginal line. Elytra not wider than the thorax, humeri entirely obliterated, no umbone, sides arcuate, gradually wider posteriorly, obliquely truncate at apex, leaving the entire pygidium exposed, disc convex, sparsely, finely and indistinctly punctate. Body beneath piceous, shining Abdomen sparsely, indistinctly punctate. Legs piceous, posterior femora bronzed, the tibiae pale brown or testaceous. Length .06 inch.; 1.5 mm.

This species, which is one of the smallest in our fauna, is readily known by the truncate elytra, bronzed and nearly smooth surface. The general appearance is that of a minute *Meloe*. The body is entirely apterous and the metasternum quite short.

Occurs in California.

The following species has been described by Motschulsky:

Teinodactyla californica Motsch.—Oblonga, testacea, punctatissima, corpore subtus capiteque piceis: femoribus rufopiceis. Long. 1 lin.; lat. .5 lin.

This Teinodactyla resembles greatly our species of Europe, such as *atricilla* and *melanocephala*, but it is considerably more elongate and more strongly punctate on the elytra.

Occurs in California.

In the preliminary remarks to the paper in which this is described Motschulsky mentions that part of the species were purchased from Dupont as collected in California. On several occasions I have had to deal with this material and have satisfied myself from the identification of nearly all the species that the series was collected in southwestern Texas.

There is very little doubt in my mind that the above species came from that region, and that it is possibly indentical with *occidentalis* Horn.

Longitarsus nigripalpis Lec. must be placed with *Malacosoma fuscula* Lec., from which it may not differ specifically.

GLYPTINA Lec.

Head inserted as far as the eyes, front not carinate, the tubercles distinct, clypeus broadly emarginate, labrum arcuate in front. Maxillary palpi moderate in length, second joint rather slender, conical, third much shorter and stouter, fourth more slender, conical and acute at tip. Antennae as long as half the body, slender, very slightly thicker externally; first joint cylindrical, second more than half the length of first, conical, joints 3–7 gradually increasing in length, 8–10 shorter, eleventh longer and acute at tip. Thorax broader than long, usually narrowed in front, sides and base arcuate, apex truncate, anterior angles slightly obliquely truncate, the hind angles obtuse, disc without basal or transverse impression. Elytra oval, striato-punctate at base and sides confused at apex, often smooth at sides and apex. Prosternum moderate between the coxae, slightly dilated at apex, the cavities rather widely open behind. Ventral segments all free, the first as long as the next two. Legs moderately long. Posterior tibiae straight, terminated at middle of its tip by a moderate spur, the outer edge grooved near the tip. Tarsi moderately long, the first joint of the posterior one-third the length of the tibia and equal to the other joints together. Claws simple.

Through the kindness of Mr. Jacoby I have been enabled to study a specimen of *Batophila rubi*, and have been forced to the conclusion that Batophila and Glyptina cannot be retained as distinct, as there does not seem to be any structural difference.

All the European species are said to be apterous, this is the case also with *bicolor*, which in turn resembles Podagrica in its color. Following this *cyanipennis* has similar colors, and while the body is feebly winged, the elytra are united. The pale species which follow on have better marked humeri and well developed wings, but this is not an abrupt transition as *spuria* has but feeble humeri.

The elytral striae are confused at apex and sides in *bicolor*, while in the three following species the striae are entire and regular, while in the last two species the sides and apex are quite smooth.

It seems to me that Crotch was correct when he united Glyptina and Batophila, but he seems to have overlooked the fact that Glyptina has the right to priority.

The species may be readily distinguished by the following table:

Elytra blue, with metallic lustre.
Head and thorax reddish yellow; humeri indistinct.
Thorax somewhat wrinkled, vaguely punctate; elytral striae much confused at apex..**bicolor.**
Thorax smooth, very sparsely, finely punctate; striae entire, not confused.
cyanipennis.
Head and thorax shining black; humeri distinct...............**nivalis.**
Elytra yellowish or rufotestaceous; humeri wider than thorax.
Elytral striae of well defined punctures, the lateral striae distinct.
Lateral striae, especially the ninth, deeper than those of the disc; body beneath brown..**brunnea.**
Lateral striae faint; body beneath brownish piceous, very rarely pale.
spuria.
Elytral striae of very fine or obsolete punctures, sides and apex smooth.
Elytral striae of extremely fine punctures; body beneath always pale.
cerina.
Elytral striae of coarse, obsolete punctures near the base and scutellum only; body beneath piceous or nearly black................**atriventris.**

G. bicolor n. sp.—Oblong oval, more narrowed in front, convex, beneath piceous; head, thorax and legs pale reddish brown, elytra bright bluish green, metallic. Antennae with basal joint brown, next three rufotestaceous, outer joints piceous. Head impunctate. Thorax one-third wider than long, narrower at apex, sides arcuate, anterior angles slightly obliquely truncate, disc convex, the surface somewhat wrinkled, the punctuation very indistinct and rather fine. Elytra not wider at base than the thorax and very nearly continuous in outline, surface shining, confusedly punctate at apex, striato-punctate at base and sides, the punctures coarse, deep and moderately close, intervals flat, with smaller punctures than those of the striae. Prosternum and side pieces smooth. Abdomen shining, sparsely, indistinctly punctate, and with few hairs. Length .10--.14 inch.; 2.5- 3.5 mm.

In the specimens before me no sexual differences have been observed.

The facies of this species is that of a large Chaetocnema, and its colors are so exactly those of many Podagrica that the species was referred to that genus in the "Classification" (1883, p. 353). Notwithstanding its resemblance to the latter genus, there can be no doubt of its correct reference to Glyptina, more especially in view of the structure of the front coxal cavities.

Occurs in Georgia (Morrison), Louisiana and Kansas.

G. cyanipennis Crotch.- Oblong oval, convex, body beneath piceous; head, thorax and legs reddish yellow, elytra metallic blue. Antennae rufotestaceous, a little darker at tip. Head impunctate. Thorax about one-third wider than long, slightly narrowed in front, sides arcuate, the anterior angles obliquely truncate with a slight post-apical angulation, disc convex, smooth and shining, with a few fine scattered punctures Elytra scarcely wider at base than the thorax, humeri obliquely rounded, umbone feeble, disc striate, striae coarsely, serrately punctured, the punctures finer near the apex, intervals slightly convex, a little wider than the striae, each with a single row of finer punctures. Abdomen piceous, shining, sparsely, finely punctate. Length .08 inch.; 2 mm.

This species has very nearly the form and elytral sculpture of *rubi* of Europe, but is a little less convex. It forms a link between the species of Europe and those which follow. The body is not entirely apterous, but the elytra seem to be connate. All the European species are said to be apterous, as is the *bicolor* which precedes.

Occurs at Biscayne Bay, Florida, and in Texas.

G. nivalis n. sp.--Oblong oval, moderately convex and shining, body beneath, head and thorax piceous black, elytra metallic blue Antennae piceous, four basal joints rufotestaceous. Head smooth. Thorax one-half wider than long, not narrowed in front, sides slightly arcuate, anterior angles slightly obliquely truncate, the posterior a little prominent, disc moderately convex, sparsely finely punctate. Elytra wider at base than the thorax, humeri distinct, umbone moderate, smooth, disc regularly striato punctate, striae not impressed, punctures rather fine, moderately close, intervals flat, indistinctly, sparsely punctate, punctures less distinct at sides and apex. Body beneath shining, abdomen sparsely punctate. Anterior and middle femora brown, posterior piceous, slightly bronzed, tibiae and tarsi testaceous. Length .09 inch.; 2.5 mm.

This species recedes from the others with metallic blue elytra in having the humeri quite distinct. In this respect it resembles *cerina*, although the elytral sculpture is very like *spuria*.

One specimen collected by Prof. Snow near Hot Springs, Las Vegas, New Mexico, at an elevation of seven thousand feet.

G. brunnea n. sp.—Oblong oval, rather robust, moderately convex, shining, reddish brown above and beneath, legs and antennæ pale rufotestaceous. Head smooth, impunctate. Thorax nearly twice as wide as long, slightly narrowed in front, anterior angles obliquely truncate, with slight post apical angulation, sides feebly arcuate, disc convex, shining, the punctures extremely fine and sparse. Elytra very distinctly wider than the thorax, humeri obtuse, umbone moderately prominent, disc striato-punctate, the punctures moderately coarse and closely placed, but not serrate, the ninth stria more distinctly impressed than the discal, intervals flat, wider than the striæ, uniseriately finely punctate. Body beneath a little darker than above. Abdomen slightly rugulose and punctate, the last two segments more closely. Length .07--.08 inch.; 1.75--2 mm.

This species is the most robust of those of non-metallic color, resembling some of our Longitarsus. The reddish brown color is peculiar to it. It differs from *cerina*, to which it is more especially allied by its comparatively smooth thorax, shorter and more robust form and by the underside not of different color from the upper, although slightly darker.

Occurs in Georgia, Louisiana, Texas and Wisconsin (Chope).

G. spuria Lec. --Oblong oval, moderately convex, body beneath piceous, above rufotestaceous. Antennæ entirely rufotestaceous. Head smooth, impunctate. Thorax one-half wider than long, not narrower in front, except at the oblique truncation, behind which is a distinct angulation, sides arcuate, disc convex, the punctuation relatively coarse and sparse, but somewhat variable. Elytra distinctly wider at base than thorax, humeri broadly rounded, disc faintly striate, striæ coarsely and closely punctate, the lateral striæ less deep, intervals wider than the striæ, slightly convex, uniseriately finely punctate. Abdomen piceous, shining, scarcely visibly punctate. Legs pale yellowish testaceous. Length .06 - .07 inch.; 1.5—1.75 mm.

The punctuation of the thorax varies from relatively coarse to almost smooth. One specimen before me which I suppose to be a male, has the last ventral segment pale and more convex than the others. Rarely the abdomen may be entirely pale.

From the fact that the striæ are distinct at the sides as well as on the disc this species is more nearly related to the preceding than any other, but may be known by its less robust form and piceous underside.

Occurs from Pennsylvania to Florida, and westward to Kansas, Colorado and Dakota.

G. cerina Lec.—Oblong oval, feebly convex, entire body and members pale yellowish testaceous, the head slightly darker. Head smooth, impunctate. Thorax a little more than half wider than long, not distinctly narrowed in front, sides feebly arcuate, obliquely truncate at front angles, without distinct post apical angulation, disc moderately convex, sparsely punctate or quite smooth. Elytra distinctly wider at base than the thorax, humeri rounded, umbone scarcely prominent, disc indistinctly striato punctate, the punctures fine, feebly impressed and not close, the sides and apex quite smooth. Abdomen sparsely, indistinctly punctate. Length .08—.09 inch.; 2—2.25 mm.

By the table which precedes, it will be observed that two species have the sides of the elytra quite smooth, this and *atriventris*. In the latter the underside is normally piceous, in marked contrast with the upper surface. In *cerina* the elytral punctures, although fine, are well defined and distinct, and not vague as in the other.

Occurs in California and Arizona.

G. atriventris n. sp.—Oblong oval, feebly convex, body beneath piceous, above pale yellowish testaceous. Antennae slightly darker externally. Head smooth, impunctate. Thorax a little more than half wider than long, very little narrowed in front, anterior angles obliquely truncate, without post-apical angulation, sides slightly arcuate, disc sparsely, finely punctate or quite smooth. Elytra distinctly wider at base than the thorax, humeri obtusely rounded, umbone distinct, disc indistinctly striato-punctate, the punctures relatively large, but very vague and indistinct, intervals wider and with an indistinct series of finer punctures, sides and apex quite smooth. Abdomen slightly rugose and indistinctly punctate. Legs pale yellowish testaceous. Length .06—.08 inch.; 1.5—2 mm.

This species varies in the punctuation of the thorax as in *cerina*, although the punctures are never so distinct as in that species. The punctures of the striae are larger than in *cerina*, but more vague. Occasionally specimens are seen with a brown abdomen which might be confounded with *cerina*, in which, however, the underside is quite pale.

Occurs in Colorado, New Mexico, Texas, Arizona and California.

PHYLLOTRETA Foudras.

Head small, deeply inserted in the thorax, the eyes convex and prominent, front distinctly carinate between the antennae, the tubercles obliterated. Last joint of maxillary palpi nearly as long as the preceding, elongate conical. Antennae half as long as the body or slightly longer, slender in some species, or gradually thicker in others, in many species different in the sexes in the form of the middle joints. Prothorax always broader than long and somewhat narrowed

NORTH AMERICAN COLEOPTERA.

in front, apex not emarginate, base slightly arcuate; prosternum narrowly separating the coxæ, slightly dilated behind them, the coxal cavities open behind, angulate externally exposing the trochantin. Elytra oval, usually convex, the humeri never prominent. Legs moderately long, the posterior thighs stout, posterior tibiæ gradually broader to tip, not sulcate on the outer edge, although slightly excavate near the tip. Tarsi of hind legs shorter than the tibia, the first joint about one-third the length of the tibia and equal to the other three; claws simple.

These insects are all of rather small size, many of them marked with a yellowish white sinuous vitta on the elytra. The European species are said to depredate on various species of Cruciferæ; the same is known of several of our species, but Prof. Riley states that the larva of *P. vittata* "feeds upon the roots below the ground (Third Missouri Rep. p. 83)," the habit of those in Europe being to mine the leaves.

Our species, as well as those of Europe, may be arranged in two parallel series. In the first, the fourth joint of the male antennæ is often thickened, the fifth always so, and at the same time elongate. In the female the fifth joint is always longer than the fourth or sixth. In the second series the antennæ are alike in the sexes, the joints 2–10 not varying greatly in length.

In the vast majority of our species the antennæ are gradually thicker to tip, but in *pusilla*, *Lewisii* and *æneicollis*, the antennæ are slender, as in Systena.

The body is usually moderately convex, but several are quite depressed,—*albionica* and *pusilla*.

The males have the last ventral more or less impressed at tip, usually triangularly, but both the males and females of the first series may be known from those of the second by the fifth joint of the antennæ being longer than either of the adjacent joints.

For this genus Crotch adopted the name *Orchestris* Kby., but the reasons why it should not be followed have already been given by Dr. LeConte (Proc. Am. Philos. Soc. 1878, p. 615).

Phyllotreta may be divided into two series in the following manner:

Intermediate joints of male antennæ thickened and elongate, the fifth joint always, sometimes also the fourth; in the female the fifth joint is always longer than either the fourth or sixth. ....SERIES A.
Antennæ not different in the sexes, the joints gradually slightly stouter from the second to the tip, the fifth joint never longer than the sixth..SERIES B.

Series A.

Fifth joint of ♂ antennæ notably enlarged and thickened; species of rather
robust facies; elytra vittate, except in *denticornis* and *Ulkei*...............2.

Fifth joint of ♂ antennæ merely slightly longer and stouter; species of elongate, depressed form, without vitta, at most an indistinct posterior spot.

Head not distinctly punctate; surface with scarcely any bronze lustre;
punctuation of thorax not close; elytra with faint spot posteriorly.
8. decipiens.

Head closely punctate; surface with very evident bronze lustre; punctuation of thorax close; elytra always without spot.........9. **albionica**

2.—Elytra not vittate.

Sixth joint of ♂ antenna prolonged beneath in a spine-like process.
6. denticornis.

Sixth joint of ♂ antenna as long as the fourth and cylindrical.
7. Ulkei.

Elytra vittate; sixth joint ♂ simple......... ....3.

3.—Elytra with a simple vitta as in *Systena*........... ....1. **lepidula.**

Elytral vitta more or less dilated or appendiculate at either end and
sinuous........... ....4.

4.—Lower angle of fifth antennal joint ♂ distinctly prolonged; elytral vitta
very broad ....5. **robusta.**

Lower angle of fifth joint not prolonged...... ....5.

5.—Elytral vitta at middle as broad as the space between it and the suture; incurved at base.............................. ....4. **oregonensis.**

Elytral vitta narrow ....6.

6.—Vitta incurved at base, approaching the scutellum.............3. **vittata.**

Vitta parallel, with suture at its basal half.................2. **sinuata.**

Series B.

Elytra with vitta or spots, form more robust........... ....2.

Elytra unicolorous.

Head and thorax bright reddish yellow, elytra bluish green metallic.
16. picta.

Head and thorax not very unlike the elytra in color .... 3.

2.—Each elytron with two oval yellow spots, one humeral, the other subapical.
11. bipustulata.

Elytra with a sinuous vitta, appendiculate at each extremity 10. **ramosa.**

3.—Form very depressed and slender, surface with æneous lustre, elytral punctuation equal................. ....15. **pusilla.**

Form more robust and convex, surface of elytra decidedly blue...............4.

4.—Punctuation of elytra equal and uniform ....14. **Lewisii.**

Punctuation unequal, the coarser punctures forming striæ near base........5.

5.—Thorax æneous; hind tibiæ slender...................... ....13. **æneicollis.**

Thorax and elytra blue; hind tibiæ stouter than usual.
12. chalybeipennis.

1. **P. lepidula** Lec.—Oblong oval, moderately convex, piceous, shining.
surface with faint æneous lustre, each elytron with a narrow, simple, yellow

vitta, nearly straight, incurved at apex. Antennæ scarcely half as long as the body, piceous, joints 1–4 usually paler. Head rather coarsely and closely punctate. Thorax not quite twice as wide at base as long, sides arcuately narrowing to the front, disc convex, coarsely and moderately closely punctate, the surface faintly alutaceous. Elytra slightly wider at base than the thorax, surface more finely and sparsely punctate than the thorax, smoother at apex, the yellow vitta nearly exactly median, rather narrow, of equal width throughout, slightly incurved at apex. Body beneath piceous, with a faint æneous surface, abdomen sparsely, finely punctate. Legs similar in color, the tibiæ paler at base. Length .08–.10 inch.; 2–2.5 mm. Plate VI, fig. 17.

Male.--Last ventral segment notched each side of the median lobe and with an impressed median line extending the entire length of the segment. The antennæ have joints 2–3–4 nearly equal in length, the fourth very slightly broader. fifth much broader and equal to the two preceding, sixth small, nodiform, 7–10 equal in length, but gradually broader, eleventh longer.

Female.-- Last ventral simple. Antennæ with the fifth joint longer than the fourth or sixth, but not stouter, 6–10 equal in length, eleventh longer.

Among the species with vittate elytra this may be at once known by the form of the vitta, approaching more closely to *Systena* than any other species.

Occurs in California.

2. **P. sinuata** Steph.--Elongate oval, moderately robust, piceous, shining, æneous lustre very faint, each elytron with a narrow sinuous vitta, parallel with the suture at base. Antennæ nearly half as long as the body, piceous, the three or four basal joints paler. Head sparsely, finely punctulate. Thorax nearly twice as wide at base as long, sides rather strongly arcuate and distinctly narrowed in front, disc convex, surface very finely alutaceous, the punctures not coarse, more widely placed than their own diameters. Elytra scarcely wider than the thorax, humeri obliquely rounded, disc convex, the punctures coarser and closer than those of the thorax, finer near the apex, without tendency to strial arrangement; vitta narrow, parallel with the suture at basal half, not incurved at base, a short, broad, post-humeral branch, apical third strongly sinuous. Body beneath piceous, abdomen sparsely punctate. Legs piceous, tarsi brown. Length .10 inch.; 2.5 mm. Plate VI. fig. 15.

Male.--Last ventral slightly sinuous each side, a broad triangular impression at apex. Antennæ with joints 2–3–4 nearly equal in length, the fourth much broader, fifth longer than the preceding two and much dilated, sixth short, oval, narrow at base, 7–10 equal in length, eleventh longer.

Female.--Last ventral simple. Antennæ as in *vittata*.

This species, which seems widely spread in Europe, has been introduced and become widely spread in our Atlantic region, as far west as Missouri. It is rather remarkable that Crotch should have failed to recognize a common English species when he described *Zimmermanni*.

Occurs from the New England States to Georgia and westward to Missouri.

3. **P. vittata** Fab.- Elongate oval, moderately convex, piceous, shining, surface with slight æneous lustre, elytra with a yellow vitta incurved at base, thickened and slightly incurved at apex. Antennæ half as long as the body, piceous, the basal two or three joints testaceous. Head sparsely, finely punctate. Thorax about one-third wider than long, narrowed in front, sides moderately arcuate, convex, surface minutely alutaceous, punctures moderately coarse and close, denser at the sides. Elytra scarcely wider at base than the thorax, humeri obliquely rounded, convex, punctures coarser than those of the thorax, moderately closely placed, finer near the apex and with a tendency to a strial arrangement in the yellow vitta; the vitta is narrow at middle, incurved at base and with a broad, short, post-humeral branch, the apical third is abruptly broader, slightly incurved at tip. Body beneath piceous, abdomen faintly alutaceous, punctures numerous, but not coarse. Legs piceous, the tibiæ and tarsi brown. Length .08 inch.; 2 mm. Plate VI, fig. 14.

Male.—Last ventral not distinctly lobed, at middle slightly flattened and with a vague longitudinal impression extending two-thirds to base. Antennal joints 2-3-4 nearly equal in length, the fourth broader, fifth a little broader and nearly equal in length to 3 and 4, sixth elongate oval, 7-10 equal in length, eleventh longer.

Female.—Last ventral simple. Fifth joint of antennæ longer than fourth or sixth, sixth shorter than seventh, joints 7-11 as in the male.

This is one of our best known species of the Atlantic region, and is closely related to *sinuata* and *oregonensis*, differing from the former more especially by the antennal characters of the male, as well as by the incurved base of the vitta. From the second it differs in smaller size, narrower thorax and much narrower vitta and less robust form.

Specimens often occur with the intermediate portion of the vitta wanting, so that markings resemble somewhat *bipustulata*, but the two are readily known by the antennal characters. Occasionally specimens are seen with the front and middle legs entirely pale, also the hind tibiæ and tarsi. The vitta may be prolonged to the apex.

Occurs in the entire Atlantic region.

4. **P. oregonensis** Crotch.—Oblong oval, moderately robust, piceous, shining, surface scarcely æneous, elytra with a broad, sinuous vitta, somewhat incurved at base, strongly so at apex. Antennæ nearly half as long as the body, piceous, three or four basal joints paler. Head rather closely, not coarsely punctate. Thorax nearly twice as wide at base as long, narrowed in front, sides arcuate, disc convex, the punctures moderate and rather closely placed. Elytra a little wider at base than the thorax, humeri rounded, disc convex, punctuation a little coarser and closer than on the thorax, the vitta broad, as wide at middle as the distance to the suture, at base incurved, a broad, short, post humeral branch, apical third strongly arcuate and incurved. Body beneath piceous, abdomen sparsely punctate. Femora piceous, tibiæ pale, brown at middle, tarsi pale. Length .10—.12 inch.; 2.5—3 mm. Plate VI, fig. 16.

Male.—Last ventral slightly sinuate each side, a broad and deep triangular impression at apex. Antennæ as in *vittata.*

Female.—As in *vittata.*

This is the largest and most robust of our species. It is more especially related to *vittata*, but has a much broader vitta, is larger and of more robust form. The ventral characters of male also differ. Occurs in Oregon and Nevada.

5. **P. robusta** Lec.—Oblong oval, moderately convex, similar in form to *vittata*, piceous, surface shining, slightly æneous, elytra with a broad yellow vitta dilated at humerus and broadly dilated at tip, reaching the sides and apex. Antennæ as long as half the body, piceous, three basal joints pale. Head alutaceous, indistinctly punctate. Thorax nearly twice as wide as long, slightly narrowed in front, sides arcuate, disc convex, alutaceous, coarsely, deeply and closely punctate. Elytra scarcely wider at base than the thorax, humeri obliquely rounded, surface rather more coarsely punctured at base than the thorax, gradually more finely to apex, the yellow vitta broad, parallel with the suture the greater part of its length, incurved at the scutellum, a broad post-humeral process, the apical third broadly expanded, reaching the apex and side margin. Body beneath piceous abdomen sparsely punctate. Femora piceous, tibiæ and tarsi paler. Length .03 inch.; 2 mm. Plate VI, fig. 18.

Male.—Last ventral slightly sinuate each side, a very deeply impressed median line extending two-thirds the length of the segment. Antennæ with joints 2-3-4 very nearly equal in length, the fourth slightly broader, fifth as long as the two preceding, the apical free angle prolonged, sixth short, oval, 7-10 nearly equal, gradually broader, eleventh longer.

Female.—Has not been seen.

While not different in form from *vittata*, and therefore scarcely meriting its trivial name, the species is readily known by the very broad yellow vitta, which at its apical third reaches side, apex and suture.

The sexual characters of the male are very well marked, and will enable it to be at once distinguished.

Occurs at Garland, Colorado; collected by Mr. E. A. Schwarz.

6. **P. denticornis** n. sp.—Elongate oval, rather feebly convex, entirely piceous, shining, surface with slight æneous lustre. Antennæ half as long as the body, piceous, second and third joints paler. Head alutaceous, rather closely punctate. Thorax nearly twice as wide as long, slightly narrowed in front, sides feebly arcuate, disc convex, alutaceous, moderately, coarsely, closely punctate. Elytra slightly wider at base than the thorax, humeri rounded, surface shining, not alutaceous, the punctures less coarse than on the thorax, equally dense, but less impressed, smoother near the apex. Body beneath piceous, abdomen sparsely punctate. Femora piceous, tibiæ and tarsi brownish. Length .10 inch.; 2.5 mm.

Male.—Last ventral feebly sinuate each side, the middle with a deep, but short, triangular impression. Antennæ with joints 2-3-4 nearly equal in length, the

fourth broader, fifth still longer and more dilated, sixth short, conical, its lower
angle prolonged in an acute process, 7-10 equal in length, but gradually broader,
eleventh longer. Plate VI, fig. 19.

Female.—Has not been seen.

While this species has the strongly dilated antennal joints of the
vittate species, the form of body and uniform color approach it to
albionica. It is the only species known to me in which the male
sixth joint has any marked peculiarity.

Occurs in California ; region unknown.

7. P. Ulkei n. sp.—Oblong oval, moderately convex, piceous black, shining,
without metallic lustre ; legs, excepting the posterior femora, reddish brown.
Antennae half as long as the body, piceous, three basal joints pale. Head not
punctate. Thorax one-third wider than long, very little narrowed in front,
sides arcuate, disc convex, sparsely regularly punctate, surface alutaceous. Elytra
scarcely wider than the thorax, humeri obliquely rounded, a distinct depression
within the umbone, disc convex, more coarsely, closely and deeply punctate than
the thorax, a little smoother near the apex, surface shining. Body beneath piceous, abdomen sparsely punctate. Legs reddish brown, posterior femora piceous. Length .10 inch. ; 2.5 mm.

Male.—Last ventral segment distinctly sinuate each side, middle lobe moderately prominent, a deep triangularly oval impression extending more than half
the length of the segment. Antennae with joints 2-3-4 gradually shorter and
broader, fifth as long as the preceding two and more than twice as broad, sixth
equal to fourth, 7-10 longer and equal, eleventh longer. Plate VI, fig. 23.

This species is rather more robust than any other known to me,
recalling the form of some Chaetocnema.

There will be no difficulty in distinguishing the male of this species from any in Series A (1) by the broad fifth joint, (2) the absence of elytral vitta and (3) the simple form of sixth joint. It is,
therefore, most nearly allied to *denticornis.*

For the unique I am indebted to my friend Ulke, without whose
assistance my studies in the Halticini would have been far more
incomplete than they now are.

Occurs in Ohio.

8. P. decipiens n. sp.—Elongate oval, rather feebly convex, piceous black,
shining, without metallic lustre, elytra often with a short, indistinct yellow line
one-third from apex. Antennae half as long as the body, piceous, three basal
joints paler. Head alutaceous, obsoletely finely punctulate. Thorax nearly
twice as wide as long, slightly narrowed in front, sides feebly arcuate, disc convex, coarsely, deeply and closely punctate, the surface distinctly alutaceous.
Elytra wider at base than the thorax, humeri rounded, disc feebly convex, the
punctures coarser and deeper than those of the thorax, very closely placed and
but little finer near the apex, surface shining, not alutaceous. Body beneath and
legs piceous, abdomen almost entirely smooth. Length .08—.10 inch. ; 2—2.5 mm.

Male.--Last ventral with a feeble sinuation each side, a moderately deep, elongate triangular impression. Antennæ with joints 2-3-4 nearly equal in length, the fourth slightly broader, fifth longer and very little broader, sixth shorter than second, 7-10 equal in length, but gradually broader, eleventh longer.

Female.--Last ventral simple. Antennæ with joints 2-3-4 equal in length and thickness, fifth longer, sixth equal to fourth, 7-11 as in the male.

In two specimens before me there is a short yellow line midway between the suture and side, one-fourth from apex, a third has the elytra entirely black. The antennæ do not show the marked sexual differences observed in the vittate species, and in this respect is very like *albionica*. While this species and *albionica* are closely related by description, this is more convex, more coarsely punctate, without æneous lustre and less elongate. When immaculate it resembles *denticornis*, and the sexual characters must be relied upon to separate them.

Occurs in Oregon and Washington Territory.

9. **P. albionica** Lec.--Elongate oval, narrow, depressed, piceous, surface with very distinct æneous lustre. Antennæ half as long as the body, slender, piceous, three basal joints paler. Head moderately closely punctate. Thorax not quite twice as wide as long, narrowed in front, sides arcuate, disc moderately convex, the punctuation relatively coarse and densely placed. Elytra wider at base than the thorax, humeri obtuse, disc subdepressed, more coarsely punctured than the thorax, less dense and more shining. Body beneath piceous shining, abdomen with very few punctures. Legs piceous, tibiæ and tarsi brown. Length .06--.08 inch.; 1.5--2 mm.

Male.--Last ventral not sinuate each side, a short and broad triangular impression at the apical margin Antennæ with joints 2-3 equal, fourth a little longer, fifth a little longer and stouter, sixth equal to fourth, 7-10 equal, gradually broader, eleventh longer. Plate VI, fig. 22.

Female.--Last ventral simple. Antennæ with fifth joint a little longer than fourth or sixth, otherwise as in the male.

This species and *pusilla* are the smallest in our fauna, their form narrowest and most depressed. They are closely allied and separable with certainty by the sexual characters alone.

In Mr. Ulke's cabinet is a green-blue specimen from Colorado which is possibly a distinct species, but there are no strongly defined characters to separate it from *albionica*, it is therefore left to the future.

10. **P. ramosa** Crotch.--Elongate oval, moderately convex, piceous, with very faint æneous lustre, each elytron with a sinuous yellow-white vitta. Antennæ half as long as the body, piceous, joints 2-3 and underside of first pale. Head with very few punctures between the eyes. Thorax nearly twice as wide as long, narrower in front, sides arcuate, disc convex, the punctures moderately

coarse and rather closely placed. Elytra a little wider at base than the thorax, humeri rounded, disc convex, punctures coarser than those of the thorax, but not so closely placed, each elytron with a slender sinuous vitta, incurved at base, a post-humeral branch, near the tip the vitta joins a narrow crescentic spot, one end of which points anteriorly the other incurved toward the suture. Body beneath piceous, abdomen nearly smooth. Legs entirely piceous. Length .08 inch.; 2 mm. Plate VII, fig. 12.

Male.—Last ventral very feebly sinuate on each side, a vague triangular impression at apex. Antennæ as in *bipustulata.*

Female.—As in *bipustulata.*

This species resembles *vittata*, but may be known by the form of the apical portion of the vitta. The form of the fifth joint of the antennæ will distinguish either sex from that species.

Occurs at Lakeport, California (Crotch).

11. **P. bipustulata** Fab.—Oblong oval, moderately robust, piceous, without metallic lustre, each elytron with two large, irregularly oval, yellow spots, one humeral, the other subapical. Antennæ half as long as the body, distinctly thicker externally, piceous, the basal five joints paler. Head sparsely, finely punctate, not alutaceous. Thorax one third wider than long, narrowed in front, sides feebly arcuate, disc convex, the punctures moderate, not closely placed, surface very indistinctly alutaceous. Elytra distinctly wider at base than the thorax, humeri obtusely rounded, the punctures coarser than those of the thorax, but gradually finer toward the apex, and with a faint tendency to a strial arrangement at middle, humeral spot oval, touching the base, not including the umbone, subapical spot elongate oval, but narrower. Body beneath piceous, abdomen sparsely punctate Legs rufotestaceous, the posterior femora darker beneath. Length .08—.10 inch.; 2—2.5 mm. Plate VI, fig. 13.

Male.—Last ventral distinctly sinuate each side, middle lobe moderately prominent and with a rather deep, triangularly oval concavity. Antennæ as in *Lewisii,* but stouter.

Female.—Last ventral simple, antennæ as in the male.

This species could only be confused with some of the forms of *vittata* in which the vitta is broken at middle, but in either sex the form of the fifth antennal joint would easily distinguish it together with the pale legs. I have a specimen, given me by Mr. Ulke, without elytral spots.

Occurs from Pennsylvania to South Carolina.

12.—**P. chalybeipennis** Crotch.—Elongate oval, moderately robust, beneath piceous, above bright blue Antennæ longer than half the body, the outer joints dark brown, basal five joints rufotestaceous. Head sparsely, but very distinctly punctate. Thorax one-half wider than long, narrowed in front, sides rather strongly arcuate, disc convex, alutaceous, moderately closely, but not coarsely punctate. Elytra scarcely wider than the thorax, humeri obliquely rounded, punctuation similar to that of the thorax and equally close, with larger punctures forming quite distinct striæ near the base, five being very evident, surface not alutaceous. Body beneath piceous, abdomen sparsely punctate. Anterior and middle femora brown, the posterior piceous with bluish green surface, tibiæ and tarsi testaceous, the posterior tibiæ more dilated than usual at tip. Length .10--.12 inch.; 2.5--3 mm.

Male.--Last ventral sinuate each side, the middle lobe moderately prominent and concave, a median impressed line near the base of the segment. Antennæ as in *Lewisii.*

Female.--Last ventral with a slight longitudinal impression at apex. Antennæ as in the male.

This is the largest and most robust of all the species with simple antennæ and unicolored elytra. It is readily known by its uniform blue color and the stouter hind tibiæ.

Occurs occasionally in considerable abundance on the sea-coast of New Jersey; Massachusetts to Florida.

13. **P. æneicollis** Crotch.--Elongate oval, form rather slender, moderately convex, piceous, head and thorax with a cupreous lustre, elytra greenish or bluish. Antennæ slender, half as long as the body, piceous, joints 2-5 and underside of first rufotestaceous. Head sparsely, indistinctly punctulate. Thorax one-third wider than long, narrowed in front, sides irregularly arcuate, disc convex, the punctuation moderate in size, closely placed, the surface alutaceous. Elytra wider at base than the thorax, humeri obtuse, disc moderately convex, the punctures rather coarser than those of the thorax, but less closely placed, becoming finer near the apex, near the base there are conspicuously coarser punctures tending to form striæ, that just within the umbone quite evident. Body beneath piceous, abdomen sparsely punctate. Legs piceous, the tibiæ and tarsi brownish testaceous. Length .08--.10 inch.; 2--2.5 mm.

Male.--Last ventral slightly sinuate each side, a narrow, feeble, triangular impression at middle. Antennæ simple, as in *Levisii.*

Female.--Last ventral simple. Antennæ as in the male.

This species is especially related by the characters of the table to *chalybeipennis.* It is less robust, more elongate, differently colored, and with quite slender posterior tibiæ. The larger punctures do not form such distinct rows as in that species.

Occurs in Kansas and Texas.

14. **P. Lewisii** Crotch.--Elongate oval, moderately convex, piceous, surface with dark bluish lustre. Antennæ slender, half as long as the body, piceous, joints 2-5 pale. Head sparsely, indistinctly punctate. Thorax more than half wider than long, slightly narrowed in front, sides arcuate, disc convex, punctures moderate in size, not closely placed, surface not alutaceous. Elytra scarcely wider at base than the thorax, humeri broadly rounded, disc convex, the punctures coarser than those of the thorax, and therefore apparently more closely placed, finer toward the apex. Body beneath piceous, shining. Abdomen very sparsely punctate. Legs piceous, tibiæ and tarsi brown. Length .08--.10 inch.; 2--2.5 mm.

Male.—Last ventral distinctly sinuate each side, the middle lobe moderately prominent, slightly concave and with a broadly triangular impression. Antennæ with joints 2-10 scarcely different in length, eleventh a little longer.

Female.—Last ventral with a very faint impression near the apex. Antennæ as in the male.

Among the species with simple antennæ and non-vittate elytra two have the elytral punctuation composed of equal punctures, the present species and *pusilla*. The latter is smaller, more depressed, the surface distinctly brassy, the thorax small and the punctuation closer.

Specimens occur with scarcely any bluish surface lustre, and those from Nevada have the first five joints of the antennæ more conspicuously pale.

Occurs in Colorado, Illinois (Crotch), Texas, Nevada and adjacent regions of California.

15. **P. pusilla** n. sp.—Form narrow, elongate, depressed, piceous, surface with distinct æneous lustre. Antennæ slender, half as long as the body, piceous, joints 2-3 paler. Head scarcely visibly punctate. Thorax less than twice as wide as long, widest at middle, sides arcuate, apex slightly narrower than base, disc convex, surface shining, the punctures moderate, closely placed, but not convex. Elytra wider than the thorax, humeri obtuse, punctuation coarser than that of the thorax, closely placed, very little finer near the apex, but less dense, surface shining. Body beneath and legs piceous, abdomen sparsely punctate. Length .06—.08 inch.; 1.5—2 mm.

Male.—Last ventral with a feeble triangular impression in the apex.
Female.—Last ventral simple.

The antennæ are alike in the sexes. The joints 3-10 vary but little in length, although very slightly broader externally.

This species could only be confounded with *albionica*, which it resembles in form, size and color. It is, however, more shining, the head nearly smooth, thorax and elytra less densely punctured, the latter never scabrous.

Occurs from Dakota to Texas, Arizona, southern California and Nevada.

16. **P. picta** Say.—Oval, slightly oblong, feebly convex; head, thorax and legs pale reddish yellow; abdomen piceous, elytra bright bluish green, surface shining. Antennæ a little longer than half the body, slightly thicker externally, basal joints pale, outer joints fuscous. Head smooth, frontal carina and tubercles distinct, a vague longitudinal impression of the vertex. Thorax nearly twice as wide as long, distinctly narrowed in front, sides arcuate, slightly obliquely truncate at the front angles, disc moderately convex, the punctuation very fine, sparse and indistinct. Elytra a little wider at base than the thorax, humeri rounded, umbone smooth, not brownish, surface moderately closely,

iudistiuctly punctate ou the disc, smoother at sides and apex, the punctures fine, but intermixed. Abdomen piceous, indistinctly punctate. Legs yellowish, the posterior femora often fuscous. Length .08 inch.; 2 mm.

This species is so unlike the others in our fauna that I place it in Phyllotreta with regret, but after repeated examination I see no other course to pursue. It is true that viewed in certain light there appears to be a vague ante-basal depression, but this is purely deceptive. As the choice of position seems to be either here or in Haltica, it is preferably placed here. It was placed by Crotch in Aphthona, but the form of hind tibia is not as seen in that genus. Occurs in North Carolina, Florida, Georgia and Texas.

APHTHONA Chev.

Head inserted as far as the eyes, front carinate between the antennæ and with tubercles above it, clypeus broadly emarginate, labrum arcuate in front. Maxillary palpi moderate in length, the penultimate joint oval, truncate, the terminal joint more slender, longer and acute at tip. Antennæ slender, longer than half the body, first joint stout, claviform, second elongate oval, third more slender and a little longer, joints three to seven gradually longer, eight to ten slightly shorter, eleventh longer than tenth, acute at tip. Thorax slightly broader than long, apex truncate, base arcuate, scutellum transversely oval. Elytra wider at base than the thorax. Prosternum moderately separating the coxæ, slightly broader behind them, the cavities widely open behind. Ventral segments free. Legs moderately long, tibiæ with outer edge rounded, the posterior tibiæ depressed near apex, the lower edge at tip emarginate or bilobed, the outer lobe terminated by a spur. Tarsi moderate, the first joint a little shorter than the others together, the claws not appendiculate at base.

The essential character of this genus is in the structure of the apex of the hind tibiæ. The tip is said to be bilobed, i. e., there is a notch of the edge immediately in front of the tarsal insertion which probably enables the tarsus to move more freely to the front, while in Longitarsus the motion is confined entirely to a folding backward against the posterior edge of the tibia.

The species composing Aphthona, judging from the European monographs, seem to be much less homogeneous in aspect than the other genera of the tribe. With this fact known there seems to be reason why the species known in our fauna should not be associated.

The following species are known to me :

Form oblong oval, rather depressed, elytra blue; beneath piceous; head, thorax
    and legs pale yellowish red ....**texana.**
Form short, robust, entirely rufotestaceous, shining.
  Thorax more than half wider than long, sides arcuate; antennæ slender.
                                                                  socia.
  Thorax very little wider than long, sides nearly straight; antennæ stout.
                                                                insolita.

A. texana Crotch.—Oblong oval, not very convex ; head, thorax and legs
bright reddish yellow, abdomen and elytra piceous, the latter with bluish or
purplish lustre. Antennæ rufotestaceous, slightly darker at apex. Head faintly
alutaceous, impunctate, frontal carina well marked, the tubercles flat. Thorax
one-half wider than long, scarcely narrowed in front, sides feebly arcuate, disc
moderately convex, the punctuation rather fine, not closely placed, a little coarser
along the base. Elytra wider at base than the thorax, humeri rounded, umbone
moderately prominent, smooth, disc irregularly punctate, becoming much
smoother at apex, and with much coarser punctures forming irregular striæ near
the base. Abdomen piceous shining, very sparsely punctate and pubescent.
Length .08—.10 inch. ; 2—2.5 mm.

The males have the first joint of the anterior tarsi slightly dilated,
the last ventral segment obtuse at apex and the antennæ a little
stouter. Chapuis states that the sutural angle is also more obtuse,
but this is scarcely evident in our species. By its form and elytral
sculpture this species represents the *ovata* Foud. of southern France.

Occurs in Texas, Colorado and Nebraska.

A. socia n. sp.—Oval, slightly oblong, convex, rufotestaceous, shining. Antennæ slender, longer than half the body, rufotestaceous, the second joint a
little longer than the fourth, third a little shorter. Head extremely finely alutaceous, impunctate. Thorax one-half wider than long, not narrowed in front,
sides rather broadly arcuate, anterior angles obliquely truncate, with distinct
post-apical angulation, hind angles distinct when seen from above, base arcuate,
disc convex, the punctuation fine and indistinct, almost obliterated in front and
at sides. Elytra distinctly wider at base than the thorax, humeri obtusely
rounded, umbone distinct, sutural angles well marked, disc convex, a slight depression divided by the suture very near the apex, punctuation extremely fine,
confused with vague indications of strial arrangement near the suture at base,
a very distinct stria of punctures at the sides a little distance from the margin.
Body beneath and legs colored as above. Length .08 inch. ; 2 mm.

The unique specimen before me is a female, and has the terminal
half of the last ventral segment paler, so that it appears at first
sight to be two segments.

The very shining surface of this species will render it easily known
among all the species of the group, in connexion with the antennæ.

Occurs at Columbus, Texas.

I have before me a specimen which I am quite convinced is the male of the above. It differs in having the elytra very distinctly alutaceous so as to be subopaque with a greasy aspect, the punctuation less distinct. The apices of joints 8–9–10 of the antennæ are prolonged on their lower edge so as to be acutely serrate. In other respects the two specimens agree, the former being the female, the latter a male. Occurs with the preceding. Pl. VII, fig. 19.

A. insolita Mels.—Oval, slightly oblong, convex, rufotestaceous, shining. Antennæ longer than half the body, stout, the first and last two joints testaceous, the others brown. Head smooth, impunctate. Thorax one-fourth wider than long, not narrowed in front, sides nearly straight, anterior angles obliquely truncate, with distinct post-apical angulation, base feebly arcuate, disc convex, smooth and polished. Elytra distinctly wider at base than the thorax, humeri obtusely prominent, umbone distinct, sutural angles distinct, but obtuse, disc convex, the punctuation excessively fine and visible only at base near suture, where one vague stria is seen, otherwise polished. Body beneath and legs similar in color to upper surface, tarsi brown. Length .07–.08 inch. ; 2 mm.

The antennæ are stouter than usual in the group Aphthonæ; the first joint is oval, suddenly narrowed at base, second oval, narrower and about half as long, third more slender not longer, joints 4–10 gradually very little longer and broader; eleventh longer, acuminate at tip.

The occurrence of paler joints at the tip of the antennæ seems to be a rare character in the Halticini, but the extreme tip of the eleventh joint is black, although the remainder as well as the tenth is quite pale.

This insect was originally described by Melsheimer as a doubtful Sphæroderma, and later Crotch made a new genus—*Cerataltica*, and placed by him in such a position as to lead to the inference that the anterior coxal cavities are closed. The facts are, however, quite the reverse, and the only character of moment not possessed by the other Aphthonæ is found in the moderately stout antennæ.

In general appearance and color the insect resembles *Longitarsus rubidus*, but the very polished surface is like the preceding species.

Occurs in Pennsylvania (Melsheimer) and Capron, Florida (Schwarz).

The following species has not been identified:

A. subglobosa Motsch.—Nigro-picea, subtiliter punctatissima; elytris subglobosis, antennarum basi, tibiis tarsisque rufo-piceis. Length two-thirds, width three-fifths of a line.

It resembles a little *A. euphorbiæ* Fab., but it is much broader and of a browner black color.

The thorax, the sides of which are rounded, shows some sparse punctures feebly impressed. The elytra are twice as wide as the thorax, slightly globose and feebly prolonged at the extremity, they are rather strongly punctured. The base of the antennæ, the tibiæ and tarsi are of a reddish black color.

From California.

The figure given, although very poor, looks very like a Chætocnema. It is very likely that this is one of the things obtained from Dupont, and that it was collected near the Rio Grande.

Group XVI.—DIBOLIÆ.

Antennæ 11-jointed. Anterior coxal cavities open behind. Head retracted. Thorax without any ante-basal impressions. Posterior tibiæ with a long, rather broad terminal spur, which is more or less deeply emarginate at apex Pl. VII, fig. 17.

These few characters amply define the group. In fact the form of the posterior tibial spur of itself from a sufficient limitation.

Two genera constitute this group,—Dibolia and Megistops, the latter distinguished by having the eyes contiguous on the vertex. Several species were described by Boheman and credited to California, but there can be no doubt that they should be referred to South America.

DIBOLIA Latr.

Head rounded, retracted within the apex of the thorax. Eyes slightly reniform. Front carinate, the frontal tubercles distinct. Maxillary palpi rather slender, the terminal joint of slender conical form nearly as wide at base as the third joint. Antennæ at least half as long as the body, slightly stouter externally. Thorax broader than long and much narrowed in front. Elytra oval, not wider at base than the thorax, with regular striæ of punctures. Prosternum narrowly separating the coxæ, the anterior coxal cavities open behind. Legs moderate in length. Posterior thighs strongly dilated, the tibiæ slender at base, broader at the extremity, terminated by a rather long and broad spur, which is deeply emarginate at tip; the tibia grooved on its outer edge and denticulate near the tip. Tarsi slender, first joint one-third the length of the tibia, the claws appendiculate.

The males are said by Chapuis to differ from the females in having the first joint of the anterior tarsi dilated and the pygidium transversely striate.

Four species occur in our fauna:

Apices of elytra very deeply sinuous at apex..................................**sinuata.**
Apices of elytra conjointly rounded.
  Antennæ rufotestaceous; legs (except the posterior femora) rufotestaceous or brownish; thorax very distinctly punctate.
    Form more oblong; interstrial spaces with very few punctures. **borealis.**
    Form more ovate; interstrial spaces with numerous fine punctures..**ovata.**
  Antennæ and legs piceous; thorax very indistinctly punctate.
    Thorax greenish black, elytra blue green....................................**libonoti.**

D. sinuata n. sp.—Broadly oval and convex, very like a *Phædon*, beneath piceous, thorax above black bronze, elytra bluish green. Antennæ entirely rufotestaceous. Head rufescent, not distinctly punctate. Thorax more than twice as wide at base as long, narrowed in front, sides moderately arcuate, disc moderately convex, the surface slightly rugulose, the punctuation moderate in size, sparse and indistinct. Elytra not wider at base than the thorax, broadly oval, the apices deeply sinuous, the sutural angle obtuse, disc convex, disc striato-punctate, striæ not impressed, punctures moderately coarse and deep, but not closely placed, intervals flat, moderately closely, finely punctate, with a row of distant coarser punctures, finer than those of the striæ. Body beneath piceous. Abdomen moderately closely punctate and slightly wrinkled transversely. Legs brownish, tibiæ and tarsi a little paler. Length .12 inch.; 3 mm.

This species is even more broadly oval than *ovata*, resembling at first sight *Phædon viride*. It is especially distinguished by the rather deep sinuation of the apices of the elytra. This character seemed at first sight as if an accidental deformity, but the exact symmetry of the two sides, together with the other characters, have satisfied me that the species is well founded.

One specimen, Dallas, Texas.

D. borealis Chev.—Oval, slightly oblong, convex, piceous, surface distinctly bronzed, either æneous, slightly cupreous, or bluish. Antennæ pale rufotestaceous. Head shining, sparsely, indistinctly punctate. Thorax rather more than twice as wide at base as long, apex but little wider than the length, sides arcuate, disc convex, closely punctate, with coarse and fine punctures intermixed. Elytra not wider at base than the thorax, the sides of both continuous, umbone moderately prominent, disc convex, with striæ of coarse punctures, which are rather closely placed, some of the striæ rather irregular, intervals broad and flat, with but few fine punctures, the alternate intervals 2-4-6 with coarser punctures, striæ not obliterated at apex. Body beneath and posterior femora piceous, slightly bronzed. Abdomen shining, sparsely punctate. Anterior four legs and posterior tibiæ rufotestaceous. Length .12 inch.; 3 mm.

This insect is so well known as not to require special comment. The elytral sculpture is somewhat variable, the striæ being quite regular in some, although the greater number have the third and sixth striæ more or less confused.

Widely distributed over the entire eastern United States and Canada. A specimen in my cabinet from Nevada.

This species is said to occur in Mexico by Mr. Jacoby, but from the remarks it is probable that both this species and *ovata* are included under the one name. At all events the figure represents the latter more nearly as far as the form and striæ are concerned.

D. ovata Lec.—Oval, moderately convex, piceous, with æneous or cupreous surface lustre. Antennæ pale rufotestaceous. Head moderately punctate. Thorax similar in form to *borealis*, equally densely punctate with intermixed punctures. Elytra more oval than in *borealis*, the punctures of the striæ finer, the intervals flat, with numerous fine punctures. Body beneath and legs as in *borealis*. Length .12 inch.; 3 mm.

This species is closely related to *borealis*, and was considered by Crotch merely a variety, but the more oval form, the fine striæ of the punctures (which are sometimes obliterated posteriorly) and the finely punctate intervals seem to make it a distinct species.

Occurs in California and Nevada.

D. libonoti n. sp.—Oval, slightly oblong, convex, piceous, head and thorax blackish bronze, elytra blue green. Antennæ piceous. Head sparsely, indistinctly punctate. Thorax more than twice as wide at base as long, narrowed in front, sides feebly arcuate, disc convex, the punctuation indistinct, but intermixed. Elytra not wider at base than the thorax and continuing the curve of the sides, umbone small, disc convex, the striæ composed of fine, not closely placed punctures, the intervals flat, finely, but indistinctly punctulate. Body beneath piceous. Abdomen sparsely punctate. Legs piceous, the posterior femora slightly bluish. Length .10 inch.; 2.5 mm.

A smaller and less convex species than the other two and with faintly punctured thorax, which is differently colored from the elytra. The legs are entirely piceous.

Occurs in Arizona (Morrison).

Group XVII.—PSYLLIODES.

Form oblong. Antennæ 10-jointed, widely distant at base, inserted against the inner border of the eyes. Anterior coxal cavities closed behind. Ventral segments free. Posterior tarsi inserted above the end of the tibia and slightly to the outer side, the first joint very long, the last slender, not inflated, the claws rather long, slender and simple.

But one genus constitutes this group, having characters sufficiently obvious to make it easily recognized without discussion. On one point sufficient stress does not seem to be laid, and that is in reference to the insertion of the antennæ. Chapuis has indicated one group in which the insertion of the antennæ against the inner border of the eyes is made the important character. Here a similar character has been passed over in silence. The antennæ of Psylliodes are inserted as close to the eye as is possible without causing an emargination.

The fauna of Europe is more than ten times richer in species than our own, the disparity being greater than in either Chætocnema or Longitarsus.

PSYLLIODES Latr.

Head oval, deeply inserted, the front inclined, or nearly vertical, without carina, but forming a broad flat plate, tubercles not distinct, usually with an arcuate impressed line, which marks the lower edge of the tubercles (entirely absent in sublævis), clypeus truncate, labrum moderately prominent, entire. Antennæ 10-jointed, separated at base, inserted at the inner border of the eye, filiform, slightly thicker externally, first joint slender clavate, joints 2–3–4 nearly equal, 5–9 gradually slightly shorter, tenth longer, acute at tip. Maxillary palpi slender, second joint slender clavate, third obconical, acute at tip. Thorax transverse, narrowed in front, base broadly arcuate, with distinct marginal line, obliterated at middle. Elytra oblong oval, usually widest slightly in front of middle. Prosternum moderately separating the coxæ and not depressed between them, dilated at apex and with the epimera closing the cavities. Mesosternum moderately long, slightly oblique Legs moderate in length, posterior femora much thickened, deeply sulcate beneath for the tibiæ. Anterior and middle tibiæ slender, the outer edge rounded, posterior tibiæ broader toward apex, the posterior edge sinuate near apex and with a border of short ciliæ, the tip prolonged beyond the insertion of the tarsi and terminated by a short spur (Pl. VII, fig. 13). Posterior tarsi long and slender, the first joint more than half the length of the tibiæ, the third joint narrowly bilobed, the fourth slender and with moderately long simple claws.

This genus is probably one of the most easily recognized of the tribe by the structure of the antennæ and posterior tibiæ. The apex of the posterior tibia is not simply prolonged beyond the insertion of the tarsi, but is excavated slightly externally. These tarsi resemble those of Longitarsus, although the first joint is really longer in proportion to the tibia.

In the "Genera" Chapuis states that the anterior coxal cavities are open, but the error has already been noticed, and, in 1873, Crotch had placed the genus in the series with closed cavities.

The European species do not seem to exhibit any well defined sexual characters, but these are quite well marked in all our species, although less distinct in *sublævis*.

The following species are known to inhabit our fauna:

Last ventral segment of male distinctly impressed; first joint of anterior tarsi broadly dilated ....**punctulata.**
Last ventral of male convex, not impressed.
  Elytra with very distinct interstrial punctures, those of the striæ well impressed; abdomen numerously punctate; first joint of anterior tarsi male rather broadly dilated.
    Above uniform in color, dark bronze, form distinctly oblong...**convexior.**
    Above bicolored, thorax black bronze, elytra blue-green; form more evidently ovate............... ....**elegans.**
  Elytra without distinct interstrial punctures, those of the striæ fine and feebly impressed; first joint of anterior tarsi male not dilated in oval form.
                                       sublævis.

The first two species have very wide distribution, the other two are more restricted.

P. punctulata Mels.—Form elongate oval, little narrower in front, moderately convex piceous, surface dark bronzed shining. Antennæ a little longer than half the body, three basal joints pale, the outer joints brownish. Head sparsely indistinctly punctate, the surface usually slightly alutaceous. Thorax a little more than half wider at base than long, distinctly narrowed in front, sides feebly arcuate, distinctly obliquely truncate at front angles with feeble post-apical angulation, disc moderately convex, the punctures rather coarse, but not dense, the intervals usually distinctly alutaceous. Elytra not wider at base than the thorax, humeri obliquely rounded, sides moderately arcuate, widest in front of middle, disc moderately convex, punctato-striate, striæ feebly impressed, punctures coarse, rather close, but not serrate, intervals slightly convex, scarcely wider than the striæ, each with a single series of fine punctures. Body beneath piceous, shining. Abdomen distinctly punctate and alutaceous, the punctures coarser, more deeply impressed and sparser along the middle, denser at the sides, sparsely pubescent. Anterior and middle femora piceous, the posterior distinctly bronzed, the tibiæ rufotestaceous, darker at middle. Length .08--.10 inch.; 2--2.5 mm.

The male has the first joint of the anterior tarsi broadly dilated. The last ventral segment is sinuate each side, the middle of disc near apex with a semi-oval depression.

This species is the commonest form taken everywhere in the eastern region. It is the most elongate of the species. The thorax is usually comparatively coarsely and closely punctate with the intervals distinctly alutaceous, but the specimens from the warmer regions are scarcely alutaceous. Specimens rarely occur with the thorax rather finely and sparsely punctate. The punctures of the elytral striæ are always closely placed, almost crenate, and by this means (in the absence of the ♂) the species may be separated from *convexior*.

Widely distributed : Massachusetts and Canada, westward to Washington, Vancouver and California, Nevada, Utah, Kansas, Colorado and Texas.

P. convexior Lec.--Oblong oval, moderately convex, piceous, shining, surface distinctly bronzed. Antennæ piceous, three basal joints testaceous. Head shining, sparsely punctate. Thorax nearly twice as wide at base as long, distinctly narrowed in front, sides nearly straight, feebly obliquely truncate near the front angles, a slight post-apical angulation, disc moderately convex, sparsely finely punctate at middle, a little more coarsely at the sides, surface shining. Elytra not wider at base than the thorax, humeri obliquely rounded, umbone moderate, disc convex, striato-punctate, striæ not impressed, punctures rather coarse and well separated, becoming gradually finer toward the apex, in tervals flat, the inner three with numerous interstrial punctures, the outer with but a single row. Body beneath piceous. Abdomen indistinctly alutaceous, sparsely pubescent, the punctures moderate, numerous, but sparser at middle. Legs as in *punctulata*. Length .08--.10 inch. ; 2--2.5 mm.

The first joint of anterior tarsus is broadly dilated in the male ; the last ventral segment is convex, without impression, the apex rather obtuse.

This species is of rather broader and more convex form than *punctulata;* has the thorax always sparsely and finely punctured, the elytral striæ not impressed, and the punctures always well separated.

Occurs especially in the south of California, thence north to Washington and eastward to Texas, Georgia, Florida, Illinois and Missouri and District of Columbia. On the whole more southern in its distribution than *punctulata*.

P. elegans n. sp.—Oval, slightly oblong, moderately convex, head and thorax black bronze, elytra bluish green, shining. Antennæ rufotestaceous, scarcely darker externally. Head punctate, slightly alutaceous. Thorax nearly twice as wide at base as long, narrowed in front, sides nearly straight, obliquely truncate near the front angles, with slight post-apical angulation, disc moderately convex, shining, punctures moderate, not closely, but very regularly placed. Elytra not wider at base than the thorax, humeri oblique, umbone moderate, disc striato-punctate, striæ not impressed, the punctures moderately coarse, round and well separated, intervals flat, with numerous fine punctures, equivalent on all to more than a single row. Body beneath piceous, faintly bronzed. Abdomen slightly alutaceous, distinctly punctate, sparsely pubescent Anterior and middle legs rufotestaceous, the femora a little darker, posterior femora brown or piceous, the tibiæ and tarsi pale. Length .10 inch.; 2.5 mm.

The male characters are as in *convexior*.

The form of this species is still a little broader than *convexior*, and may at once be known by its colors. The elytral intervals are more numerously punctulate than any other of our species.

Occurs in Florida and Kansas (Ulke).

P. sublævis n. sp.—Oblong oval, moderately convex, piceous, shining, surface distinctly bronzed. Antennæ slender, rufotestaceous, the seven outer joints piceous at their apices. Head sparsely obsoletely punctate. Thorax one-half wider than long, narrowed in front, sides slightly arcuate, obliquely truncate at front angles with distinct post-apical angulation, disc moderately convex, the punctures small, sparsely placed, feebly impressed. Elytra slightly wider at base than the thorax, humeri obtusely rounded, umbone moderate, disc moderately convex, striato-punctate, the striæ not impressed, the punctures fine, not close, entirely obliterated at apex, intervals flat, the interstrial punctures almost entirely obliterated. Body beneath piceous, faintly bronzed, shining, with very few hairs, punctures indistinct, but when present forming a row of distant punctures along the anterior and posterior borders of the segments. Anterior and middle legs and posterior tibiæ rufotestaceous, the femora a little darker, posterior femora piceous. Length .14 inch.; 3.5 mm.

In the male the first joint of the anterior tarsus, although slightly broader than in the female, is not oval as in the other species. The last ventral is convex, the apical border slightly sinuate each side, the surface smooth.

This species is the largest in our fauna. It may be known by the comparatively smooth surface both above and below, and by the elytra distinctly broader at base than the thorax, as well as the feeble sculpture.

Occurs in southwestern Utah ; collected by Dr. Edward Palmer.

The following Halticide has not been identified :

Altica liturata Oliv. Ent. vi. p. 707, pl. iv, fig. 7.—Oval, pale yellow ; elytra with many short brown lines.

It resembles *A. atricilla* [Longitarsus] in form and size. Antennæ fuscous, with the base pale. Head testaceous, eyes large, black. Thorax smooth, pale yellow, without spots. Elytra smooth, pale yellow, the suture and four abbreviated lines fuscous. Body beneath pale.

Found in Carolina. Palisot de Beauvois.

The figure represents a rather broadly oval species, entirely pale yellow; the suture of the elytra narrowly bordered with fuscous, on each elytron two moderately long fuscous lines parallel with the suture, external to these two shorter ones; there is a short line also at the humerus. The size as nearly as can be ascertained is .12 inch. or 3 mm. Plate VI, fig. 24.

The "Catalogus" places the species in Longitarsus, probably from the comparison made by Olivier, but this is certainly not correct. I have suspected that it might possibly be either *Œdionychis texana* or *subvittata*.

Bibliography and Synonymy.

BLEPHARIDA Rogers.

B. rhois Forst., Nov. Spec. Ins. 1771, p. 21; Hübner, Naturf. xxi, p. 40, pl. 2, fig. 3; Rogers, Proc. Acad. 1856, p. 29; Riley (larva), Sixth Missouri Rep. 1874, p. 118.
  stolida Fab., Syst. Ent. p. 95; Oliv. Ent. v, p. 526, pl. 2, fig. 24 a–b; Suff. Stett. Zeit. 1858, p. 241.
  virginica Fröhl., Naturf. xxvi, 1792, p. 129.
  meticulosa Oliv., Ent. v, p. 531, pl. 6, fig. 91.

PACHYONYCHUS Chev.

P. paradoxus Mels., Proc. Acad. iii, p. 163; Crotch, Proc. Acad. 1873, p. 58 (not *Pachyonychis paradoxa* Clark).

PHÆDROMUS Clark.

P. Waterhousei Clark, Catal. B. M. Halticidæ, p. 66, pl. iii, fig. 1

HYPOLAMPSIS Clark.

H. pilosa Illiger, Mag. vi, p. 105; Clark, Cat. Halt. 1860, p. 229.
  rugosa Oliv., Ent. vi, p. 707, pl. 4, fig. 71.
  hispida Zieg., Proc. Acad. 1846, p. 47.
  Clarki Crotch, Proc. Acad. 1873, p. 57.
H. Mellyi Crotch, Proc. Acad. 1873, p. 58.

PSEUDOLAMPSIS n. g.

P. guttata Lec., Trans. Am. Ent. Soc. xii, 1884, p. 29.

HAMLETIA Crotch.

H. dimidiaticornis Cr., Proc. Acad. 1853, p. 58.
  paradoxa Clark (*Pachyonychis*), Halt. B. M. p. 67, pl 2, fig. 7.

ŒDIONYCHIS Latr.

1. Œ. gibbitarsa Say, Journ. Acad. 1824, p. 83; edit. Lec. ii, p. 225.
2. Œ. flavocyanea Crotch, Proc. Acad. 1873, p. 62.
3. Œ. thoracica Fab., Syst. Ent. App. 821; Oliv., Ent. vi, p. 678, pl. 1, fig. 16.
   flava Gmel. Edit. Linn. i, 4, p. 1691.
4. Œ. vians Illig., Mag. vi, p. 83.
   abdominalis Oliv., Ent. vi, p. 679, pl. 1, fig. 17.
   scripticollis Say, Journ. Acad. 1824, p. 84; edit. Lec. ii, p. 226; Lec., Proc. Acad. 1860, p. 321.
   thoracica var. Clark, Journ. Ent. ii, p. 166.

5. Œ. concinna Fab., Syst. El. i, p. 499; Oliv., Ent. vi, p. 679, pl. 1, fig. 18.
6. Œ. violascens Lec., Proc. Acad. 1859, p. 81.
7. Œ. lugens Lec., Col. Kans. 1859, p. 24.
8. Œ. interjectionis Crotch, Proc. Acad. 1873, p. 61 ; Harold, Berl. Zeit. 1881, p. 129.
     gracilis Jacoby, Biol. Cent. Am. vi, 1, p. 420, pl. xxiv, fig. 14.
9. Œ. fimbriata Forst., Nov. Spec. Ins. i, 1771, p. 25.
     saturella Say, Journ. Acad. v, p. 300; edit. Lec. ii, p. 344.
     circumcincta Crotch, P. Acad. 1873, p. 62; Harold, Berl. Zeits. 1881, p. 151.
10. Œ. æmula n. sp.
11. Œ. petaurista Fab., Syst. El. i, p. 495; Oliv., Ent. vi, p. 674, pl. 2, fig. 7; Harold, Berl. Zeit. 1881, p. 150.
     var. *brevilineata* Horn, supra.
12. Œ. tenuilineata n. sp.
13. Œ. miniata Fab., Syst. El. i, p. 495; Oliv., Ent. vi, p. 685, pl. 2, fig. 29
     fallax Mels., Proc. Acad. iii, p. 162.
     jocosa Harold, Col. Heft. xv, p. 124 ; Berl. Zeit. 1881, p. 141.
14. Œ. Horni Harold, Berl Zeit. 1881, p. 142.
15. Œ. Ulkei n. sp.
16. Œ. longula Harold, Deutsche Zeit. 1877, p. 434 ; Berl. Zeit. 1881, p. 141.
17. Œ. Jacobiana n. sp.
18. Œ. flavida n. sp.
19. Œ. indigoptera Lec.
20. Œ. texana Crotch, Proc. Acad. 1873, p. 63.
21. Œ. thyamoides Crotch, Proc. Acad. 1873, p. 63.
22. Œ. limbalis Mels., Proc. Acad. iii, p. 162.
23. Œ. sexmaculata Illiger, Mag. vi. p. 104.
     palliata Rand., Bost. Journ. ii, p. 47.
24. Œ. suturalis Fab., Syst. El. i, p. 499; Oliv., Ent. vi, p. 692, pl. 3, fig. 42.
25. Œ. quercata Fab., Syst. El i, p. 495; Oliv., Ent. vi, p. 687, pl. 2, fig. 32.
     obsidiana Fab., loc. cit. p. 499; Oliv., loc. cit. p. 691, pl. 2, fig. 40.
     circumdata Rand., Bost. Journ. ii, p. 48.
26 Œ. scalaris Mels., Proc. Acad. iii, p. 163.
     lobata Lec., Col. Kans 1859, p. 24.

HOMOPHŒTA Chevr.

Asphæra Chev.

H. æquinoctialis Linn., Syst. Nat. ed. x, p. 374.
     quadrinotata Fab., Oliv. Ent. vi, p. 682, p. 2, fig. 23.
     octomaculata Crotch, Proc. Acad. 1873, p. 60.
H. lustrans Crotch, Proc. Acad. 1873, p. 60.
H. abdominalis Chev., Col. Mex. Cent. 1, No. 65.
     opacior Crotch, Proc. Acad. 1873, p. 60.

PHYDANIS n. g.

P. bicolor n. sp.

DISONYCHA Chev.

D. pensylvanica Illig., Mag. vi, p. 146.
     var. *limbicollis* Lec., Pacif. R. R. Rep. 1857, p. 67.
     var. *pensylvanica* Illig. loc. cit.
     uniguttata Say, Journ. Acad. 1824, p. 88 ; edit. Lec. ii, p. 229.
     vicina Kby., Fauna Am. Bor. iv, p. 217.
     procera Casey, Contributions, p. 182.

var. *pallipes* Crotch, Proc. Acad. 1873, p. 64.
var. *conjugata* Fab., Syst. El. i, p. 495; Oliv., Ent. vi, p. 686, pl. 2, fig. 30.
D. quinquevittata Say, Journ. Acad. 1824. p. 85; edit. Lec. ii, p. 227.
puncticollis Lec., Pacif. R R. Rep. 1857, Ins. p. 67.
fumata Lec., Proc. Acad 1858, p. 86.
pluriligata Lec., Journ. Acad. 1858, p. 27; Col. Kans. 1859, p. 25.
punctigera Lec., Col. Kans. 1859, p. 24.
capitata Jacoby, Biol. Cent Am. vi, pt. 1, p. 316.
var. *pura* Lec., Proc. Acad. 1858, p. 86.
D. crenicollis Say, Bost. Journ. 1835, p. 200; edit. Lec. ii, p. 668.
D. caroliniana Fab., Syst. Ent. 1775, p. 122; Oliv., Ent. vi, p. 684, pl. 2, fig. 27.
quinquevittata Fab., Syst. Ent. p. 118.
alternata Illig., Mag. vi, p. 144.
pulchra Casey, Contributions, p. 51.
D. arizonæ Casey, Contributions, p. 52.
D. glabrata Fab., Spec. Ins. i, p. 156; Illig., Mag. vi, p. 144; Oliv., Ent. vi. 685,
      pl. 2, fig. 28.
D. maritima Mann., Bull. Mosc. 1843, ii, p. 311.
D. abbreviata Mels., Proc. Acad. iii, p. 163.
D. tenuicornis n. sp.
D. discoidea Fab., Ent. Syst. i, 2, p 25; Illig. Mag. vi, p. 143.
D. funerea Randall, Bost. Journ. ii, p. 47.
D. triangularis Say, Journ. Acad. 1824, p. 84; edit. Lec ii, p. 226.
puncticollis Kby., Fauna Bor. Am. iv, p. 218, pl. 7, fig. 9.
D. xanthomelæna Dalm., Analecta Ent 1823, p. 79.
collaris ‡ Illig. Mag. vi, p. 126.
D. politula n. sp.
D. cervicalis Lec., Col. Kans. 1859, p. 25.
D. mellicollis Say, Bost. Journ. i, p. 199; edit. Lec. ii, p. 668.
semicarbonata Lec., Col. Kans. 1859, p. 25.
D. collata Fab., Syst. El. i, p. 463; Oliv., Ent. vi, p. 702, pl. 4, fig. 64.

HEMIPHRYNUS n. g.

H. intermedius Jacoby, Biol. Cent. Am. vi, pt. 1, p. 293.

ARGOPISTES Motsch.

A. scyrtoides Lec., Proc. Am. Philos. Soc. 1878, p. 416.

SPHÆRODERMA Steph.

S. opima Lec., Proc. Am. Philos. Soc. 1878, p. 417.

HALTICA Geoffr.

H. bimarginata Say, Journ. Acad. 1824, p. 85; edit. Lec. ii, p. 226.
plicipennis Mann., Bull. Mosc. 1843, ii, p. 310.
prasina Lec., Pacif. R. R. Rep. Ins. 1857, p. 67.
ambiens, subplicata Lec., Col. Kans. p. 25.
H. chalybea Illiger, Mag. vi, p. 115.
ritivora Thomas, Sillim. Journ. 1834, p. 113.
H. nana Crotch, Proc. Acad. 1873, p. 72.
nanula Lec., Trans. Am. Ent. Soc 1884, p. 29.
H. ignita Illiger, Mag. vi, p. 117.
kalmiæ Mels., Proc. Acad. 1847, p. 164.
inærata Lec., Proc. Acad. 1860, p. 317.
H. vicaria n. sp.

H. **carinata** Germ., Ins. Spec. Nov. 1824, p. 610.

erapta Say, Ins. Louisiana, 1832, p. 6; edit. Lec. i, p. 302.

torquata Lec., Journ. Acad. 1858, p. 27 ; Col. Kans. p. 26.

H. **californica** Mann., Bull. Mosc. 1843, ii, p. 310.

H. **obliterata** Lec., Col. Kans. 1859, p. 26.

H. **evicta** Lec., Proc. Acad. 1859, p. 286.

H. **æruginosa** Lec., Proc. Acad. 1859, p. 286.

H. **obolina** Lec., Pacif. R. R. Rep. 1857, p. 67.

H. **amœna** n. sp.

H. **marevagans** n. sp.

H. **tombacina** Mann., Bull. Mosc. 1853. iii, p. 259.

cuprcola Lec. MSS.

H. **tincta** Lec., Proc. Acad. 1859. p. 286.

H. **punctipennis** Lec., Col. Kans. 1859, p. 25.

H. **lazulina** Lec., Pacif. R. R. Rep. 1857, p. 67.

H. **foliacea** Lec., Proc. Acad. 1858, p. 86.

H. **polita** Oliv., Ent. vi, p. 706, pl. 4, fig. 68.

H. **fuscoœnea** Mels., Proc. Acad. 1847, p. 165.

H. **opulenta** n. sp.

H. **floridana** n. sp.

H. **Burgessi** Crotch, Proc. Acad. 1873, p. 71.

H. **rufa** Illiger, Mag. vi, p. 153.

scutellaris Oliv., Ent. vi, 699, p. 3, fig. 56; Harold, Heft. xiv, p. 20; Jacoby (*Lactica*). Biol. Cent. Am. vol. vi, pt. 1, p. 273, pl. 16, fig. 6.

LACTICA Erichs.

L. **tibialis** Oliv., Ent. vi, p. 697, pl. 3, fig. 52.

ocreata Say, Ins. Louis. 1832, p. 7 ; edit. Lec. i, p. 303.

xanthochroa Harold, Heft. xiii, 1875, p. 89.

L. **iris** Oliv. Ent. vi, p 702, pl. iv, fig. 62.

specularis Harold, Col. Heft. xiii, p. 89 ; xiv, p. 17.

DIPHAULACA Clark.

D. **bicolorata** n. sp.

TRICHALTICA Harold.

T. **scabricula** Crotch, Proc. Acad. 1873, p. 71 ; Harold, Heft. xv, 1876, p. 2.

HEMIGLYPTUS n. g.

H. **basalis** Crotch, Trans. Am. Ent. Soc. 1874, p. 80.

ORTHALTICA Crotch.

O. **copalina** Fab., Syst. El. p. 466 ; Oliv., Ent. vi, p. 720, pl. 5, fig. 92.

forticornis Illig., Mag. vi, p. 111.

O. **melina** n. sp.

CREPIDODERA Chev.

C. **rufipes** Linn., Syst. Nat. ed. x, p. 373.

erythropus Mels., Proc. Acad. iii, p 165.

C. **longula** n. sp.

C. **Helxines** Linn., loc. cit. p. 373.

nana Say, Journ. Acad. iv, p. 86.

violacea Mels., Proc. Acad. iii, p. 164.

areola Lec., Pacif. R. R. Rep. 1857, p. 68.

opulenta Lec., Proc. Acad. 1858, p. 86.

C. **robusta** Lec., Proc. Bost. Soc. N. H. 1874, p. 274.

C. **Modeeri** Linn., Faun. Suec. 1761, p. 167 ; Oliv., Ent. vi, p. 724, pl. 5, fig. 98.

maucula Lec., Proc. Acad. 1861, p. 358.

C. atriventris Mels., Proc. Acad. iii, p. 165.
C. nitens n. sp.

EPITRIX Foudras.

E. fuscula Crotch, Proc. Acad. 1873, p. 72.
E. lobata Crotch, loc. cit.
E. cucumeris Harris, Journ. Agric. 1851, p. 103.
pubescens (pars) Illig., Mag. vi, p. 58.
seminulum Lec., Proc. Acad. 1861, p. 358.
E. brevis Schwarz, Proc. Am. Philos. Soc. 1878, p. 367.
E. subcrinita Lec., Pacific R. R. Rep. 1857, p. 68.
E. parvula Fab., Syst. El. i, p. 468.
hirtipennis Mels., Proc. Acad. iii, p. 165.

LEPTOTRIX n. g.
L. recticollis Lec., Proc. Acad. 1861, p. 358.

MANTURA Steph.
M. floridana Crotch, Proc. Acad. 1873, p. 73.

EUPLECTROSCELIS Crotch.
E. Xanti Crotch, Proc. Acad. 1873, p. 75.

CHÆTOCNEMA Steph.
C. perturbata n. sp.
C. cribrata Lec., Proc. Am. Philos. Soc. 1878, p. 419.
C. irregularis Lec., Pacific R. R. Rep. 1857, p. 69.
rudis Lec., Proc. Am. Philos. Soc. 1878, p. 615.
C. subcylindrica Lec., Proc. Am. Phil. Soc. 1878, p. 419; cylindrica || l. c. p. 417
C. protensa Lec., Proc. Am. Philos. Soc. 1878, p. 417.
C. brunnescens n. sp.
C. denticulata Illig., Mag. vi, 163.
semichalcea Mels., Proc. Acad. iii, p. 167.
americana Mots.. Schrenks Reise, ii, p. 235.
texana Crotch, Proc. Acad. 1873, p. 74.
C. cribrifrons Lec., Bull. U. S. Geol. Surv. 1879, v. p. 517.
C. pinguis Lec., Proc. Am. Philos. Soc. 1878, p. 417.
C. æmula n. sp.
C. opacula Lec., Proc. Am. Philos. Soc. 1878, p. 418.
C. minuta Mels., Proc. Acad. iii, p. 167.
C. alutacea Crotch, Proc. Acad. 1873, p. 74.
C. subviridis Lec., Col. Kans. 1859, p. 27.
C. opulenta n. sp.
C. obesula Lec., Proc. Am. Philos. Soc. 1878, p. 418.
C. ectypa n. sp.
C. parcepunctata Crotch, Proc. Acad. 1873, p. 74.
pauperula Casey, Contrib. i, p. 53.
C. pulicaria Mels., Proc. Acad. iii, p. 167.
æneola Lec., Bull. U. S. Geol. Surv. 1879, v, p. 518.
C. crenulata Crotch, Proc. Acad. 1873, p. 74; Schwarz, Proc. Am. Philos. Soc.
1878, p. 368.
C. confinis Crotch, Proc. Acad. 1873, p. 75.
flavicornis Lec, Proc. Am. Philos. Soc. 1878, p. 418.
C. elongatula Crotch, Proc. Acad. 1873, p. 75.
C. dispar n. sp.
C. quadricollis Schwarz, Proc. Am. Philos. Soc. 1878, p. 368.
C. decipiens Lec., Proc. Am Philos. Soc. 1878, p. 418.

SYSTENA Clark.

S. hudsonias Forst., Nov. Spec. Ins. 1771, p. 26.

   frontalis Illig., Mag. vi, p. 155, pars.

S. frontalis Fab., Syst. El. i, p. 300; Oliv., Ent. vi, p. 694. pl. 3, fig. 46.

S. collaris Crotch, Proc. Acad. 1873, p. 68.

S. senilis Say, Journ. Acad. iv, p. 87; edit. Lec., ii. p. 228; Crotch, Proc. Acad. 1873, p. 70.

S. subaenea Lec., Pacific R. R. Rep. 1857, p. 68.

S. pallipes Schwarz, Proc. Am. Philos. Soc. 1878, p. 367.

S. elongata Fab., Ent. Syst. Supp. p. 99; Oliv., Ent vi, p. 694, pl. 3, fig. 45.

S. taeniata Say, Long's Second Exped. p. 294; edit Lec. i. p. 195.

   blanda, Mels., Proc. Acad. iii, p. 164.

   Egata Lec., Pacific R. R. Rep. 1857, p. 68.

   ochracea Lec., Proc. Acad. 1858, p. 87.

   mitis Lec., Proc. Acad. 1858, p. 87.

   bitaeniata Lec., Col. Kans. 1859, p. 36.

   pallidula Boh., Eugen. Resa, p. 192.

S. marginalis Illig., Mag. vi, p. 150.

   oblonga Lec., Ann. Lyc. i, p. 173.

GLYPTINA Lec.

G. bicolor n. sp.

G. cyanipennis Crotch, Proc. Acad. 1873, p. 65.

G. nivalis n. sp.

G. brunnea n. sp.

G. spuria Lec., Col. Kans. p. 26.

   lissotorques Lec., loc. cit. p. 27.

G. cerina Lec., Pacific R. R. Rep. 1857, p. 68.

G. atriventris n. sp.

APHTHONA Foudras.

A. texana Crotch, Proc. Acad. 1873, p. 67.

A. socia n. sp.

A. insolita Mels., Proc. Acad. iii, p. 168; Crotch (*Cerataltica*), Proc. Acad. 1873, p. 73.

A. subglobosa Motsch., Bull. Mosc. 1845, iv, p. 381. pl. 7, fig. 7 (unknown).

PHYLLOTRETA Foudras.

SERIES A.

P. lepidula Lec., Pacific R. R. Rep. 1857, p. 68.

P. sinuata Stephens, Illust. Brit. Ent iv, p. 297.

   Zimmermanni Crotch, Proc. Acad. 1873, p. 66.

P. vittata Fab., Syst. El. i, p. 469

   striolata Fab., Illig., Mag. ii, p. 293; vi, p. 148.

P. oregonensis Crotch, Proc. Acad. 1873, p. 66.

P. robusta Lec., Proc. Am. Philos. Soc. 1878, p. 614.

P. denticornis n. sp.

P. Ulkei n. sp.

P. decipiens n. sp.

P. albionica Lec., Pacific R. R. Rep. 1857, p. 68.

SERIES B.

P. ramosa Crotch, Trans. Am. Ent. Soc. 1874, p. 80.

P. bipustulata Fab., Syst. El. i, p. 464; Oliv., vi, p. 723, pl. 5, fig. 97.

P. **chalybeipennis** Crotch, Proc. Acad. 1873, p. 67.
P. **æneicollis** Crotch, loc. cit.
P. **Lewisii** Crotch, loc. cit. p. 66.
P. **pusilla** n. sp.
P. **picta** Say, Journ. Acad. iv, p. 87; edit. Lec., ii, p. 228.

LONGITARSUS Latr.

L. **Heliophyti** n. sp.
L. **subrufus** Lec., Col. Kans. 1859, p. 26.
L. **turbatus** n. sp.
L. **oregonensis** n. sp.
L. **traductus** n. sp.
L. **postremus** n. sp.
L. **repandus** Lec., Proc. Acad. 1858, p. 87.
L. **livens** Lec., Proc. Acad. 1858, p. 87.
L. **vanus** n. sp.
L. **occidentalis** n. sp.
L. **bicolor** n. sp.
L. **alternatus** Ziegler, Proc. Acad. 1846, p. 271.
   rubicunda Mels., Proc. Acad. 1847, p. 166.
   rubidus Lec., Col. Kans. 1859, p. 26.
L. **montivagus** n. sp.
L. **erro** n. sp.
L. **pygmæus** n. sp.
L. **testaceus** Mels., Proc. Acad. iii, p. 166; Lec., Proc. Acad. 1858, p. 87.
L. **melanurus** Mels, Proc. Acad. iii, p. 166.
L. **rufescens** n. sp.
L. **insolens** n. sp.
L. **perforatus** n. sp.
L. **solidaginis** n. sp.
L. **nitidellus** Cockerell, First Rep. Colorado Biol. Assoc. 1888, p. 4.
L. **mancus** Lec., Proc. Acad. 1858, p. 87.
   apterus Lec., loc. cit
L. **californicus** Motsch., Bull. Mosc. 1845, iv, p. 382 (unknown).

DIBOLIA Latr.

D. **sinuata** n. sp.
D. **borealis** Chev., Guér. Icon. Règne Anim. 1845, p. 307, pl. 49 bis, fig. 12 ; Jacoby, Biol. Cent. Am. vi, pt. 1, p. 357, pl. xxi, fig. 10.
   ærea Mels., Proc. Acad. iii, p. 167.
D. **ovata** Lec., Proc. Acad. 1859, p. 286.
D. **libonoti** n. sp.

PSYLLIODES Latr.

P. **punctulata** Mels., Proc. Acad. iii, p. 166.
   parvicollis Lec., Pacific R. R. Rep. 1857, p. 69.
   extricata ♂ Casey, Contributions 1884, p. 54.
   ærnescens Casey, loc. cit. p. 55.
P. **convexior** Lec., Pacific R. R. Rep. 1857, p. 69.
   interstitialis Lec., Proc. Acad. 1858, p. 67.
P. **elegans** n. sp.
P. **sublævis** n. sp.

320 GEO. H. HORN, M. D.

EXPLANATION OF PLATE V.

Figs. 1-5. —Œdionychis petaurista Fab. and its variations; fig. 5 may be longula
  Harold.
Fig. 6.—Œdionychis interjectionis Crotch.
" 7.--   "   æmula Horn.
" 8.—   "   fimbriata Forst. (typical)
Figs. 9-12.— " texana Crotch and varieties.
Fig. 13.—   "   miniata Fab.
" 14.—   "   tenuilineata Horn.
" 15.—   "   Ulkei Horn.
" 16.—   "   Jacobiana Horn.
Figs. 17-20. -- " scalaris Mels. and its varieties.

————o————

EXPLANATION OF PLATE VI.

Fig. 1.--Œdionychis quercata var. obsidiana Fab.
" 2.--   "   quercata Fab.
" 3.--   "   sexmaculata Illig.
" 4.--   "   quercata var.
" 5.—   "   suturalis Fab.
" 6.--   "   suturalis var.
" 7.—   "   limbalis Mels. var. subvittata Horn.
" 8.--   "   thyamoides Crotch.
" 9.—Hamletia dimidiaticornis Crotch.
" 10.--Phydanis bicolor Horn.
" 11.--Leptotrix recticollis Lec.
" 12.--Phyllotreta ramosa Crotch.
" 13.--   "   bipustulata Fab.
" 14.—   "   vittata Fab. and ♂ antenna.
" 15.--   "   sinuata Steph. and ♂ antenna.
" 16.—   "   oregonensis Crotch and ♂ antenna.
" 17.—   "   lepidula Lec. and ♂ antenna.
" 18.—   "   robusta Lec. and ♂ antenna.
" 19.—Antenna ♂ of P. denticornis Horn.
" 20.—Antenna ♀ of species of Series A.
" 21.--Antenna ♂ and ♀ of species of Series B.
" 22.--Antenna ♂ of P. albionica Lec.
" 23.--Antenna ♂ of P. Ulkei Horn.
" 24.--Altica liturata Oliv.. enlarged after Olivier (unknown).

————o————

EXPLANATION OF PLATE VII.

Fig. 1.—Pachyonychus paradoxus Mels.
" 2.—Hemiglyptus basalis Crotch.
" 3.—Euplectroscelis Xanti Crotch.
" 4.—Argopistes scyrtoides Lec.
Figs. 5-8.--Systena tæniata Say.
Fig. 9.--Posterior tibia of Chætocnema, seen from beneath.
" 10.— "   " Sphæroderma.
" 11.-- "   " Œdionychis.
" 12.— "   " Homophœta (Asphæra).
" 13.— "   " Psylliodes.
" 14.— "   " Longitarsus.
" 15— "   " Argopistes.
" 16.-- "   " Disonycha.
" 17.-- "   " Dibolia.
" 18.--Antenna and claws of Blepharida.
" 19.--Antenna ♂ Aphthona socia.
" 20.—Elytra of Œd. limbalis Mels. from a specimen in the LeConte cabinet,
   intermediate between the subvittate form (Pl. VI, fig. 7) and the
   typical, which resembles fig. 2, Pl. VI.